GOOD SPIRITS

ALSO BY EDGAR M. BRONFMAN

The Making of a Jew

GOOD SPIRITS

THE MAKING

OF A BUSINESSMAN

EDGAR M. BRONFMAN

G. P. Putnam's Sons   *New York*

G. P. Putnam's Sons
Publishers Since 1838
a member of
Penguin Putnam Inc.
200 Madison Avenue
New York, NY 10016

Copyright © 1998 by Edgar M. Bronfman

Library of Congress Cataloging-in-Publication Data

Bronfman, Edgar M., date.
Good spirits : the making of a businessman / by Edgar M. Bronfman.
p.   cm.
ISBN 0-399-14374-2
1. Bronfman, Edgar M., date.   2. Executives—Canada—
Biography.   3. Liquor industry—Canada—History.   4. Conglomerate
corporations—Canada—History.   5. Seagram Company—History.
I. Title.
HD9390.C22B713   1998
338.7'6635'092—dc21   97-23932 CIP
[B]

Printed in the United States of America

1   3   5   7   9   10   8   6   4   2

This book is printed on acid-free paper. ♾

BOOK DESIGN BY LAURA HAMMOND HOUGH

To my wonderful wife, Jan Aronson

———◆———

And to my seven loved and loving children,

Sam, Edgar, Holly, Matthew, Adam, Sara, and Clare

CONTENTS

CHAPTER 1

— ◆ —

A DEFINITIVE DECISION

We're between a rock and a hard place," Harold Fieldsteel, Seagram's chief financial officer, said to me that Monday morning in July 1981. A sensible realist and a fully seasoned businessman, Harold had remarkable financial instincts, and he never panicked. So when he said we were in trouble, I knew he was not exaggerating.

As he continued, the problem became clear: unless we changed the terms of our tender offer for the Conoco oil company, we were headed for inevitable defeat. If we changed the bid, however, we faced the frightening risk of spending millions of dollars and ending up with a relatively illiquid asset worth less than what we'd paid for it.

Though the offer was for Conoco, the real focus of our efforts was Du Pont, which also was bidding for the oil company. We knew we couldn't outbid Du Pont; instead, we were trying to get in on the back end of their deal. This would make us a significant shareholder in both Conoco and the much larger Du Pont.

The gravity of the situation could hardly be overstated. If I made the right decision, Seagram would likely become a massive, powerful company. If I made the wrong one, our future opportunities outside the liquor industry would certainly be curtailed, and our chances of becoming a major factor in the business world greatly reduced.

My kids call me an instinct operator, because I rely more on my intuition than on anything else. But they tend to forget that these instincts have been honed by a great deal of experience, both my own and that passed on to me by the extraordinary men and women I have worked with (and occasionally against) in my long career. No doubt I also inherited some of that instinct from my remarkable father, Samuel Bronfman, who founded the Seagram empire. Certainly, I grew up with his business dicta constantly ringing in my ears.

Instinct *and* experience had brought me to this critical moment. Now both would be put to their greatest test.

The origins of the Conoco/Du Pont drama actually date back to 1947, when Imperial Oil Ltd., a subsidiary of what was then Standard Oil of New Jersey, discovered the Leduc field in Alberta. Suddenly Canada became an oil-producing country, which awakened the ambitions of countless people. One of those people was Samuel Bronfman.

My father was not a gambler in the normal sense, but he most certainly was a risk taker. He also could sense an opportunity and had the guts to claim it. He loved the oil business. "If it's good enough for the Rockefellers, it's good enough for me," he used to say.

Oil can be glamorous, but you have to be willing to take risks. You never know what will happen when you spud in the well. In a sense, gushers are like western movies—full of romance, but not based on much fact. People on the periphery forget that, beyond all the excitement, oil exploration is a business with a simple rule: the earnings from selling oil have to be greater than the costs of finding it. If not, you'll slide down a greasy pole to oblivion.

Unfortunately, while Father was immensely shrewd, he was a surprisingly poor accountant. Though he pretended to understand everything about finance, he was actually very naive on the subject. As a result, our oil-exploration business was foolishly placed into various trusts that had been set up to pass on some assets owned by my father and his brother, my uncle Allan, for the benefit of their children. If we succeeded in finding oil, we would reap no tax benefits from depletion allowances; if we didn't succeed and lost money on drilling, we couldn't lower our taxes by writing the losses off against other income.

I am still surprised that Father, surrounded as he was by the ablest accountants and lawyers, could have embarked on such a poorly structured venture. The reason, of course, was that it was very difficult to tell Sam Bronfman that he was wrong. No one ever wanted to be on the receiving end of his violent, epithet-laden outbursts. Even Philip Vineberg, a brilliant lawyer whom Father trusted and respected, was a little afraid of him. "If your father wants to do it this way, who's gonna say no?" he asked me.

I was about twenty-two years of age and was working at Ville LaSalle as an assistant blender at the time. As young as I was, I might have seemed the least likely person willing to confront Father. But even then I knew enough about tax law to see the absurdity of the situation, and I could not let it continue. With considerable temerity, I sat down and explained to him the tax implications. Carefully, I argued that the better place to explore for oil was in the United States, and that if the exploration were done by a taxpaying corporation, there could be huge tax advantages. I pointed out that, even if he wanted to continue looking for oil in Canada, our tax benefits would be greater if we arranged for a U.S. company rather than a Canadian one to handle our oil explorations in both countries.

Fortunately, Father saw the point at once and agreed. It struck me then (and often later) that, although other people were scared of contradicting him, he was *sometimes* willing to listen to me—even when I was telling him that he was wrong.

Of course, part of the reason that Father agreed to relocate his oil business to the United States was that he could do so without admitting that he had made an error. We were still involved in the Canadian oil and gas business through an investment he had made earlier in Royalite, so moving to the United States could be seen as an expansion of his interests, not as a retreat from his decision to invest in Canadian oil.

We decided to use Frankfort (a company Father had bought in 1943 for its liquor brands, Four Roses and Paul Jones inter alia) as the operating company. Thus, the oil operation became known as Frankfort Oil.

—•—

When they first went into their own oil business, Father and Uncle Allan had hired Ray Shaffer, an Oklahoma oil man, and brought him to Canada. Later, when I persuaded Father to move the business to the United States, Ray set up our offices in Bartlesville, Oklahoma.

Shaffer managed to be singularly unsuccessful: he didn't find any commercial oil in Canada, and he found little in the United States. He kept puttering around and Seagram kept losing money, although not in large amounts. But Father—who had an ego beyond belief, and the success to go with it—liked Ray because Ray kissed his ass with considerable panache and also was an amusing fellow. One of the things he taught me was the meaning of an "Oklahoma guarantee." He'd say, "I'll be a son of a bitch if there isn't oil here." When you asked him what that meant, he'd say, "If there isn't any oil, why, you can call me a son of a bitch!"

In spite of Ray's broken "guarantees," we stayed in the oil business. One reason was our eventual success in Forrest Oil, a company I had come across during a period in 1953, when I worked at the Empire Trust Company. Forrest Oil had a program to drill for petroleum with outside investors. At my recommendation, Seagram invested some money in a drilling deal with Forrest, and made out quite well.

The other reason we stayed in the business was that Ray Shaffer was very clever at being charming. The first deal he dreamed up was one he knew would have enormous appeal for Uncle Allan. A company was established to do the drilling for Frankfort Oil, but it was owned by the family, not by Seagram (and, of course, Shaffer had a piece of it). Thus, whether or not Seagram was making money, the

Bronfman family was. As soon as I read about this arrangement in Seagram's proxy statement, I realized that, though it was legal, it was nevertheless a clear conflict of interest. At the time, the parameters of business ethics were not as clearly defined as they are today. But I've always had a strong sense of fair play, and I put a stop to it immediately. In the course of my career, I've found that you don't have to abandon your principles in order to make money.

Even after this arrangement ended, we persisted, although the oil business was only limping along. From time to time, Shaffer would report a success. But nobody ever accused Ray Shaffer of being a trustworthy reporter, and I'm not sure those successes were real. In fact, I think the true reason for the high level of activity was that, by the terms of our agreement with Shaffer, he got 1 percent of all the oil found under his direction. It was a terrible deal for us because there was no penalty for failure; he was encouraged to drill on as many prospects as he could. And drill he did.

In the spring of 1957, by which time I was chairman of the Administrative Committee, a Shaffer deal to buy a building in Bartlesville crossed my desk. I had always been suspicious of Shaffer, but this really smelled. A little operation like ours certainly didn't need a building. It seemed to me that Shaffer had finally gone too far, and I promptly called Father to report his latest escapade.

"Send him a telegram saying that the Seagram board of directors won't authorize any such deal," Father ordered. (He could use the board when it suited him! When I first went on the board of the parent company, I asked Father what directors did. "Why, declare a dividend and have a drink.")

I did so promptly, and also decided that it was time to send in the auditors. While they didn't find any smoking guns, the investigation raised more than enough questions for me. I fired him and he disappeared from view, never to be heard from again. It's interesting to note that Ray never made a point, neither then nor later, about his 1 percent. I came to the conclusion that while I knew we hadn't found much auditing the operation, he didn't know that and was more than prepared to let sleeping dogs lie.

Now I needed someone to run the oil business, so off I went to see my friend Mark Millard, then a senior executive at Carl M. Loeb, Rhoades & Company and my father-in-law John L. Loeb's partner. I had enjoyed many successful business dealings with Mark over the years, and I trusted him deeply. Originally named Metznetsky, he was a Hungarian Jew, tallish, very broad and thick, with dark, almost black hair and laughing eyes. Of all the people I had met in connection with our oil investments, I thought most highly of him. A brilliant man, he had great vision and clarity of thought, as well as great integrity.

I told Mark everything I knew or suspected about Shaffer and explained that I needed someone I could trust to head the oil company and clean up the mess. It took him very little time to find the solution. He recommended Carroll M. Bennett, an economist from Dallas with plenty of oil experience. Carroll made an excellent impression on me, and then on Father, and I promptly hired him.

One of Carroll's first ideas was to move the company from Bartlesville to Dallas, where he lived. He pointed out that it would be easier to start from scratch there than to try to turn around the awful reputation that Frankfort Oil had earned in Bartlesville.

Carroll did a first-rate job, and built a strong organization around him. Carroll was a good, decent man, someone I could trust. We found some oil and the company grew slowly, making a deal here and there and becoming an entity of which we could all be quite proud.

But all that hardly amounted to more than an early learning experience for me in the oil business. It was several years later when my intuition first played a decisive role, setting in motion the series of events that eventually led to the Conoco/Du Pont nail-biter.

On January 10, 1963, I was having lunch with Mark and Carroll. Halfway through the meal, Mark proposed that we bid for Texas Pacific Coal and Oil. I agreed that it would be an excellent deal, but of course I had to convince Father.

The matter was complicated by the tricky nature of oil bids. In trying to fix on the proper bid, experts make a huge to-do about analyzing the reserves. But this is never an exact science. Since properties are often put up for secret bid (for example, when the federal government leases offshore properties), if some of the bidders think there are large reserves while others doubt it, the winning bid is often way over the next highest.

As it turned out, Father wasn't afraid of spending the money. But he was very concerned that, if he bid too much for Texas Pacific and left a lot on the table, he would look foolish—or at least less than the genius he was supposed to be. His ego couldn't have stood for him to be in that position.

Somehow I became convinced that the bid Father had authorized was just a little too low. I was determined to get him to go up. It took a lot of effort—as well as the help of Mark, Carroll, and oil attorney Dick Loftus. But eventually I persuaded him to bid another $0.25 a share. Our bid beat the next highest by about a nickel!

The purchase was financed by the ABC system of buying natural resources. This acronym refers to the corporate setup to make it work—"A" sells to "B" and "B" sells to "C." This meant that we put up $65 million in equity, and the remaining $215 million was financed by the oil itself. The debt, none of which appeared on the balance sheet, was to be retired and the interest was paid as the oil flowed. As far as I know, this was the last oil deal done this way. Interestingly enough, the last natural-resource deal using this system was Conoco's purchase of Consolidation Coal a year or so after. Then the IRS changed the rules.

The Bankers Trust Company, which had been Seagram's principal bank from the time we started doing business in the United States, immediately told me that it wanted a major role in the financing. So when Bill Moore, the new chairman of the bank, asked to visit, I assumed this was to be a courtesy call. I couldn't have been more wrong.

Imagine my shock and surprise when he came to my office and told me that Bankers Trust had decided not to lend us the money after all. Their oil people, he explained, had estimated that the deal wouldn't pay out in twelve years, as it was required to do by their rules; they thought it might take thirteen or perhaps even fourteen.

I was dumbfounded. I quickly decided that someone with influence over the bank must be trying to foul up our deal. Surely the bank couldn't be stupid enough to pull out of its own accord and risk losing all the business it did with Seagram. Besides, to take that risk because it might require an extra year or so for their money to be repaid beyond the twelve years of their theoretical model was totally absurd. How could Bill Moore think his oil analysts were this accurate?

However, it turned out that he was, indeed, that stupid. As a result, I took away every piece of business we did with Bankers Trust and gave it to those who had helped us. John Loeb, then my father-in-law, implored me not to be vengeful, probably because his good friend Louis Lapham was an officer of Bankers Trust. But I was angry, and I would be just as angry today; nobody does that to us and gets away with it.

Now we were really in the oil business. We changed the name to Texas Pacific Oil Company, and Carroll brought in some very talented people. However, I was soon to learn just how capital intensive the oil business really is.

(There is a story about the time that Esso, now Exxon, decided to go into the rubber tire business—remember Atlas tires? The idea was to supply consumers through its vast network of service stations. The boys in Akron got together and sent their spokesman to talk to Esso's chairman and CEO. The spokesman said that if Esso insisted on going forward with its plans to enter the tire business, a consortium of tire companies would invest $100 million in the oil business to compete with Standard Oil of New Jersey. "Do that," the chairman was reported to have said. "You will discover that in the oil business $100 million is one white chip.")

Texas Pacific Oil under Carroll Bennett, and later his successor Al Hrubetz, continued to do well. But it was always looking for more capital. For example, they had come up with a new proposal to buy carbon dioxide (God knows from where—Indiana, maybe), pipe it all the way down to our fields in west Texas, and inject it into the wells, thus achieving a higher rate of secondary oil recovery. The deal made economic sense, but it would cost us another $50 million—and at that time, $50 million was a great deal more than it is today. Proposals like this came up constantly.

Not long after Father's death, I became truly disturbed by the oil business's capital requirements. Perhaps I was wary of all the decision-making, since my knowledge of oil didn't compare to my expertise in Seagram's base liquor business. I did know enough to be nervous about the accuracy of the figures upon which we were relying. The Seagram debt was climbing, and the Seagram dog was now in danger of being wagged by the Texas Pacific tail.

The other thing that bothered me about our ownership of Texas Pacific was the rising price of oil. It was selling at just over thirty dollars a barrel, and many pundits were predicting it would go to fifty or sixty dollars a barrel. The results of such a climb in the costs of energy could have been disastrous for the Western democracies, especially the United States. Surely the government would have to intervene, which would be bad for small, independent oil companies like ours. I didn't want to do business in that kind of an environment.

I discussed these concerns with my brother, Charles, and with Phil Beekman, our president and COO. Charles shared my concerns and was inclined to sell. Phil, however, was worried about replacing the earnings if we left the oil business, and I agreed that this had to be a consideration in anything we did.

I called Mark Millard and said, "Let's see what we can get for Texas Pacific."

I have often thought, *What would Father have done?* He didn't like selling businesses—it somehow worried him that others would conclude that he had made a mistake in buying them in the first place.

For example, we had owned a company named Pharmacraft (it had come with Frankfort distillers in 1943, and Father didn't know we owned it until ten years later), which marketed Fresh deodorant and Allerest allergy treatment. I realized one day that it was a seasonal business, because what you shipped out often came back. I went to Father and told him that we should sell that company. I could have spoken the words before they left his lips.

"I don't sell businesses, I buy businesses."

"This is not a business," I said. "We ship out tons of stuff and then it comes back."

"What? You ship out tons of stuff and then it comes back?"

"Dad, we ship Fresh deodorant in the summer because that's when it's hot. If they don't sell it off during the summer, what's left comes back. And Allerest, that's only for hay fever season. If it doesn't sell during hay fever season, then they ship back what they didn't sell."

"What kind of a business is that?" he said.

"You're right, that's not a business," I answered. Only then was I free to sell it.

My decision to sell the oil business was still pending. Once again, I proved that it is better to be lucky than smart.

The astonishing news reached me on Easter Sunday, April 6, 1981. I was in the library of my Virginia farm when Mark Millard called to tell me that the Sun Oil Company was willing to pay us $2.1 billion for Texas Pacific.

The size of the offer took my breath away. Between the purchase price of $65 million and the later investments we had made, Texas Pacific was on our books for $566 million. Of course, I knew it was worth a lot more than that, but this offer was amazing. I hardly knew what to say. I could analyze oil and I knew what it was worth. About 80 percent of this oil was secondary-recovery oil, not nearly as valuable as primary reserves. So $2.1 billion, which worked out to be some twelve dollars a barrel in the ground, was a huge sum.

Somehow my bargaining instincts prevailed, and I replied that it was not nearly enough. In response, Mark went back to Sun Oil and actually managed to get them to increase the price to $2.3 billion, plus a reversionary interest on all unproven land (this meant that, after the purchaser's investment had paid out, part of the future profit would revert to us).

When I had worked at the Empire Trust Company in 1953, we'd calculated that oil in the ground was worth one dollar a barrel. This was now 1981, and the price of oil had almost quadrupled since then. But twelve dollars a barrel? To this day, no one has received that much per barrel of oil in the ground. As Morgan Stanley senior executive Barry Good said, it was the best example he'd seen of having your cake and eating it too. And as the leader of the negotiations, Steve Banner (then a partner at Simpson Thacher & Bartlett and later, until his untimely death in May 1995, a very senior Seagram executive), put it, "Edgar, it's like stealing candy in a candy shop."

Apart from my decision to sell, the credit for this coup goes to Mark Millard, who negotiated the whole deal. In fact, the only time I ever met the chairman of Sun was when he came to our Montreal headquarters with the check in his pocket. Charles and I picked him up at the airport and brought him back to the office for the signing ceremonies and celebration lunch.

In hindsight, I clearly chose the right time—and the right person—to sell the company. I've since learned that the right time to sell anything is when everybody thinks the price is going to keep going up, as was the case with oil in 1981. In fact, the price of oil soon started to drop. My instincts had served me well once again.

———

We sat on that bundle of cash for some time, trying to figure out what to do with it. During the Carter administration, interest rates were over 20 percent—which meant that Phil Beekman did not have to worry about Seagram's income flow! Indeed, the amount of interest we earned was almost sinful. We paid full taxes on that income, however, and clearly these interest rates would not last forever. Sooner or later, we would have to reinvest the money (before we eventually did, it grew from $2.3 billion to $3 billion). In the meantime, our superb treasurer, Richard Goeltz, obtained a standby loan so that we would be ready to move.

To help us decide where to put the funds, we formed a committee chaired by Harold Fieldsteel. The group's mission was to look into various industries and, based on its general conclusions, investigate specific companies that we might acquire. We quickly discovered that it was not going to be easy to place our money well. The companies that appeared most promising tended to be overpriced, with unreasonable price-to-earnings multiples. And, of course, if we sought to buy them, it would likely start a bidding war that would drive the prices even higher.

To camouflage our intent, we played a few games and invested in a number of companies, and made quite a bit of money in those transactions. I liked natural-resource companies, probably in part because natural resources were very much on everyone's mind during the early eighties. But I was also interested in buying value and, surprisingly, the natural-resource companies were relatively inexpensive.

We looked at many other opportunities. For example, we seriously considered acquiring the Union Pacific Railroad. I asked W. Averell Harriman, who had been Harry Truman's secretary of commerce and was a major shareholder in that railroad (as well as my neighbor in Yorktown Heights), whether he would have any objections. He said no, but told me that he didn't hold a controlling interest and that management probably wouldn't want to sell. In the end, we shied away from the railroad on the advice of our investment bankers, who indicated that an unfriendly takeover would be terribly difficult.

Then we came across St. Joseph Lead, a company knee deep in natural resources, including gold, lead, copper, and zinc, as well as phosphates and other minerals essential to fertilizers.

Our usual bankers, Goldman Sachs & Company, made a practice of refusing to act for hostile bidders. (They had made a lot of money by becoming Wall Street's Oliver Cromwell—"The Great Protector.") Since buying St. Joe would be an unfriendly takeover, we asked Lazard Frères, under the able leadership of my good friend Felix Rohatyn, to act for us in this matter. Felix had a long relationship with our family— he had once dated my sister Phyllis, and had gone into the mergers and acquisitions business at the urging of Father. He's a very bright, decent man, and I knew I could trust him.

Our Montreal boardroom became the scene of several meetings to determine the bid. Finally, on March 11, 1981, we offered forty-eight dollars a share against a market price in the low thirties. I was sure we would prevail—but again, I was more lucky than smart, for we did not.

In fact, our bid was too high, and the management of St. Joe should have leapt at it. For example, we calculated gold at $500 an ounce, and we've never seen such a price since. Instead, their chief executive, John Duncan, refused to meet with me, even though he served on the board of Goodrich, as did our board member John Weinberg. But as it turned out, Duncan's bluff worked, because the Fluor Corporation came up with a higher bid. We wished them luck and backed off.

(I was so sure that Fluor had made a mistake that I wanted to short their shares. Steve Banner, our lawyer, asked me not to, saying I could be accused of trying to rig the market. For a few thousand shares? I'm still annoyed when I think about this—it would have been like shooting fish in a barrel.)

Later, a reporter from *Fortune* asked me why we hadn't upped the bid for St. Joe, saying, "You're a rich company and a rich family."

"Maybe we're a rich company and a rich family because we don't throw our money away," I answered. "We bid everything we thought we could and we had no further appetite."

It would have been only ego that would have made us compete. In my view, that sort of pride is not only stupid, but sinful. We must always bear in mind that we have associates and shareholders. It is our duty to protect their interests as much as our own.

I do believe that if we had bought St. Joe it would have done much better than it has. We had cash to put into the business, and probably could have expanded it. But it never would have been a great investment.

Moreover, I'm not a miner, and I feel that you shouldn't get into a business unless you understand how it operates and thus can improve it. Knowledge doesn't always translate into profits, but it's an important ingredient in the recipe for business success.

—◦—

I had been lucky—or perhaps intuitive—three times in a row. Persuading my father to add an extra quarter to our Texas Pacific bid had made us players in the oil business. Judging the right time to sell had given us an enviable hoard of cash. And *not* upping the bid for St. Joe had allowed me to keep that hoard intact. But the question remained, how should we invest the money?

The answer came, as it often does, from left field. It started when a smallish Canadian oil company, Dome Exploration, made a tender offer for a portion of Conoco stock. Dome had a limited objective, namely to trade the stock it acquired for Conoco's Canadian operations. The bid was enormously oversubscribed, and Dome succeeded in its goal. However, Mark Millard realized that the number of shareholders who had been willing to sell to Dome indicated that Conoco was quite loosely held and represented a golden acquisition opportunity, which he was quick to point out. Clearly, Conoco was up for grabs, and the stock was relatively cheap.

As Mark well knew, when you evaluate oil companies, first you decide how many units of oil and gas they have, then you put a number on what you think each unit is worth, and finally you do some simple multiplication. In this case, the numbers were convincing. Conoco was a company with great expertise in discovering oil. It had found "black gold" not only in the United States, but in Libya, Dubai, the Norwegian and British North Seas, and in Asia, principally Indonesia.

Considering all this, Mark strongly encouraged us to bid for Conoco, even though he knew that, only a year earlier, I had definitely wanted Seagram out of the oil business. In fact, when he first brought up Conoco, my visceral reaction was, "My God, we're out of the oil business, why would we want to go back into it again?"

But the deal made sense. I had led Seagram away from oil because I thought it was too capital intensive and because I feared possible government intervention. However, as Mark correctly pointed out, Conoco was big enough to generate its own cash flow; Seagram would not have to invest any money beyond the initial acquisition. As for government intervention, I was no longer concerned, since the price of oil had receded from the dizzying heights of a few years earlier.

Moreover, here my instinct set in. Even as I was considering whether or not we should get back into oil, my gut was saying, "This looks good, it really looks awfully good." So I agreed to try our hand at a friendly bid, and Goldman Sachs was happy to work with us.

As a first step, my brother Charles and I decided to meet Conoco's CEO, Ralph Bailey. The meeting was held May 29, 1981, at Conoco's head offices, which were in Stamford, Connecticut. The setting made me a bit uneasy—there seemed to be no need for these luxurious offices when the company's oil operations were run from Houston and their coal operations from Pittsburgh.

Bailey was a tall, overweight man with bushy eyebrows and a midwestern, all-American air about him. He loved to play golf, which may have explained the Connecticut offices (lovely golf courses in the Stamford area!).

During this meeting, we suggested that, rather than buying Conoco outright, we would acquire 25 percent as an investment and agree not to extend our ownership for at least five years. Had they asked us, we would have been willing to lengthen that time period, possibly to ten years. Our goal was to make a sound investment, not necessarily to take over operating control.

Bailey was cordial enough and asked us to come back to meet their board. We did, but the meeting was not a propitious one. The board members took it upon themselves to grill me for a good half hour, asking a battery of what I felt were dumb questions. There was a lack of dignity about it. *Why do I have to go through this?* I kept wondering. There was such an evident lack of trust and faith underlying the whole process. (Perhaps anti-Semitism, too?)

What really irritated the hell out of me, however, was the chairman's duplicity. You see, we had found out that while he was talking to us, Bailey was also running back and forth to Du Pont.

We happened upon this knowledge quite by accident. Both our planes were kept at the Westchester Airport, and we could easily monitor where their planes were going by listening to the control tower on the radio. Their aircraft kept flying to Wilmington, Delaware. Well, what else is in Wilmington but Du Pont?

After keeping us dangling for a while, Bailey finally came to my office, accepted a drink, and told me that they were not going to go along with our proposal. Evidently, he had decided it would be more lucrative for him and his fellow executives, who all had shares in Conoco, to sell outright than to take in a minority partner.

Two days later—very much to Bailey's surprise, I think—we made a tender offer for Conoco.

There were now three players involved in the fight to acquire Conoco: Du Pont, Seagram, and Mobil. Mobil made the outlandish bid of $125 a share, but Mark Millard kept telling us that this offer was meaningless, since neither the Federal Trade Commission nor the Justice Department would allow Mobil to buy Conoco without hearings, and probably not even then.

Du Pont's final bid was ninety-seven dollars a share. This was getting extremely rich for our blood, and we decided to back off. I was disappointed, but hardly upset. We had stayed in the bidding up to what we thought the stock was worth; a competitive bidder had offered more; so that was that. I went on vacation to the south of France with my wife and our two little girls.

———•———

The Conoco deal, however, continued to occupy my attention. Then I received two telephone calls that profoundly changed the fate of Seagram.

The first call came from Mark. If we concentrated on the "back end" of the Du Pont deal, he explained, it was very possible that we could acquire a large share of Du Pont.

This would be a brilliant business deal: Du Pont was one of the finest companies in America and, in my judgment, had a great future before it. If we could somehow become a major Du Pont shareholder, Seagram would become a huge enterprise.

Here's how it would work: Du Pont had offered ninety-seven dollars cash per share for 51 percent of Conoco, and a fixed number of Du Pont common shares for the remaining 49 percent. Mark reasoned that the arbitrageurs, who by now held almost all the Conoco stock, would much prefer cash to Du Pont stock, which would probably fall a bit as a result of the dilution. Mark therefore felt—and I agreed—that we didn't have to compete with the Du Pont bid. We only had to be close enough to make our cash more appealing than their stock, especially after brokerage fees.

However, we would have to own at least 20 percent of Du Pont. That way, we could consolidate our Du Pont earnings into Seagram's and show the full profitability of the combined company. Also, with a share of 20 percent or more, we would play a meaningful role in the strategic direction of Du Pont.

The second fateful call was from Charles, who urgently asked me to fly back to Montreal for a board meeting, where we would decide what to do about Conoco and Du Pont.

On July 22, 1981, the Seagram G-III flew nonstop from Nice to Montreal, a record distance for us. By this time, company planes were by no means a novelty at Seagram, but a daily working tool. But it had not always been so.

———

Originally, our fledgling oil company had owned a small Aero-Commander, a two-engine propeller plane used to visit drilling sites. Once in a while, I used it to go to an island in the St. Lawrence River for a weekend of hunting. Father knew that I used the plane, and sometimes asked about its safety. I think he had a vision of string and chewing gum. I finally told him that he just didn't understand. "I'm not so stupid as to put my life in that kind of danger," I had said. We agreed not to discuss it again.

Eventually, I ordered a jet for Seagram. Not long thereafter, Father called to say that he and Mother had to go to Charlottetown (the capital of the Canadian province of Prince Edward Island, where the

Articles of Confederation had been signed). It was a difficult place to get to commercially, he explained, but fortunately Miss Shanks, his Montreal secretary, had found a charter plane that was quite reasonable. The clear implication was that I should be proud of my father for being willing to fly on a private plane.

I told him not to fly on chartered planes because you never know how good their maintenance is. "But it doesn't matter," I said, "I'll send the corporate jet to fly you there."

"The corporate *what?*" he yelled.

I told him we had just purchased a Sabreliner, and that I thought he would be pleased. Then, to stop further argument, I quickly added, "I have to run now. Let's discuss it after the flight."

That evening, he interrogated everyone around his table in Montreal. Who knew Edgar had bought a jet? It appeared that everyone was in on the plot. Why, he inquired, had he not been told? Mother saved the day by replying that it was because everyone thought he would cancel the order. He heartily agreed.

Nevertheless, the next morning he and Mother flew to Charlottetown on Seagram's first corporate jet. After that, except for overseas flights, there were no more commercial flights for Sam Bronfman. He loved it so much that at one point he came into my office wanting to know why he couldn't have the plane that day for a trip. I told him that it was in St. Louis being serviced, and nothing ever interfered with that.

"Where's the flea?" he wanted to know, referring to the plane the oil company was now using, a Beechcraft 18.

I sent for it, as he requested. It took almost two hours to fly him to Montreal versus an hour in a commercial plane. But that was what he wanted.

Some years later, we were having lunch with Father's friend Sir Ronald Cumming, the chairman of the giant Scottish spirits combine DCL. Much to my amusement, Father gave Ronnie a half-hour lecture on why he, the chairman of such a great company, should have his own airplane. A man in his position, Father said, "shouldn't fly around with the common herd."

It was fortunate now that I had prevailed on the matter of corporate airplanes so long before. Only because I had the right craft at my disposal was I able to arrive at 1430 Peel Street, Seagram's Montreal headquarters, in plenty of time.

The atmosphere was tense, but somehow the pressure of these situations rarely affects me, and this occasion was no different. I had had a smoked-meat sandwich, a glass of red wine, and a nap.

(Smoked-meat sandwiches were part of my childhood. My Grandpa Rosner used to take us to Ben's Delicatessen, a small restaurant that specialized in this delightful dish. It's basically brisket of beef, lightly smoked with garlic and other spices and served with a mild mustard on rye bread. To this day, when I'm in Montreal for a board meeting, I always have one and a half smoked-meat sandwiches. One time in the early seventies, I missed a board meeting, and Charles neglected to order smoked meat. The American directors put up a fuss, and from then on we've always had them at meetings. It's a tradition!)

The meeting commenced in the late afternoon. The people from Lazard Frères explained that if we wanted to stay in the running for the back-end deal, we should increase our bid from ninety to ninety-two dollars. Their figures showed that, for many sellers, ninety-two dollars in cash would be just enough to be preferable to the Du Pont stock. Offer any less, they told us, and most Conoco shareholders would decide that Du Pont stock was the better value. Halfway through the explanation, Charles and Leo Kolber arrived.

Leo Kolber had been a lifelong friend of Charles and mine. Leo's own father had died when he was a kid, and his mother had struggled to bring up Leo and his younger brother, Sam, and educate them as best she could. Leo was a lawyer, but his claim to fame would come as a real estate magnate. He was ambitious, but not to a fault. Father was very fond of him, and would point out to Mother—and, of course, to Charles and me—that we were fortunate to be influenced by a guy like Leo who had to count his pennies and earn a living.

While we were still in college, Leo, Charles, and I went into business together, investing in real estate. The sums were relatively small,
but we did well, and much of the credit goes to Leo. He had therefore
earned our trust very early on, and felt quite free to say whatever he
thought.

I took them to one side to explain where we stood. Then the
other directors arrived. It was now perhaps eight P.M., and time to call
the meeting to order. I explained why our goal should be not to acquire
Conoco, but rather to end up with a significant position in Du Pont.
Our two leading experts, Mark Millard and Felix Rohatyn, were peppered with questions. Gradually, however, everyone understood our intention, and they agreed. Only the price remained an issue. Should we
bid ninety or ninety-two dollars?

Leo Kolber interrupted the debate. "Edgar," he said, "why don't
you put the question to a vote?"

"Because," I replied, "I am not sure whether Charles has agreed to
a figure."

Charles put up two fingers. That was all I needed. We promptly
passed a resolution to bid ninety-two dollars for the stock of Conoco.

However, there was an important proviso to our offer—that we
would not be obliged to take any stock unless we received more than 50
percent of the total shares outstanding. We should have set it at 20 percent since that was our goal, because the worst thing that could happen
would be for us to receive, say, 5 percent of the outstanding Conoco
shares and be obliged to sit on a meaningless minority of Du Pont equity, but the 50 percent slipped through the cracks.

———————

Everything progressed smoothly until that fateful moment when I entered Harold Fieldsteel's office. Typically solemn, almost taciturn, his
face was even longer than usual. Through constant conversations with
the "arbs" and the investment funds who now held most of Conoco's
stock, Harold had come to realize that our so-called safety net of 50
percent was working against us. Investors were not going to commit

their stock to us unless they knew we were going to accept it. Many of them preferred our cash to Du Pont stock. But if our cash did not materialize, they would lose a chance to be prorated between Du Pont stock and Du Pont cash, and would end up with only Du Pont stock. They wouldn't risk that.

"If we drop the net, we might be forced to take less than the 20 percent we need for equity accounting," Harold said. "But if we don't drop the net, we have virtually no chance of picking up much stock at all."

I called our advisers at Lazard Frères and Shearson, two of the shrewdest, toughest firms in the oil investment business.

"Keep the net," they both insisted. "Otherwise, the risk is too great."

There was no time to seek further advice or to contact the board. It was decision time.

I dropped the net.

Once again I had trusted my instincts, even in the face of contrary advice from the experts. Would my luck hold up, or had I overreached myself this time?

Before I had an answer, both of our investment bankers called back to advise that we should drop the net after all. They were surprised to learn that we had already done so (and no doubt chagrined when I pointed out that they couldn't charge us for this advice).

When the dust settled, we were the proud owners of just over 20 percent of the Du Pont shares. As Ed Jefferson, then the chairman and CEO of Du Pont, said later, "Edgar, the day you dropped the net, I knew we were going to have a new, big shareholder."

It had been a long but enormously profitable journey from Seagram's original investment in Texas Pacific Coal and Oil. With our 20 percent share of Du Pont, we now owned 20 percent of Conoco, which represented far more oil and gas in the ground than all of Texas Pacific's reserves when we had sold it to Sun Oil. And we owned 20 percent of the rest of Du Pont to boot!

Nevertheless, most of the press was highly critical. *Business Week,* for example, claimed that, when the news was announced, one Du

Pont senior executive boastfully ordered "Seagram on the rocks." But the truth was quite different. Only the inimitable Malcolm Forbes really understood the deal. "Who Lost the Battle for Conoco?" the headline of his article demanded. "Certainly Not Seagram." For the foreseeable future, Du Pont dividends would be extremely important to Seagram, and as Du Pont grew, so would our shares appreciate enormously.

I didn't lose any sleep over what the pundits had to say. I've learned that once a deal is made, there's no point in worrying about it. In fact, one of the worst mistakes managers make is that they try to make a bad decision look good.

In this case, I knew the decision was right. The dividend and cash flow would be great, and with the influence we now had over management decisions at Du Pont, I was confident we could help make the company even more profitable.

As I prepared to meet the Du Pont executives with whom Seagram and I would be so closely associated, it was clear that I had made the right choice in dropping the safety net. But I had no inkling that, with this single decision, I had set off a series of events that would ultimately make Seagram larger, more powerful, and more diverse than even my father could ever have imagined.

How had I reached my decision? Informed intuition, plain good luck, or the solid judgment of an experienced businessman? Probably a mixture of all three. In a sense, my whole life had been a training ground for making this sort of decision—and getting it right.

CHAPTER 2

———◆———

THE LITTLE PRINCE

M y father was an empire builder. And, true to the customs of his times, the emperor needed a male heir. As the first son among four children born to my parents, I was destined to be that heir.

In truth, Sam Bronfman wanted a clone. This fact goes a long way toward explaining why my childhood was more of an endurance test than a time of nurture. Father's dreams of passing on his empire were eventually realized, but at a high cost.

I've written briefly about my early life in my first book, *The Making of a Jew*, but in order to explore the making of a businessman, it will be useful to examine it here and to enlarge on it in other ways. I grew up in Montreal, where my parents had moved from Winnipeg, Manitoba, in 1922, seven years before I was born. At that time, Montreal was the largest, most cosmopolitan city in Canada. More important, Quebec was the only province that had not yet taken control of the wholesale liquor business, and therefore was the logical place for Father and his brothers to pursue their ambitions.

Montreal was overwhelmingly French, but unlike today, the

French-Canadians had little influence. Though English speakers accounted for only about one-third of the city's million-plus population, the largest subgroup, white Anglo-Saxon Protestants, ran most of the institutions and called most of the shots. Next came the Irish Catholics, followed by about 65,000 Jews. Not all that well established, Montreal's Jewish community was always speculating about who would be the first Jew to be a senator, to be on the board of a major bank, to be on the board of McGill University, and so on.

The Bronfmans were easily the city's most prominent Jewish family and enjoyed a lifestyle consistent with that status. My childhood home was 15 Belvedere Road, a beautiful estate in the suburb of Westmount. We had a large staff: a butler, a cook, a kitchen maid, a parlor maid, a "lady's maid," a laundress, a gardener, a chauffeur, a "mademoiselle" for the girls, and a nanny for the boys. In the material realm, we wanted for nothing.

Conspicuous by its absence, however, was love. This most essential gift was not to be had from Father, whose business obligations and emotional predisposition left little time or room for paternal tenderness. Nor was it forthcoming from Mother, with whom I was to enjoy a close relationship only in later years.

My parents' inability to provide a loving environment rendered our home, already made gloomy by the heavy furniture and poor light, even more oppressive. Small wonder that I have little nostalgia for the place, or for Montreal itself, to which I return only for meetings of the Seagram board of directors.

To understand my mostly unhappy childhood, you must know something about Father, and the experiences that shaped him. A short, stout man with blue eyes, thinning hair, and a round, babyish face, Sam Bronfman was unremarkable in appearance. In all other respects, he was anything but ordinary.

Throughout his life, Father was a driven, insecure person, the dominant force in his own family as well as those of his brothers and sisters. His lifelong ambition was to "be somebody"—a status he achieved early on but, in his own mind, could never quite attain.

This deeply ingrained insecurity no doubt stemmed from his

modest roots. He had grown up in Saskatchewan, and later Brandon, Manitoba, the third son in a family of eight children. Though he claimed to have been born in Canada, a passport I discovered after his death proved that, in fact, his native country was Russia. Mindful of the anti-Soviet feeling that prevailed for so long in the West, he simply hid the truth about his birth, and was never betrayed by his siblings.

Much to my regret, I know very little about Father's childhood— the subject was taboo among both him and his siblings. I was never even told what kind of work my grandfather did (although, according to family lore, he arrived from Russia with a sack of tobacco seeds, which of course were of no use to him in the harsh Canadian climate). But it is clear that my grandfather did not earn much, and that there were few material comforts; indeed, as a six-year-old boy, Father had to wear torn clothing to school.

Such deprivation filled young Sam with shame and instilled in him a fierce aversion to poverty. This almost primal reaction to the hardships of his youth found expression in his dogged pursuit of financial fortune and social recognition, which in turn had a profound influence on how his own children were reared.

Father's initial commercial venture was in the hotel business— "hotel" being a euphemism for a bar, a pool table, a kitchen, and a couple of rooms upstairs. When Canadian prohibition was enacted and each province took over all retailing of beverage alcohol, the Bronfman family began shipping on an interprovincial basis, which was perfectly legal. Province after province took over the wholesale business as well as the retail, and the Bronfmans relocated to Quebec, the last province to do so. When that province also took over control of the wholesale business, the family went into the distilling business.

In 1924, the Bronfmans opened a plant in Ville LaSalle, outside Montreal. Father and his younger brother, Allan, took the boat to England and managed to convince the Distillers Corporation Limited to be a full partner in the new enterprise. They shipped bulk malt whiskey in barrels to Ville LaSalle, where it was blended with product from a Coffey still—named for the man who had invented it—and the resulting product was called Highland Whiskey and sold to the provinces. Four years later, Father and his brothers bought a second distillery from the Seagram family, and Distillers Corporation–Seagrams Ltd. was born. In 1992, I was in New Delhi at the residence of the Canadian high commissioner. Frank Wisner, the American ambassador, was there. Hearing the story of where the name Seagram had come from, he asked, "Why would anyone sell a distillery in 1928?" I could come up with only one answer, which almost forced the wife of the Israeli ambassador to fall off her chair with laughter. I said: "*Goyim.*"

How much business Father and his brothers did with bootleggers was never clear, although Father insisted that everything they did was perfectly legal. One thing was certain: when American Prohibition was lifted, the Bronfman name was tarnished by lawsuits brought by the U.S. government against Canadian companies that had dealt with bootleggers. Though Father didn't let it stop him from building his empire, he was deeply and permanently wounded by the impugning of his reputation.

Sam Bronfman was not the type of man who licked his wounds quietly. If he was upset—and he often was—someone was going to hear about it, and in the most profane language imaginable. Those who knew him, including his family, lived in fear of his legendary outbursts.

As we grew up, it became apparent that Father always had a target at which he could rail. Frequently it was his brother Allan. I recall one time, during an annual meeting of shareholders, when Father first cursed out Uncle Allan, and later during lunch threw a glassful of ice water at him.

This incident notwithstanding, Father was never physically abusive. And his outbursts, though monumental, were usually short-lived. I even used to kid him about his temper. One day I walked into his office while he was talking to a government official named Simms who was in charge of corn allocations in Ottawa. "Never mind my goddamn blood pressure!" he screamed into the phone. When we returned to the house, I got everybody to start singing "Corn is busting out all over." By that time he was calmed down, and he smiled somewhat ruefully.

For my siblings and me, Father's frightful specter loomed more as a threat than as a reality, since he was rarely at home. Long before commercial air travel, he boarded the train in Montreal every Sunday night, stayed in New York City during the week, and returned by train the following Saturday morning. He then went not to synagogue like the rest of us, but to the Montreal office. After all, he had an empire to build.

Father did make time for what he called his "lessons in life." Perhaps homilies would be a better description. He loved to lecture us nonstop whenever he was home. Though he was not an educated man, he read voraciously and thus could sprinkle his sermons with literary allusions. If talk about sex had not been taboo, "lessons in life" could have been interesting, but neither Father nor Mother would even speak of anything to do with sex, let alone explain it.

Instead, a man named Ben Raginski was hired to teach the girls about sex. Ben was a doctor of psychosomatic medicine whom my parents knew from Winnipeg. Eventually, he became a kind of all-purpose counselor for my siblings and me.

Almost despite himself, Father did teach us the importance of high moral values. I say despite because, great pontificator that he was, we learned right from wrong through his actions, not his words.

I'm the first to admit that Father was a deeply flawed man, but at the same time, he abided by a core set of principles rooted in his Jewish faith. These principles were evident in the way he ran his business, as well as in his prodigious fund-raising efforts on behalf of numerous Jewish and non-Jewish charities. Perhaps a greater testament to Father is that, even with all the time spent away from home, there was never so much as a rumor about infidelity. Throughout his life, he remained faithful to Mother, as well as to his business—and, in his very imperfect way, to his kids.

Though Father wasn't around much during my early years, I certainly felt his presence when he was. The opposite is true of Mother: while physically present, to me she was remote and inaccessible.

Saidye Rosner (she picked that strange spelling to be different) was a beautiful young woman, the second daughter of Samuel and Priscilla Rosner of Plum Coulee, Manitoba, and later Winnipeg. Tall for her generation—a shade over five feet six—with brown eyes, thick black hair, and a full figure, she smiled easily and was always very popular. (Her dream in high school was to be a cheerleader, an unattainable ambition for a Jewish girl from a religious family.) I'm told she had a great sense of humor, though I didn't witness it growing up. She was socially much more at ease than Father and was always quite happy in her own skin, something I did recognize and admire.

Between them, Mother and Father seemed to have decided that she was responsible for the girls and he for the boys. For practical purposes, that meant that they dealt with us via separate surrogates, he with our nanny and she with the "mademoiselle." The girls lived on the same floor as Mother and Father, while we lived on the top floor with the nanny. In fairness, Mother didn't leave everything to the proxy and spent some time with the girls, including listening in on their telephone conversations.

With regard to Charles and me, Mother was remote. Indeed, our diminutive Scottish nanny, Helen MacDonald, whom we called Cutie, played a greater role in our early lives. A real martinet, she was constantly threatening us with impending punishment. "Wait until I tell your father," she would say, and though the punishment never came, I still felt the sword of Damocles ever present.

Perhaps what I wanted was to have Mother intercede with Father, or more likely to comfort me when Cutie's ominous words were uttered. But she had decided not to interfere, and she never did. Hers were the sins of omission, not commission.

One occasion best sums up this maternal void. I had been caught throwing torpedoes—water balloons—at passing cars and got the usual "Wait until I tell your father . . . " from Cutie. When I told Mother that I was going to run away from home, she replied, "What will you do for money?" and started to give me some cash. I rushed off to my room in tears. I felt that she wasn't there for me.

Indeed, I was probably closer in some ways to the family chauffeur than to either Father or Mother. He was a real hero to me, filling the parental void.

———

As for my siblings, I was really close only with my younger brother, Charles, who arrived two years and seven days after me. I learned later that Father actually persuaded Mother to take castor oil to see if they could coax him into the world on my birthday, which coincidentally fell on their wedding anniversary. Charles, bless him, held out for a week. Father had this fetish of having things happen on the same day. After his first child, Minda, was born, he had decided to celebrate his birthday on hers. He had someone calculate that his birthday on the Jewish calendar coincided with hers, the fourth of March. At one time he was toying with creating a family crest with the slogan "March Forth." Just as he had stolen Minda's birthday, he wanted my brother to steal mine!

Charles was not only the baby in our immediate family, but also brought up the rear behind cousins Edward and Peter, who lived next door. As a youngster, he looked frail. At the end of World War II, when he was fourteen, we used to joke that he would make a perfect model for the "Milk for Britain" ads showing starving, pale British kids in need of nutrition. He actually did suffer from a series of illnesses as a child, and was saved from a bout of double pneumonia by sulfa and then penicillin.

Charles was treated as a love object. I have early recollections of Father always squeezing his hand and fondling him. As time went on, I thought he was regarded as an insurance policy, in case something should happen to me.

If I resented the love he received, I'm certain Charles must have struggled with growing up in the shadow of both Father and me. Still, there was always great affection between us. Thankfully, we never engaged in competition over our eventual position with Seagram. Somehow, it was just understood that I would be in charge.

It was different with my sisters. When I arrived, my older sister, Minda, was four and quickly became jealous of the attention I received. Who could blame her? I was the prince. Even without me, it wouldn't have been easy being father's firstborn, the daughter of a man who made Queen Victoria look like a swinger.

My entry as first son didn't bother my sister Phyllis in the slightest. At two and a half, she was already rebelling. When she was young, she would hold food in her mouth for hours rather than swallow something she didn't want to eat. She was also a bit of a bully, particularly toward Charles, though she's always been short of height (a trait inherited from our grandmothers). But for the most part, she paid little attention to either of us until we were old enough to play ice hockey, and only then because she wanted to play, too. By the time I reached twenty, however, Phyllis and I had become good friends.

While my early years held little joy, they weren't entirely bleak.

Though Father was seldom there, I have warm memories of Friday-night dinners, the time when observant Jews welcome the Sabbath. Passover also was very special. My maternal grandparents would visit and, in addition to having the two seders (the traditional Passover meal) at home, we would gather for lunches at Uncle Allan's and Uncle Harry's.

It was at a family seder that I got drunk for the first time when I insisted on following the custom of drinking four cups of wine.

Then there was my bar mitzvah, which came right in the middle of World War II. As I approached the great day, I suddenly became very conscious of my Jewishness, going so far as to ask to be called "Edgar Moses," the translation of my middle name.

Saturday, June 20, 1942, was a handsome day. I was in good voice even though it was changing, and I belted out my portion of the service with vigor.

The night before, Father had stayed up late writing me a bar mitzvah letter. It was full of "lessons in life," but he also included some poetic phrases and references to his own father that moved me. My parents' gift was an ambulance in my name for the war effort. I was very pleased, since all of us on the home front were eager to contribute in any way we could.

The bar mitzvah luncheon at 15 Belvedere was wonderful, with a garden party and a forty-pound fruit cake baked especially for me by my older cousin, Allan Bronfman Jr. I'm not at all sure how he got that name. In Ashkenazi Judaism one does not name a child after a living relative—only after one who has passed on—yet Allan Jr. was Harry Bronfman's firstborn, and Allan Sr. was Harry's youngest brother. In home movies of the festivities, you can read the cursing on my lips as I struggled to move the knife through Allan's massive creation. That evening was reserved for my parents' anniversary celebration. I had been born on their seventh anniversary; this, then, was their twentieth, and we were allowed to stay up very late to celebrate with them. I can still hear the songs—"Moonlight Cocktails," "A Sleepy Lagoon," "Don't Fence Me In"—and see the guests dancing under a starry sky.

—•—

Odd as it may seem, Father and Mother had a wonderful relationship. They loved each other until his death and trusted each other absolutely. They shared one bank account, and Mother, who ran a large household, could write as many checks as she wanted. Later on I was amazed to discover how many business matters Father had discussed with Mother. In deference to his ego, she never revealed her involvement in his professional life.

Father's relationship with Mother, of course, was the exception to the rule. He was always having a war with somebody. He saved his biggest war for Uncle Allan. Uncle Allan brought some of it on himself by always speaking in terms of "we," as if he and Father were equal partners and equally responsible for the family's success. They weren't—a fact I had to explain as a teenager to my dismayed cousins Peter and Edward, Allan's sons. (Of the four boys—Peter, Edward, Charles, and me—I was the only one who knew something about the financial relationship between Father's family and Allan's family.)

The truth was that Father had total control over Allan's shares in Seagram through a holding company. All of Sam and Allan's Seagram shares had been placed in trusts for the benefit of their children and grandchildren. The Sam family trusts owned a company called CEMP Investments Ltd. (Charles, Edgar, Minda, Phyllis) and CEMP in turn owned 67.8 percent of Seco Investments, Ltd. Edper Investments Ltd. (Edward, Peter) owned the remaining 32.2 percent of Seco, which in turn owned all the Seagram shares that had previously been owned by Sam and Allan.

(CEMP itself was divided 30 percent each for the boys and 20 percent each for the girls. This allotment became a bone of contention in later years, but for 1942, it was quite liberal. At that time, the business was almost always left to the sons, while the daughters received cash.)

———

Shortly after my bar mitzvah, our family went to stay at Ste.-Marguerite, as we did every summer and on weekends year-round.

I have fond recollections of this place. Our house was on a beautiful estate some sixty miles northwest of Montreal in the Laurentian Mountains. The property was two square miles, and had five lakes. One was stocked with fish, and the butler, a Finn we called Silver, used to go out early in the morning to catch a fish for Father's breakfast. The estate also had two cows and a separator, the device that separates cream from milk. To this day, I recall the wonderful taste of the ice cream from that rich cream.

The house was large, with ten or more bedrooms, lots of bathrooms, and a living room so gigantic that its dining area, which seated twelve, was a mere nook. During the winter, I would ski, no matter the temperature. Afterward, I liked to sit in one of the comfortable chairs that ringed the huge fireplace and gaze deeply into the fire, dreaming and dozing as the flames danced above the burning logs.

———

During the summer of my fifteenth year, I received a telephone call from Hugh Reid, who was the Alpine Inn's golf pro in the summer and who ran the ski tow at Hill 60, that hotel's ski place, in the winter. I had caddied for the last two weeks of the previous summer, and he wanted to see me. I rode my bike down the mile and a half to the golf course, and he asked me if I would caddy for a Mr. Kenny from New York. In those days, golfers were at a premium, and Mr. Kenny insisted on having an English-speaking caddy or he would play elsewhere. Mr. Kenny paid a dollar a bag for fourteen holes, except sometimes his daughter also would play—she had a very light bag, and then it would be three dollars, a munificent sum. Sensing a negotiating possibility, I seemed reluctant at first as I thought it over. Then I announced that I would caddy in the afternoons only if I wanted to, and that I would not caddy for women. "Why not?" I was asked. "Because they're too slow and they don't tip very much."

Mr. Reid had no problem with that, so then I asked that if I didn't caddy, could I play golf—for free? A reluctant "Yes," and then I stated that I didn't know how to play golf and asked for six free lessons. "Will you pay the boy who shags the golf balls?" was his now-angry retort—I had gored *his* bull—and I left well enough alone. When I got home, I told Mother with some pride that I had agreed to be a caddy. Her reaction, and I was always proud of her not being the typical Jewish mother, was that of a typical Jewish mother. You're not strong enough, she said. I haughtily told my mother that I was very strong and that I had already agreed to caddy. She relented somewhat, but said that I should not caddy in the afternoons. "What do you mean, not caddy in the afternoons—I have agreed to be a caddy!" "I'll pay you what you make in the morning, dear, but don't caddy in the afternoons." So I played for free in the afternoons and got paid by Mother to do so.

———

One summer stands out in my memory, no doubt because it was so different from the rest of my youth. The year was 1945, and at the age of sixteen I got a job in Montreal as an office boy at Holt, Renfrew and Company (a store similar to New York's Bergdorf Goodman), which was run by a friend of the family, Alvin J. Walker.

These were to be the best months of my childhood. Father's car dropped me off in the morning. At the end of the day, I would walk to the Seagram office a couple of blocks away and work the switchboard while I waited for him. Then the two of us would go home together and eat out on the veranda. I don't remember any lectures, only pleasant conversations. He also gave me the money to take the chauffeur's daughter to the movies once a week.

For once, I had time with my father alone. And, for once, I felt loved.

Perhaps the defining moment that summer came one day when I saw a watch I wanted to buy. I asked Father for a loan, and after agreeing on how I would repay him, he gave me a signed blank check.

I was overwhelmed. Somehow, the trust he placed in me felt like the greatest gift I had ever received from him.

———————

My childhood was marked by a tension between privilege on the one hand, and emotional dysfunction on the other. Adding another element of confusion was the role of Jewish identity in our lives. The fact of our Jewishness was never in doubt but the contradictory ways in which it found expression created a deep ambivalence in me that took many years to resolve.

Giving their sons a Jewish education was clearly important to my parents. Twice a week, a Lithuanian woman named Luba Gordon taught Charles and me to read Hebrew by translating the Bible with us. They also insisted that Charles and I go to junior congregation on Saturdays and to Sunday school the next day, though we usually played hooky from Sabbath services with our cousins Edward and Peter. Ultimately, we received the same rudimentary knowledge of the Jewish religion as our parents had, and were taught very little Hebrew. I wish now that the two hours a week had been spent on real Jewish studies rather than Bible translation, which to a child is little more than nonsense.

Father, meanwhile, was a great Anglophile, a fact reflected in our daily education. Charles and I did not go to Jewish schools, but instead were enrolled at the Selwyn House School, where we were among a tiny handful of Jewish boys.

Going to Selwyn House during the week and religious school on the weekend created great confusion in our lives. We had two sets of friends: the WASPs at Selwyn, and the Jews from synagogue, whom we saw only on Saturdays and Sundays (when we deigned to attend). I don't know if Father ever understood the puzzlement this fostered, though I doubt he did. It was an arrangement that, in my eyes, made our Jewish friends second class. Even today, I still find myself wondering why I regarded the Jews we saw on the weekends as less fun and less important than the elite Protestant group we went to school with every day. The answer may be that our parents felt this way.

One thing's for sure: Father had a real love for Canada, a country that had welcomed his family and so many other Jews looking to start a new life. He believed that Canada, following in the tradition of English libertarianism, had made it possible for Jews to live as *almost* first-class citizens under the Union Jack.

Of course, during World War II, Canada was no better than the United States in opening its doors to Jews who were trying to escape the death camps. Nevertheless, as president of the Canadian Jewish Congress, Father threw himself into rallying Jews to the support of the British Empire. (He did get the Canadian government to accept 1,000 orphans, with the assurance that they would be self-supporting or supported by the Jewish community.)

By virtue of his position in the CJC, Father knew early on that the Nazis were murdering Jews. Thus, he and the entire Jewish community were very supportive of the war. Both he and Mother played leading roles in raising money and organizing support for the war effort. In fact, in 1943, Mother was made an officer of the Order of the British

Empire for her work. (Father's efforts would surely have been recognized as well had it not been for the residual damage done to the Bronfman name during Prohibition. In one of his truly great gestures, he eloquently congratulated his wife without showing a trace of envy.)

Yet before the war was over, my parents' conflicting impulses as proud Jews on the one hand, and empire builders on the other resulted in the worst educational decision they ever made—sending me to Trinity College School (TCS).

This was the fall of 1944. By then, news of the Nazi slaughter of Jews was becoming common knowledge. Having come from Selwyn House, where I encountered no prejudice, I was shocked by the anti-Semitic episodes I experienced at TCS, a high Anglican Church school.

No one said anything to my face, but I constantly overheard comments denigrating Jews. I was the first Jew ever to attend TCS, whose headmaster, Philip Ketcham, was the first in school history not to have been a bishop of the Anglican Church. Both Charles and I were forced to spend two unhappy years in this den of intolerance.

At TCS, students were required to attend chapel every day and twice on Sunday. As a Jew, I was allowed to skip one Sunday service—an exception as illogical as my parents' decision to enroll me there in the first place.

The confusing nature of my tenure at TCS is perhaps best exemplified by the food I ate. Like everyone else, I consumed whatever was served, including bacon and ham and pork—foods that were strictly off limits in my parents' kosher house. Somehow, I guess they thought I could eat *treyf* (non-kosher food) away from home. The hypocrisy of this situation, like so much surrounding our identity as Jews, seems to have escaped them. It echoed Father's practice of going to the office on Saturdays. I didn't, and don't, fault him for working on the Sabbath, only for his inconsistency. Why, I would ask myself, could my parents demand from us what they didn't ask of themselves? Wasn't attending temple supposed to be a family affair? Not in our family.

Experiences like these left me angry and resentful, and contributed to my later rejection as a young man of Jewish observance and ritual.

———

Besides the far from negligible issue of religious affiliation, my educational experience was characterized by above-average academic performance and, as I got older, rebellious behavior.

At Selwyn House, we were graded every week. All Father wanted to know from me was how well I had done; I don't remember any conversation about anything else related to school. If I came in second, he asked why I hadn't placed first. "Build the foundations for your future," he would lecture. My response was to make a habit of coming in second, knowing that if I finished first more than once, I would be expected to do so all the time.

I was a reasonably good athlete, and my favorite sport was hockey. I skated well, and during my last two years at Selwyn House I played defense for the school team.

Selwyn House, of course, was a boys' school. In my last year there, some other kids and I organized a dance class with some girls at the nearby Trafalgar School. This was a delicate matter, since my parents already suspected that I was not only dabbling in sex, but doing so with non-Jewish girls. Eating non-kosher food was one thing, but getting involved with a *shikse* was a whole other matter.

In fact, I knew nothing about girls at this point, and would remain ignorant at TCS, where my teenage rebellion took on different forms. TCS was a prep school designed to be as much like the public schools of England as possible. Aside from the Jewish problem, I did not take well to the demands placed upon "new boys." I was paddled by the prefects once for no particular reason—just for my general attitude. (The greater indignity was that new boys had to make the paddles for the prefect in the workshop.)

It was at TCS that I took an aptitude test, which under different circumstances might have changed my life. My law scores flew off the charts—rarely had the school officials seen such a marked aptitude for one area as compared with all others. I duly reported this to Father, who, taking a minute or two to recover, told me that lawyers make very good businessmen, and that if I wanted to go to law school he would certainly not object.

In truth, I never considered it, certain I could learn more about business under Father's tutelage. But had there been a combination law-and-business degree, which there is now, I might have taken it.

By the time I finished TCS, career decisions were the last thing on my mind. At seventeen, I was a very frustrated young man, headed for trouble.

Once again, my parents facilitated my plunge into the abyss by enrolling me at Williams College in Massachusetts. Thus began a chapter in my life I wish I could rewrite, though in hindsight it was probably a necessary brush with disaster.

The year was 1946. Most of my classmates were ex-servicemen home from the war who were taking advantage of the G.I. Bill. At seventeen, I was much younger than 90 percent of my classmates—and, thanks to my sheltered upbringing, more immature than most of those my age.

In his welcoming address, the college president urged us not to let our studies interfere with our education. For two and a half years, I took him at his word.

Later, I could see what happened. I had gone from a highly structured home and a highly regimented boarding school to the wonderfully permissive environment of a liberal-arts college. Williams had rules, but compared to where I had been, I felt as free as a bird.

During my freshman year I set about getting the grades I needed to qualify for unlimited class cuts, a well-intended policy that no doubt claimed many casualties. Thereafter, everything went downhill. I learned to party, discovered the girls at Bennington (just seventeen miles north on U.S. Route 7), and stopped caring about my studies. The Delta Phi fraternity house, where I lived, was far off the beaten track and even less supervised than other fraternities.

I became competitive, especially about my drinking capacity. By the beginning of my junior year, I was in a steep decline. My work was barely adequate and my partying was constant. I was out of control.

My recklessness came to the attention of my parents when I proposed marriage to a young woman one weekend during a house party at Williams. Father and Mother were in Europe, and I cabled them the news. After their initial shock and puzzlement, I was brought back to Montreal and spent time with Ben Raginsky.

I now realize that my cable was a cry for help. I was eighteen; I didn't want to get married. What I wanted was help in figuring out my life. Unfortunately, Father and Mother saw only the symptom and not the illness.

Ben didn't get it, either, even though I had been seeing him off and on over the years. I was sure that he would understand, and I did everything I could—except tell him outright—to get him to persuade Father that I shouldn't go back to Williams. I thought he would see that I was too immature to handle the freedom, the booze, the girls at Bennington, and that I was getting into serious trouble. He didn't, and he later knew that I never forgave him for that lack of insight.

Eventually, though, I got my wish, thanks to a motorcycle accident that easily could have cost me my life. Father had made me promise never to use a motorcycle. When I called home that Sunday to report my accident, he came straight down to Williamstown, and that was the end of Williams for me. Father arranged for me to resign from the college rather than being kicked out, and two months shy of my twentieth birthday, I headed home to Montreal.

———

My confused rebellion had taken me to the brink of self-destruction. Now, living once again at 15 Belvedere Road, I felt a sense of relief to be back home. The stultifying confines of my youth had become a refuge from the emotional trauma of the past few years.

As real as that trauma was, I somehow knew that I would get through it. Early on, I developed an ability to stand outside myself. "You know," I would say to myself, "five years from now, you're going to look back at this and laugh." This detachment proved to be an invaluable coping mechanism.

That fall I went to McGill, and two years later would graduate with honors. Mother decorated a room for Charles and me on the third floor of the house, which we outfitted with a state-of-the-art sound system, a bar, and some easy chairs, in which we could sit and enjoy the house's commanding view of the city. Mother also bought some very old muskets to be used as lampposts. Father yelled, "There will be no guns in my house!" They had to go—a petty tyrant with a whim of iron!

It was during this time that Charles and I went into business with his close friend Leo Kolber. We put up the money—Father had arranged for Charles and me to have a certain amount of tax-free money deposited into our account from the trusts he had set up for his four children—and Leo bought small pieces of real estate for a carried interest. Though they were small, practically all of our deals were successful. We also invested in the stock market and did quite well.

It might seem that, by giving us the means to start our own business at such a young age, Father was quite lenient with his sons, and in certain respects that was true. But there is little doubt that the king was also testing his callow princes in a harmless way to see whether they had inherited any of his instincts. Strangely enough, he really believed that because we were his sons, we would not fail: "Blood counts!" was one of his favorite expressions. When I asked him once how he explained the apparent shortcomings of his brothers, whom he was forever castigating, there was no response other than the familiar glare.

In any case, we had passed this first test, though if he was proud of us, he certainly didn't let on. One thing I never saw Father do was give a compliment.

If there was any way of gauging how Father felt about us, it was by winning his trust. For trust, we had learned early on, equaled love.

In the late spring of 1950, Charles and I told Father that we wanted to take a road trip through the United States and Canada. Despite all my vehicular accidents, Father actually agreed to allow his two sons—the inheritors of the empire he was building—to travel by car for thousands of miles. At first he asked us to take his chauffeur along, but we refused. We finally agreed to send him a collect telegram every night letting him know where we were and that we were okay.

To this day I can recall our itinerary. It took us from Montreal to Vancouver via Galveston, Texas. I celebrated my twenty-first birthday in San Francisco, listening to Mel Torme perform at the Fairmont Hotel's Venetian Room.

The trip represented a major milestone for both of us in our relationship with Father. The next summer, after graduating from McGill, I got an even bigger boost. While working for Seagram at Ville LaSalle, I began to pay serious attention to Father's stock market account. He and Uncle Allan had a joint account, two-thirds belonging to Father, and, having put all their Seagram stock in trusts for their children and grandchildren, both of them lived off this capital, which was invested in the stock market.

Allan was a lousy investor and was of no help to Father. However, I had a flair for the market, which did not go unnoticed by Father. To facilitate my handling of his account, Father gave me his power of attorney, an enormous expression of confidence that left me deeply gratified.

Soon after, I suggested that the brothers split the account and go their own way. Uncle Allan operated on tips from less-than-intelligent people, and his influence on the account was negative. I operated on instinct, along with the premise that the market was on the way up because the world was still recovering from World War II and had a long way to go. My promise to Father was that I would buy and sell, but always on the understanding that, if he didn't approve, I would cancel the order. (That never happened.) I was astonished, given my age, that he took my advice and left his account in my hands.

Perhaps he had been emboldened by an incident the previous summer. Charles and I were debating which was the better buy, Seagram stock or the stock of a small oil company based in Alberta called Royalite, of which the Sam and Allan Bronfman families had bought control. I advocated Seagram because the stock was too low; Charles said Royalite because it was oil.

We decided to ask Father to arbitrate our dispute. "For the long pull, Seagram, but for the short run, Royalite," he declared.

I told Charles that Father was wrong. "Who should I listen to, you or him?" he said rhetorically. Agreeing that his position was reasonable, I suggested that he buy some Royalite, I buy Seagram, and at the end of the summer we compare notes. Of course, I won, or I wouldn't be telling the story.

Another monumental development was also set in motion after I graduated from McGill: my courtship of Ann Loeb, a Bennington girl whom I would later marry.

By now I was free. The trust Father had placed in me had augmented my own sense of self-worth, making me feel that I was ready to be an adult. But I had no idea what great adventures lay ahead.

CHAPTER 3

LEARNING THE ROPES: EARLY YEARS AT SEAGRAM

Though Father groomed his sons from the cradle to take their place in the company, he had no clear idea of a career path for either Charles or me, and left it up to us. This may sound uncharacteristically benevolent. In truth, because Father was a very unorganized man, he found it impossible to create a career path, or to ask someone else to do so. It just wasn't in his nature.

Father did ask me on many occasions if I wanted to do something other than run the business—even though it would have killed him if I had said yes. But there was never really any doubt in my mind as to what my life's work would be. I started with Seagram the day I was born, and always felt that I was part of the company.

It was different for my siblings, particularly the girls. Before I embark on the story of my Seagram career, I'd like to tell you a little more about them. For my life, both personal and professional, has always been inextricably bound up with that of my family.

All four of us knew from an early age that one day Father would pass the mantle to me. But while Charles and my younger sister, Phyllis, understood and accepted this, Minda did not, and her resentment marred our relationship right from the beginning.

Minda was an interesting woman. Slim, with thick black hair, she stood at five feet seven inches and had a hauteur that made her seem taller. Though she looked more like Mother, Minda had the classic Bronfman nose (which gave her character), as well as Father's temper.

Minda graduated from Smith College and got her master's at Columbia University. She worked at Lehman Brothers for a time and later at Time Inc., where she was eventually listed on the masthead.

The super-Victorian atmosphere of 15 Belvedere Road caused all of us considerable angst, but as the oldest child, Minda suffered the most. For her generation, she married late in life, entering matrimony just before the age of thirty. She and her husband, Baron Alain de Gunzburg, lived in Paris, where she fashioned an interesting life for herself. I have always speculated that she chose exile in order to escape her stifling existence as Sam Bronfman's daughter.

I visited Minda occasionally through the years, and whenever I had dinner at her home, the closed doors to the library would suddenly burst open and the butler would say, "*Madame la baronne est servie!*" Despite her husband's title, however, I believe that she was frustrated because she wanted him to outdo Father. Alain is a perfectly decent man, but that was asking too much.

Minda, unreconciled to the fact that I was to be Father's successor, had hoped that Alain would be looked upon as a full partner. Indeed, after Father died, I think Minda blamed Alain for not taking what she saw as his rightful place. Every once in a while, he would make some effort to assert himself, such as the time he proposed that he become chief executive of CEMP Investments Ltd., the family holding company. I rejected the idea, perhaps too brusquely (though I refrained from quoting Browning, who once said, "Ah, but a man's reach should exceed his grasp, or what's a heaven for?").

Minda also resented that Father had bequeathed the boys 30 percent of his estate each, while the girls received only 20 percent apiece.

This bothered Phyllis as well, but to a much lesser extent, and in principle rather than personally.

I had a difficult time with Minda. It always seemed that she was intent on undermining me, and I wasn't about to allow that. The truth is, she made it impossible for me to like her. I could admire her, but I couldn't let down my guard.

Her frustrations eventually led her to hire a French lawyer to extricate her from the rest of the family. She started selling Seagram stock, which put a lot of strain on an already taut relationship and for a time created some unfortunate tension between her children and mine. Because she lived in Paris, I saw her infrequently, which contributed to the distance between us. She named her second son Charles Samuel, perhaps to tell me what she thought of me, though her choice was consistent with the Jewish tradition of naming the first son after the father's father and the second after the mother's. (Father actually tried to get Charles Samuel de Gunzburg to change his name to Samuel Charles—what an extravagant ego!)

It's hard to say whether the relationship between us would have improved had she lived. It's possible that both of us would have mellowed. Her son Charles, of whom I am very fond and who lives in America, might have helped bring us closer.

When Minda learned that she had liver cancer, she took it bravely. Unable to tolerate the pitying stance many people assume when they learn that someone has a fatal illness, she refused to tell anyone with the exception of her husband and sons. Phyllis, Charles, and I didn't know it until well after the diagnosis. She especially didn't want Mother to know, thinking that Mother might die before her and be spared having to bury a child. But her time ran out, and we mourned her death together, as we still do.

Fortunately, my relationship with Phyllis is far different. We have been close all of our adult lives, and I am extremely proud of her achievements. She has more honorary degrees than most U.S. presidents and has become a great citizen of Canada and the world.

Phyllis studied first at Cornell and then at Vassar. She was the first among the four of us to marry, wedding Jean Lambert, an Alsatian Jew whom neither Father nor I trusted. (Mother persuaded Father to give his consent, saying that Phyllis would have married Jean anyway. I agreed with that analysis, but I wasn't so sure that Jean would have gone through with it if Father had been adamant.) He had dated Minda earlier and, while I didn't hold that against him, I was convinced he was a fortune hunter. Whenever he entered the room, I would move to the piano and pick out with one finger Cole Porter's "I've Come to Wife It Wealthily in Padua." I would have loved to have a physical confrontation.

They ended up divorcing amicably, after which Phyllis moved out of the apartment she had bought and eventually settled in Paris. Father and Mother were very worried about their little girl living in that wicked city, and they managed to lure her back by enlisting her talents in the construction of the Seagram Building (I'll describe that episode in chapter 4).

After brilliantly completing that job, she studied architecture at Yale, then got her degree in architecture from the University of Chicago, and went on to create an impressive career for herself.

Thereafter, Phyllis chose to stay in Montreal and, while no longer a working architect, she broadened her horizons to encompass the whole of architecture, its history and impact on the human race, and the preservation of architectural sites. She involved herself in many projects, and was so busy that she resembled the one-armed paper hanger, the difference being that Phyllis got things done. (In the spirit of the late Hurricane Andrew, she was once described to an audience she was about to address as Hurricane Phyllis.) She formed the Save Montreal Society, and in large part because of her efforts that city now has a preservation code. She managed to get along well with the feisty and popular mayor, Jean Drapeau, and even convinced him, as he indulged himself in his edifice complex, to do the proper ecological thing upon occasion.

Phyllis is now the director of the Canadian Center of Architecture, which is a dream come true. She has told Charles and me that, being childless, this is her baby, and she has certainly devoted herself to it. The Center is constructed around a glorious old stone home built by a venerable Montreal family called Shaughnessy. Phyllis had owned the Shaughnessy mansion for many years before the Center was built and always had the idea of transforming it into a community resource. When the Center first opened, the *New York Times* gave its architect, Peter Rose, rave reviews.

Phyllis has always felt that each of us should be able to do his or her own thing. She was upset with Minda for wanting Alain to be the third wheel in running the business side of the family. She felt it was being well managed, and expressed the sentiment that "if the clock works, don't fix it." She suffers fools not at all, and is singularly impatient, but while these attributes might remind one of Father, she is no egomaniac.

Phyllis lives a reasonably simple life. Her friends are for the most part academics and, like herself, they are doers. She spends her time in a part of the city called Old Montreal, which she has helped restore and make fashionable through wise investment and clear-sighted vision.

Some years ago, just before his death, I had a conversation with President Anwar Sadat of Egypt about a peace initiative which would bring the three great monotheistic religions together. After Sadat's assassination, I discussed it further with then–Foreign Minister Boutros Boutros-Ghali. As a result, I agreed to pay for the restoration of the Ben Ezra synagogue in Cairo, the oldest synagogue outside Israel. It is located near both the oldest Coptic Christian church in the world, where some hold that the Holy Family sought safety, and a famous mosque where, legend has it, Mohammed hid when his life was in danger. I suggested that the work be entrusted to my sister Phyllis. She accepted the challenge and did a beautiful job. It is just one more contribution to what will one day be a formidable legacy.

I have also been blessed to have a lifelong friendship with my brother, Charles. There is a gentleness about him (there always was), humor in his eyes, and a sense of goodness when he speaks.

Although Charles, like me, was sent to Trinity College School, where he became the second Jew to attend (he was not at all robust, which partially explains why he had such a bad time, and his hatred of those years is with him to this day), he did not follow me to Williams College. Instead, he stayed home and went to McGill University. He did well in his course work but froze during examinations, so in his junior year he dropped out and started working at Seagram. After toiling away for a long time, he finally took over the entire Canadian business.

Father believed in the old British foreign policy of divide and conquer. While Charles was in Canada and I was in the United States, he told each of us uncomplimentary things about the other and deliberately kept us apart. His insecurity was such that he had a fear that we might combine and throw him out. Our friendship survived, thank the Lord.

Canadian operations are less complicated because the distribution and sales systems within the ten provinces are clear-cut, and eventually Charles might have become bored. But then he became involved in Mayor Jean Drapeau's efforts to get a Major League Baseball franchise for Montreal. Initially, ten or twelve of the city's leading businessmen expressed interest. But when Drapeau brought home the prize, one after another dropped out. Charles, meanwhile, kept writing checks until he owned more than 50 percent of the franchise.

I believe that Charles's newfound enthusiasm for baseball stemmed from two reasons: one, it would get him out from under Father's thumb; and, more important, he felt that it would be good for Montreal, and would give that divided city a common cause. He stuck it out for thirty years, then finally sold the team to a local group in 1993. He could have made much more money if he had been willing to sell to a party that wanted to move the franchise, but he felt a moral obligation to keep the team in Montreal.

Charles has worked hard on behalf of Canadian Jewish organizations as well as other philanthropic groups. He had a personal war in 1976 with René Levesque, Quebec's leading proponent of separatism, and was embarrassed when Levesque's political party won the election. He has spent a great deal of money trying to convince Canadians that the Dominion is worth keeping together. He has received many honorary degrees, and was named a member of the Privy Council and Commander of the Order of Canada, the highest distinction the Canadian government can bestow.

Today, Charles is co-chairman of Seagram. For many years, his main responsibility was as the liaison with Du Pont's management, an important role given our 25 percent share in the company. (During the course of our relationship with Du Pont, they initiated a share-repurchase program, which brought our percentage of ownership to just shy of 25 percent.) When it comes to the large decisions at Seagram, such as major acquisitions of Martell, Tropicana, and MCA, Charles and I are partners; we both have to agree before the project is presented to the board of directors. Charles has played the major role in selecting and securing members for what many consider the most talented and outstanding board in Canada, and perhaps in North America.

Charles married Barbara Baerwald, with whom he had two children, Steven and Ellen, both good kids. They were eventually divorced, and Charles married Andrea Morrison. Andy has three children, and Charles is a great stepfather to them just as Andy has a great relationship with Charles's kids.

Charles has moved his office out of the Seagram Building in Montreal and now spends much of his time working with his children and Andy on projects of the CRB Foundation, which he established. He and Les Wexner have put together an international group of prominent Jews who meet three or four times a year and discuss important issues. He's the leading donor to the Federation/Canadian Jewish Appeal in Montreal, carrying on a tradition Father started long ago. He has invested well in Israel, and takes much satisfaction in helping the Jewish state move toward economic autonomy. He's involved in numerous projects, but his biggest interest is in getting young North American Jews to visit Israel. Indeed, during a 1991 magazine interview, when asked how he would like to be remembered, he said, most generously, that Edgar would be remembered as a great president of the World Jewish Congress, and that he would like to be remembered "as a person who built a bridge between Diaspora youth and Israel." And he will.

—•—

At the end of the summer of 1951, I began working full-time for Seagram. I knew I needed to learn something about accounting, so I started as a clerk in the Montreal office on the accounts-payable ledger while also taking a correspondence course on the subject. Harry Cox, the comptroller of the Canadian companies, was a great help in the basics of double-entry bookkeeping. But I was now twenty-two, and a little accounting went a long way. After learning the rudiments of the system, I suggested to Father that I become more acquainted with the product. He heartily agreed, so I commuted to Ville LaSalle, where our original plant was located, to study the arts of manufacturing and blending. Even at that age, I was resolute in my feeling that if I was going to run the company one day, I had to know the product inside and out. I had a fervent desire to learn the process from step one, and the knowledge I was to gain would prove invaluable. The importance of understanding the product is something I cannot overemphasize—it is one of the foundations of becoming a successful businessman.

I had spent part of one summer working at the distillery, so I knew something about production. My job was working in the control lab and checking each phase of the operation. We even tested the grain coming into the distillery to make sure that it was the right humidity— no more than 14 percent moisture was allowed. When the grain (mostly corn) was ground, it was put into a large container, where it was boiled. This converted the starch to sugar. Then the yeast could convert the mash into alcohol, CO_2, and what we call spent mash. Our job was to monitor each procedure until the "beer"—the name generally given to the resultant product—went into the primary still. After each fermenter was dropped (meaning that its contents were transferred into a waiting tank before being sent to the primary still), an employee would descend into the fermenter, scrub out the remains, hose it down, then lime it to kill all bacteria before the next fermentation could begin. During the summer when I worked in the control laboratory, I would descend into the fermenter to clean out the remains of the spent mash. I did so because I was curious about the conditions. Knowing that CO_2 was heavier than air, I was concerned about breathing and sweating. It wasn't at all difficult to breathe, although it was hot.

I began working under Roy Martin, our chief blender. Roy was a wonderful man. Tall and thin, he had wavy hair and enthusiastic, gleaming eyes. Long before Father bought Seagram, Roy, then in his early teens, had started with the company in Waterloo, Ontario, as an office boy–accountant.

As chief blender, Roy was probably the most underpaid person in the history of the firm. I can't remember his salary, but he was the most vital guy in the whole organization—the one who planned everything, from production to inventory. While much of blending is accounting and inventory planning, the rest is a keen sense of taste and a good imagination, and Roy had both.

Considering the importance of the job he was doing, Roy's staff was tiny. He not only made every blend for every product we produced in Canada (including Seagram's VO, Crown Royal, and all the other whiskeys sold in Canada and abroad), but he was also in charge of inventory control, which was one of the keys to our profitability, then as now.

I learned an unbelievable amount about production from Roy. Indeed, on that subject, he taught me more than Father did, though in a sense he was Father's disciple.

One of Roy's invaluable lessons was to impress on me the importance of inventory control. When we'd look at a bad production sample, and we'd look at every one, he'd teach me to ask the next question: "Okay, this isn't good—why?" Sometimes we'd find a bad sample of a mature whiskey. What could possibly have happened? It could have been the result of a barrel left outside and possibly some rain had gotten in it, forming acetic acid. So we decided to put all our barrels under the roof. Sam Bronfman had put the words "Make finer whiskeys—make them taste better" into Joseph E. Seagram's litany, and we took them seriously.

I spent a good deal of time learning how to approve the quality of new production before it was barreled. This is extremely difficult because you have to know what a distillate will taste like four years or more down the line, and the only way you learn that is from experience. Fortunately, we had samples of old distillates on hand, and Roy taught me to compare them with the aged product.

It is difficult to describe flavors in words. Pick up a glass of your favorite whiskey and try to explain exactly how it tastes. Blenders therefore created a language of their own, and if I heard Roy say "fruity" or "musty" or "rough," I came to understand what he meant.

Perhaps the most important thing Roy taught me was the importance of the dignity of work. He was so proud of VO and how it tasted, proud to have that kind of job and do it well. That's something I carry with me to this day.

We traveled together a great deal. I remember when we bought a company named United Distillers, which had a brand called Harwood. We were desperate for inventory, and they had it. Roy and I went out there to taste it so that we could determine what was usable and what we had to redistill. By the time we were through, we had tasted every single barrel in the whole inventory. It was a turning point for me, because we were working as equals—there wasn't time to ask Roy what he thought of each sample.

Though I was learning from the best, it didn't take me long to initiate a major change at Ville LaSalle. In order to check the uniformity of our blends, girls from the bottling line were relieved from duty and asked to test the new samples. They were given three diluted shots to taste (and spit out): one of the current production, one of the proposed blend, and one of the standard. In theory, 50 percent would agree on one match and 50 percent on the other, indicating that there was no difference between the three samples. This was called the psychometric system.

I didn't trust this method and proposed a change. Under the new system, blenders would taste the new blend and compare it to the standard, thus determining whether they were consistent. Roy agreed, and from that time on product uniformity became the responsibility of the quality-control department.

Roy decided which whiskeys each of the distilleries would produce, and how much. I soon became deeply involved in his work, and together we planned to increase the size of the inventory, because we felt that both VO and Crown Royal would grow if we had the stock to back them up.

One evening, I went to Father and told him that I knew what I wanted for my birthday. He looked up over his glasses, just the way Arthur Schatz photographed him for *Fortune* magazine. I answered his unspoken question: "A new warehouse."

When I explained why we needed more space so that we could expand our inventories, he was delighted that I was already so involved in the business. "A good son asks for such a birthday present," he told Mother.

Interestingly enough, I didn't have to provide him with spreadsheets or the fifties equivalent. He probably knew the figures anyway. Nevertheless, I presented enough to be convincing. Inventory has to be based on sales projections, plus about 3 percent annual evaporation. I based my case on increasing sales, and proved to be right.

———

I stayed at Ville LaSalle for over three years. Not only was I learning, but Roy was so shorthanded that my help was truly needed.

The fact that I was the boss's son never presented a problem. Indeed, I was even asked to join the union when I was working at the plant. What I discovered is that people treat you the way you want to be treated. If you're friendly and humble, you'll be accepted. If you stick your nose in the air and constantly remind others of who you are, you'll be kept at arm's length. It's up to you.

In my case, the rarefied upbringing at 15 Belvedere Road had fostered a desire in me to be a regular guy. Father was forever telling me how special I was—in other words, that I wasn't normal. He meant well, but no kid likes to be taken out of his peer group. This was something I remembered when it came time for me to raise my own family.

Moreover, from an early age I had seen how Father was treated with fawning respect by everybody around him, and I didn't like it. He had great power over their lives, and he used it to his advantage. He knew that if he flew into a rage against his employees, they weren't in a position to fight back.

From day one at Ville LaSalle, I made sure not to throw my weight around. The fact was, I loved the people at the plant, and I felt accepted by them.

I also loved the challenge of the work. One day I walked into the blending room and saw that Roy was not well. After consulting with a doctor, I proposed to Father that Roy take some paid time off.

"Who will do the blending while Roy is away?" Father asked.

"I will," I said.

"Can you do it as well as Roy?"

"No, sir," I said, "not when he is well. But when he is sick, yes, sir."

Soon after Roy and his wife left for Florida, I found myself saddled with a major problem. In the course of normal checking, I discovered that the taste was off in the last blend of Seagram's VO that Roy had made. At first I thought it might have been a slight mistake in the dumping of barrels, so I requested that another dump be made into a separate tank. That, too, was a bit off, and I realized that the formula itself was at fault.

I was in a bind. We were dealing with a finite quantity of whiskey. There was no way I could toss out the batch and start again: this was all the six-year-old whiskey we had on hand at that time. To make matters worse, it was October, our heaviest shipping month because of Christmas, and the pressure to get the product out would be enormous. But I had been trained by both Father and Roy that quality preceded everything.

Somehow I had to add something to make the batch taste right. I made up my mind to shut the bottling hall and let the 1,000 line workers go home. It was not my concern how the union would react; I simply told the plant manager that there would be no more VO to bottle until I could correct the formula.

But first I decided to call Father. Maybe he would rush home from New York and help me. On the contrary, he simply approved my decision and stayed exactly where he was while I struggled to resolve the dilemma.

Four days later, after working until I could hardly taste anything at all, I finally found the answer. By adding a quarter of a percent of a Maryland rye whiskey and a half percent of a Kentucky bourbon to the batch, it finally tasted to me like the VO of old. The bottling hall reopened, and VO flowed once again.

Looking back, it was a gutsy play on Father's part. True, he didn't know the inventory like I did, so it would have been a waste of everyone's time for him to come to Ville LaSalle and pitch in. And he couldn't tell me to ship anyway; that was not the Seagram tradition. On the other hand, he could have sent someone from New York or Louisville—after all, I was a kid. But he chose not to and to let me handle the situation, chalking up whatever it might have cost to the education of the prince.

———

My fascination with production ran deep, and I gradually took over responsibility for all Canadian production.

I had a surprisingly easy time gaining this responsibility. It gradually dawned on me that as a rule people do not like responsibility. They are perfectly willing to let someone else assume it, as long as they don't feel threatened.

I traveled across Canada, evaluating each distillery to see if we could increase efficiency and improve quality. At our plant in Waterloo, Ontario, I discovered that we stored some used barrels out in the open. As I had discovered with Roy, when barrels are left in the rain, acetic acid can easily develop and later ruin any whiskey put in those containers. If one bad barrel slips into a blend, it can ruin the entire batch. Initially, I arranged for temporary covering; then I had structures built to shield the barrels from the elements.

On one trip, when tasting current distillates at the New Westminster plant in British Columbia, I noticed a pronounced "off" smell in a sample that had been rejected. No one seemed to know what was causing the difficulty, but I thought I knew where the problem lay. I had the plant manager and the distiller come with me to the "yeast room." There yeast is grown prior to being put into the fermenter, where sugar is converted into alcohol and carbon dioxide. Sure enough, one of the yeast tubs had a sour smell. It had gone bad.

This period provided me with important insight into the conflicting demands of production management and quality control. The former is concerned with volume, while the latter is interested only in quality. This is why quality control must report to the CEO, not to production management. At Seagram it was ever so. To this day, I will raise Cain if I taste something amiss in one of our products. Everyone throughout the organization knows and respects this.

Quite recently, for example, I tasted a new product called Bolshoi vodka, which was being made for us in Russia. I was concerned that the product had too many "heads and tails"—what comes off the alcohol still first and last. I got the production team together, we sampled the product, and then agreed on what had to be done: distill the product at a slightly higher level, thus reducing some of the congeners (a fancy name for the alcohols that give the product character, some good, some bad). A few weeks later, I tasted and approved the new edition.

I learned early on from Father that there was no compromising on quality. I once asked him what gave him the most satisfaction. He thought for a second, then replied, "When a man walks into a store, points to a bottle of Seven Crown, and says, 'Give me that.' That's something I make, and he wants it."

Though I was living and working in Canada during these years, I still came down to New York fairly often. Mother and Father had a summer home in Tarrytown, New York, which I visited occasionally. I discovered a Polaroid camera in one of Father's drawers while looking for a shirt. He was the world's least mechanical man, and had no idea how to use it. Apparently, Jack Dreyfus, the creator of the Dreyfus Fund, had given it to him, and Father asked me to call him and arrange to pay for it. But when I called Mr. Dreyfus, whom I had never met, he invited me to lunch. He told me the story of Edwin Land and Polaroid. I was so impressed that I bought five thousand shares for Father's account at about thirty dollars a share. It has split something like sixteen to one in the ensuing years!

However, the main motive for my trips to New York was a girl named Ann Loeb. From the time I first met Ann in November 1950, winning her affection was the first item on my agenda. To me, she was the most beautiful girl in the world.

Let me describe Ann as I first saw her: She was almost five feet seven, with a delicious body—strong, perfectly proportioned, with rather large, full breasts, powerful calves, and thin ankles. She had great carriage and seemed taller because she was so erect. Her thick, long hair was brown with a touch of auburn, her eyes blue, her nose a little large but straight and almost Roman.

Not only was she physically stunning, but Ann's pedigree was also impressive. Her parents were John and "Peter" Loeb (her mother had picked up the nickname Peter as a child). Peter was the granddaughter of Adolphe Lewissohn, and was related to the Altschuls as well as quite a few other famous "Our Crowd" Jews. John was the oldest son of Carl M. Loeb, founder of the important Wall Street brokerage house Carl M. Loeb, Rhoades & Co. "C. M.," as he was called by my generation of in-laws and business associates, had made his money in the metals business.

Father had always talked to me and Charles about the importance of marrying a girl from the right family. I can almost hear his voice, driving home from Lake Placid, where we used to go for weekends. "What happens if you fall in love with a poor girl?" I asked. "Don't go out with any," was his answer. That the girl would be Jewish was already a given, so he didn't even mention it. I don't know whether Father's instructions influenced my decision to go out with Ann, but her lineage certainly didn't hurt.

Our first date was a kind of fluke. Ann had been invited to a chic New York party and had to bring two dates. Since she had once gone to the theater with my brother, she called Father's suite at the St. Regis

Hotel to see if Charles was available. Mother, who happened to be in New York, answered the phone and told Ann that, while Charles would be in Montreal over Thanksgiving, her other son, Edgar, might be in New York. I agreed to be the other date, and so began our court-ship.

My pursuit of Ann lasted for two years, with many ups and downs along the way. I was always overanxious, and tortured myself when she was being cool.

Ann's parents were probably against her marrying a Russian Jew (though Ann once said that she thought the infusion of a new blood-line would do her family good). Indeed, the Loebs seemed to feel that even in New York City it would be much easier not to be Jewish, and thus they encouraged their own children to assimilate. The only Loeb child married at the time was Ann's elder sister, Judy, who had wed Richard N. Beaty, a hero of the Battle of Britain.

When the chase finally ended, we were having dinner together in a restaurant that had a wing called the "Yes Room." Just after we fin-ished the meal, Ann looked straight at me and said "Yes!" At first I didn't get it, but when it finally penetrated my thick skull that she was accepting my proposal of marriage, I rushed her over to 730 Park Av-enue to tell her parents before she could change her mind.

We were married in the Loebs' apartment. The service was per-formed by Rabbi Pearlman of Temple Emanu-El, where John Loeb was a trustee. (John's role in the temple may sound odd, given the Loebs' attitude toward Judaism, until you understand that at one time mem-bers were told to remove their yarmulkes in that "cathedral," as it was derisively referred to by more religious Jews. The majority of the tem-ple's original congregants were German Jews whose greatest dream was to assimilate.)

The wedding was a great affair filled with good humor. My brother, Charles, who served as best man, was particularly funny, as only he can be. But it was Carl Loeb who had the best line: "At my age," he quipped, "I am not sure I can adjust to the idea of being the poor relation."

Afterward, we spent a two-week honeymoon in Nassau playing

tennis and drinking martinis. "I'll Get By" became "our song," and every time we got to the line "Poverty may come to me . . . ," we'd both shudder and say, "No way!"

We also managed to get pregnant.

———◆———

Sam, the first of five children born to Ann and me, arrived on October 23, 1953, nine months and thirteen days after we were married. His name, Samuel Bronfman II, had been established one Friday evening in Montreal when a very pregnant Ann and I went to 15 Belvedere Road for dinner with other members of the family. I knew that, according to Jewish tradition, it was considered bad luck to name a child after a living relative. Instead, children are supposed to be given the name of a deceased family member to keep that person's name and memory alive.

"I know you cannot answer yes to what I'm about to ask," I said to Father, "so if you say nothing, I will assume the answer is yes. If it's a boy, I'd like to name him after you."

I had two reasons in mind. One, I really wanted to please Father. Two, I liked the idea of flouting tradition, of being above that type of superstition.

My question was greeted with silence. But I knew that Father was tickled pink, and Mother's silence let me understand that she, too, was pleased. So Samuel Bronfman II it was. In the synagogue in Montreal, he was registered as Shalom after my mother's father, who was no longer living, which made it all kosher.

I was so relieved that both Sam and his mother were okay that I went to Van Cleef & Arpels and bought Ann a sapphire/diamond bracelet. She showed it proudly to her grandfather, C. M. Loeb, and asked what would have happened if the baby had been a girl. "The stones would have been a little smaller," C. M. replied.

When we first married, I had told Ann that we were going to have five children: two boys, a girl, a boy, and a girl, in that order. Don't ask what lunacy had possessed me.

Over the next ten years, Ann gave birth to two boys, a girl, and two boys. Between the last two boys she was also pregnant, but because she had had German measles, a D & C was performed. In my madness, I used it as an excuse for my forecast going astray.

When Edgar Jr. was born on May 16, 1955, I was already an expert on Ann and her childbearing, the very definition of cool. Peter and John were away, and I stayed in their apartment. I changed Ann's hospital room for a more comfortable one, then called the Loeb residence to order dinner for seven-thirty.

Overhearing me, Ann's nurse quite properly said that the birth could take hours. Snotty ass that I was, I replied that the baby would be born between six and six-thirty, that I would be home in time for cocktails at seven and dinner at seven-thirty, and that I would then return to the hospital.

The nurse was disgusted with me, and even more so when Edgar was born at 6:17. I also remember telling Ann on the night of his conception that the date of his birth would be May 16, and I was right.

Just before our daughter, Holly, was born on August 28, 1956, John Loeb asked Ann what sex the baby would be, expecting the usual "I don't care, as long as it's healthy" response. But Ann promptly replied, "A girl." When John asked why she was sure, he was justifiably annoyed when Ann said, "Edgar said so."

Matthew was born three years later, on July 16, 1959, so I was right again. My prognostication skills inspired me to create a slogan: "I was wrong once. I was six. Father was very annoyed." I intended it as a joke, but perhaps I began to believe it. When Adam was born on March 22, 1963, upsetting my prediction of a girl, I blamed it on Ann.

People who don't allow themselves to be wrong not only do harm to themselves, they inflict emotional damage on those around them. Now I can see that because I was so intolerant of the young man I was then, I was hard on everybody else. Great expectations had been placed upon me in my youth, and as I strove to live up to them, I also started to believe my own press releases. That is dangerous indeed.

When Ann was pregnant with Sam, I began devoting myself more rigorously to learning the family business. While continuing in the production department at Ville LaSalle, I took time out for two special jobs during the summer of 1953. What I learned from each proved invaluable in the years ahead.

Even though I was still on the payroll of our Canadian company, I spent a month with the Empire Trust Company (now part of the Bank of New York), a small bank with expertise in the oil business. Our family was interested in oil, and I wanted to know more about it.

At Empire, I learned how to evaluate oil companies. Among them was an outfit called Louisiana Sulphur and Oil. I studied all the available information about their reserves and, basing oil in the ground at one dollar a barrel and natural gas at three cents an mcf (1,000 cubic feet), I established a value for the stock.

Things can, indeed, come back to haunt us—or bless us. Much to my surprise, my father-in-law, John Loeb, proposed some time later that our families buy a block of that stock from the Burden family. When I asked whose evaluation he was using, he said that it was Empire Trust's.

"John," I said, "I wouldn't trust that evaluation if I were you." This annoyed him, as he was a director of the company and very loyal to it, so I explained that I was the one who had written the evaluation. (We did buy the stock, and we all did very well, thank you.)

The rest of that summer I worked at John Loeb's firm, Carl M. Loeb, Rhoades & Co., where I had the good fortune to work under Sam Stedman, one of the partners. Sam was perhaps the most brilliant analyst I have ever met. Blessed with a quick, incisive mind, he was a tremendous asset to the company.

Under Sam's tutelage I learned to analyze companies in a different way: for their potential. He had unique methods for determining potential, and was right far more often than he was wrong, which is not easy in that business. Father recognized his genius, and later asked him to run the Samuel Bronfman Foundation, the Seagram charitable conduit.

In the summer of 1954, Ann and I had our second honeymoon, an old-fashioned wedding trip. As they so often do, business and pleasure were bound to mix—though in an unexpected way.

After crossing the Atlantic on the U.S.S. *United States* and landing in Le Havre, we spent a few days in Paris, then rented a Ford Vedette and started tooling around Europe. Upon our return to Paris, I got a call from Father. He wanted us to come immediately to London, where he and Mother were spending some time. The purpose was to meet the "DCL crowd."

The DCL was the scotch whiskey combine that owned countless brands, including Dewar's, Johnnie Walker, Black and White, White Horse, Haig & Haig, and other, lesser-known brands. It was a funny company. All the brands had their own offices with fancy addresses in London. They simply shipped to agents throughout the world and then took orders like clipping coupons; they didn't get involved with the marketing and advertising. Basically, it was a very sleepy organization. In fact, the management of that company got worse and worse, and it was finally taken over in the mid-eighties by Guinness, PLC. I would have loved to have bought it, but we were prevented from doing so by antitrust laws.

We arrived at the Savoy Hotel, where Father always stayed, and proceeded to wine and dine with members of the DCL management team. I particularly remember Sir Graham Heyman, chairman of the management committee, and Ronnie Cumming, who was later to become chairman of the entire company.

Before we took the train to Southampton to catch our boat back to the States, Father finally explained why he had asked me to come. He thought we could merge Chivas into the DCL, thereby becoming its largest stockholder, and he wanted my opinion.

Now remember, Father was a real Anglophile, and he had enormous respect for the DCL. "Distillers in America were indicted, while in England they were knighted," he told me. Thus it became clear: Father thought that, if I was intrigued with the people I met, I might want to come to England, then eventually take over the chairmanship—*and get knighted.* (He didn't say this in so many words, but the implication was clear to me then, and later confirmed.)

"How much would we own?" I asked. Not a big percentage, Father said, but there were no large shareholders.

I demurred, saying that, for one, the DCL was badly managed; that it would take an enormous effort to make a dent in the way it operated, especially given the fact that we wouldn't own enough of the company to call the shots; and that I didn't really want to move to England.

Besides, I pointed out, Chivas Regal was such a jewel that I didn't think we should give it up. Father finally agreed, if reluctantly, saying, "You may be right. Maybe someday we might sell half a million cases of Chivas." In 1996, we sold almost 4 million.

I had always thought that Father did exactly as he pleased, and here he had decided to forgo a deal based on my advice. Looking back, I should have been highly pleased that Father valued my opinion, and that he had asked me and Ann to come over from Paris so that he and I could consult on the matter. Unfortunately, it didn't occur to me until years later that he gave a damn what I or anybody else thought. If I had realized this, it might have changed our relationship for the better.

———

Although I was always eager to move to New York City, Ann and I were destined to remain in Montreal until my twenty-sixth birthday, which would put me beyond the draft age for the U.S. armed forces. I didn't want to go to New York only to be drafted. In the meantime, I felt I still had a lot to learn about the production side of the business, so I stayed at Ville LaSalle.

Then, in the fall of 1954, Father decided he wanted me to come to work with him at the head office at Peel Street in Montreal. I protested, arguing that there was so much to do in production. This was true, but I also liked being the boss and having no interference. I knew that by moving to the head office, this freedom would come to an end.

Father replied that he hadn't brought me into the world to be a production manager, and there was no refuting his logic. So I reported for duty at 1430 Peel Street, where I unhappily shuffled his papers while feeling that my career had reached a dead end.

I had no responsibilities whatsoever at the head office. I sat at my desk and listened while Father talked to Max Henderson, Seagram's secretary-treasurer, or spoke on the phone to various company ex-ecutives in New York. I watched him fiddle with label designs, listened as he screamed at his brother-in-law for having the temerity to bring him an ancient Talmudic book, watched while Uncle Allan dozed off, and observed mundane meetings with Phil Vineberg, the brilliant attorney.

One thing I did learn was that the real business was not in Mon-treal, but in New York, which made me even more anxious to move there. Looking back, I think that Father wanted me to have an overall view of the company before I moved across the border. He probably felt that I could improve Seagram's U.S. operations, but thought I should first learn something about business structure.

Of course, I couldn't learn much about that from such a totally unstructured man. Father resented the need for an organization, let alone having to work with it. Uncle Allan was supposed to oversee ad-ministration—which was under the supervision of James Friel, a very able Irish banker cum manager—because Father had no interest in the day-to-day details of the business.

Moreover, Father did not believe in market research. He decided what people wanted: what advertising would grab their interest, and how prices should be set so as to optimize image—which was every-thing to him because it was *his* image.

In addition, while he pretended to Charles and me that he was a great accountant, in fact he knew very little about the subject. I recall an instance when we were looking for more profit to put in the year-end closing. It was suggested that the profits of Fromm & Sichel, in which Seagram had an 80 percent interest, should be consolidated. Father refused on the basis that Alfred Fromm and Franz Sichel would have to pay taxes. That wasn't true—we weren't advocating paying dividends, just making a book entry—but who could tell Mr. Sam that he was wrong?

All in all, my stint at 1430 Peel Street didn't offer much of an education. Fortunately, I was at the head office for less than a year when I talked my way into a transfer to New York.

———

Ann, Sam, Edgar Jr., and I moved to the United States in December 1955. We took over the house being vacated by Dick and Judy Beaty, Ann's sister and brother-in-law, who were moving into what had been the home of C. M. and Adeline Loeb, their grandparents. Ann and I bought some twenty-three acres of that estate (at a very favorable price) and commenced to build our home there.

I had always dreamed of living in New York, and now here I was, in the pulsing heart of the United States. Frank Sinatra was the "Chairman of the Board," having been so dubbed by William B. Williams, the famous disc jockey. Rodgers and Hammerstein's *Carousel* was packing in audiences on Broadway. Zoot suits and hand-painted ties were now déclassé and Lena Horne was the thrush.

In the arena of American politics, Adlai Stevenson accused Ike of "gazing down the fairways of indifference," which might have been a bit true, but Americans continued to like Ike. McCarthyism was seen as the great evil by the eastern Liberal establishment, and eventually Eisenhower took care of that, too. The Korean War had come and gone, while Vietnam was a remote place in an even more remote continent.

America was still rather innocent, and Europe was still rather dilapidated. The dollar was supreme, and though American cigarettes didn't buy "virgin sisters," the American age was in full force. Wall Street analysts made a distinct difference between "real earnings" and "overseas earnings": you didn't get a full multiple on any profits earned outside the U.S.A. (although Canada was grudgingly considered part of America).

While I loved my new home, it was not like finding the promised land. True, New York was (and is) the best place outside of Israel for a Jew to live: except for the banks and some investment houses, there were few doors closed to Jews. But I still felt the reality of my minority status, and the Loebs' pandering to Gentiles reinforced my sense that New York wasn't all that different from Montreal.

I joined the Century Country Club, whose entrance is almost exactly opposite the entry to the Loeb home in Purchase, and we went to club parties. We were invited to many homes on weekends, and our social life was pretty conventional. In those days, people of our age group drank a lot, and so did we.

I went to work for Joseph E. Seagram & Sons, Inc., the holding company for all Seagram's U.S. companies. My new job was to establish clear lines of authority so that everyone in the organization knew what they were supposed to do—in other words, to become the organizer Father didn't want to be.

His motto could well have been "If you want something done right, do it yourself." But the company had far outgrown such a philosophy. While Father might have been a better purchasing agent or production manager or advertising director or sales executive than anyone working for him, he couldn't be all of them at once, although he sometimes tried.

A title had to be found for me. Curiously, when I was running the Canadian plants, I had no title. Presumably, "Edgar Bronfman"—or, more likely, "Sam Bronfman's son Edgar"—was title enough. I was named "chairman of the administrative committee," which meant that I was in charge of everything but sales and marketing. James Friel, who for years had been in charge of everything but sales, was now in his seventies. Not only was he happy to have me there, he made every effort to reinforce my authority by sending others to me when they came to him with their agendas.

Father had turned over to me the areas which did not interest him. He knew instinctively that there were serious problems in administration, and wanted them resolved, but he had no time for them.

Meanwhile, he kept control over the things that really mattered to him (aside from quality, which he also turned over to me because of my Ville LaSalle experience and my talent in this field). These were packaging, advertising, distribution, and sales. Father was the total tsar of all products to be sold as well as of packaging and advertising. Vic Fischel was in charge of all distribution and sales, and reported directly to Father.

Fischel was a strong, unattractive, red-haired man who had started his career with Seagram as a distillery guide. Father had taken a shine to him and brought him to New York shortly after he began operating in the United States. He was a force in the industry—the classic example of the adage "You shouldn't ask who made Seagram's 7 Crown, but rather how many people Seagram's 7 Crown made."

Fischel was a good sales manager but a very poor corporate manager. He knew how to spend money, but not how to save it or make it. He also didn't know the first thing about advertising, and relied on an in-house advertising expert, a vice president named George Mosley.

For many years, Mosley was very good at what he did. But times were changing. For example, when David Ogilvie put women in the advertisements for the Rums of Puerto Rico, Father was aghast and tried to persuade the entire distilled-spirits industry not to countenance this novel idea. I think he worried that someone would suggest that by feeding a woman beverage alcohol it would be easier to get "one's way" with her. I guess if you're on top, it is only natural to resist anything new. I'm reminded of Lestoil, which tried a different approach—buying low-cost advertising time late at night—and achieved a remarkable market share before anyone really took notice. The ads were persuasive, but the competition ignored them, until it became necessary to buy out this upstart at a handsome price.

Vic and Father went back a long way. He was a Montreal boy and had driven Father home from the hospital after my birth. The bonds between them were close, and indeed Vic was a loyal servant. During World War II, when the tremendous shortage of whiskeys and resultant rationing made distributor relations very important, Vic had been quite effective. When it was time once again to market brands, however, he was not in his element.

At one time, I had thought Vic a possible successor to Father should, God forbid, anything terrible happen. (When we were kids, Charles and I occasionally discussed the matter; Charles's candidate was Bill Wachtel, the suave, handsome, speechifying president of Calvert, a Seagram subsidiary.) But after a few months in New York, I realized that, while Fischel was a decent man, his skills were very limited. I had traveled with Father when I worked in Montreal, and had witnessed Fischel in action. His basic philosophy was that distributors sold whiskey, and if you had a great relationship with the distributors, they would break their necks selling your brands. Thus, he spent a great deal of time playing gin rummy and poker with the distributors. It was always table-stakes poker, and I'm sure that Vic, in good conscience, put his losses on the expense account.

Before long, I came to see Fischel as the sole obstacle preventing me from taking control of Seagram's entire American operation.

———◆———

CHAPTER 4

SETTING THE STAGE: PERSONNEL BATTLES AND THE CALVERT EXTRA CAMPAIGN

W hen I think about Vic Fischel, even now in the fullness of time, I know that I would do the same thing: take him on directly rather than wait for him to retire.

But it was not quite time yet. Although sales and marketing were the essence of our business, it was too soon for me to take on those re-sponsibilities. For one thing, when I became chairman of the adminis-trative committee, I didn't know anything about marketing. For another, I had yet to achieve credibility at Seagram itself and within the industry. Instead, over the next two years I focused closely on the areas I did control: administration and production. I didn't want to be accused of neglecting them.

———◆———

Theoretically, Uncle Allan was in charge of administration. Jim Friel, however, was the real boss.

To fully understand the chain of command, one must know some-thing more about the difficult relationship between Sam and Allan

Bronfman. Uncle Allan was essentially weak. Afraid of Father (who wasn't?), he would never act on his own. He was not nearly so compulsively consumed by the business, and was content to sit in Father's office, looking down his nose at everyone while his brother made all the decisions.

Father, on the other hand, was jealous of Allan for having the education he so desperately felt he lacked. Father always insisted that he had paid for both Allan's law school education and his training at the firm of Andrews and Andrews in Winnipeg.

He kept Allan at his side for two reasons. First, as strange as it may sound, he really loved him. More pragmatically, since Allan could use the King's English, Father felt that his brother made a better impression than he did. But as time went on, Father realized that he really didn't need Allan. I know he would have forced the issue much earlier except for the fraternal bond between the two.

Allan was given to deceptions. During our childhood fishing trips to Gananoque with Allan and his family, I remember that in the late afternoon he would have lengthy telephone conversations with Jim Friel in New York. Later I learned that those calls were made only to impress his wife and children with his importance to the business.

The biggest deception Allan perpetuated, of course, was that he and Father were equal partners. This led to unrealistic expectations on the part of Allan's sons, Edward and Peter, who assumed that they, like Charles and me, would take their place at Seagram.

I had no feelings of competition toward my cousins since I knew deep down who was going to be running Seagram someday. In fact, I had always thought that Edward and Peter would go to work for Royalite, the Canadian oil company controlled by trusts that Sam and Allan had established for their children. Edward (and perhaps Peter) did spend time in Calgary, Alberta, where Royalite was based, but nothing ever came of it.

Later Allan tried to put Peter into Seagram as an assistant to Merle Schneckenburger, who ran advertising in Canada. I called Father and told him that there was a plot afoot to bring Peter into the business. He asked my view, and I told him that it was a terrible idea.

Peter's ability was not the issue. The fact is, no large public company can survive with too many relatives at the top, because it becomes impossible to hire good people. Moreover, one should never hire anyone one can't fire.

It seemed Peter became obsessed with the idea that we had somehow euchred him out of Seagram, and actually gave serious thought to competing with us. All because Uncle Allan couldn't tell the truth to his kids. Indeed, he even lied about one of the great tragedies of the Bronfman family, the suicide of his daughter, Mona. Allan told Edward, Peter, and everyone else that she had died from a heart attack. Years later, Peter dug out the truth, which only deepened his bitterness toward his father. Unfortunately Peter died of liver cancer in the spring of 1997. By then he had become totally adjusted to life, and some months before he died, wrote me a charming letter of congratulations for what I had accomplished at Seagram and at the World Jewish Congress.

<hr />

Between his lies and his laziness, Uncle Allan was not much use at Seagram. Which leads us back to Jim Friel and the administrative problems I inherited.

Before I became chairman of the administrative committee, our auditors, Price Waterhouse, did a study of the company to help us improve our systems. Price Waterhouse was particularly concerned about the concentration of administrative power in the hands of Friel, and had recommended that the company hire a comptroller, who would report independently to the president. (Unfortunately, our president, General Frank Schwengel, was an elderly figurehead who did little more than represent the company to trade associations and such groups as the American Legion.)

Sitting on the board of the parent company, Distillers Corporation–Seagrams Ltd., was Thomas McInnerney, who had orchestrated the amalgamation of the dairy companies, which first became National Dairies, and later Kraft. He had just been through a reorganization and had a comptroller to spare.

His name was Herb Brown, and we got him. Father figured that if McInnerney had recommended him, he must be good, somehow not realizing that McInnerney considered him expendable.

Brown sat around and did little. In all fairness, this was mostly because Jim Friel wouldn't give him the time of day. Jim was getting older, and Father would not interfere so the system didn't work very well. In truth, this area of the business was neither Father's forte nor his real interest.

Take John Handy. When we were about to start construction on the Seagram Building, someone hired him and gave him the title of comptroller. It wasn't clear what his organizational relationship was to Brown or Friel, and he seemed to be relegated to watching the bills on the building. By the time I became chairman of the administrative committee, I could see that Handy, a very nice man, had been given a lousy deal. He had no credibility within the organization and had no chance of advancing. I suggested in the friendliest way that, through no fault of his own, his future at Seagram was in jeopardy, and that he would do himself a big favor if he found another job, which he did. (We parted amicably, and to this day he sends me a Christmas card.)

Then, in February 1956, Jim Friel died.

Friel's passing did not solve our problems, however. Herb Brown was certainly not the man to take Friel's place. I needed an exceptionally smart financial executive who understood numbers and had imagination and judgment. I went to my friend Sam Stedman, a partner at Loeb, Rhoades. Being the diligent analyst he was, Sam knew a great number of people in corporate life, and didn't suffer fools gladly. He introduced me to Sidney Fread, whom I hired as chief financial officer.

In the meantime, I had to do something with Herb Brown. When I told Father I wanted to retire him, his reaction was typical: "Not Herb Brown!"

I pointed out that in trying to streamline the company, we were letting a number of people go. But because Father saw Herb Brown in the bar on the fifteenth floor (the executive floor) at the end of the day, he didn't want to drop the ax on him. Nevertheless, he agreed with my reasoning, so the next day I went in to see Herb and offered him a deal that I thought was eminently fair. We would pay his bonus and his salary until the end of the year, then retire him as if he were sixty-five, even though he was a few years younger.

He agreed to the package, and I thought that was that. But about an hour later, he asked to see me again. He sat down and, with notebook in hand, began a recitation of all the things he had done for the company since he had come on board.

"And just what," I asked, "do you think we were paying you to do all that time?"

I called Father's secretary to tell her that Herb Brown would be in to see him, and to let me know immediately when she saw him coming down the hall. Herb did indeed go to Father's office, and I walked in just behind him. I sat on a window ledge, out of Father's sight but looking directly at Herb with a hard stare.

Herb immediately got the picture: any complaint and we would renegotiate. He told Father that he and I had come to a very satisfactory understanding, and that as a result he would be leaving the company in the near future.

After Herb left the office, Father asked me what that was all about. Nothing, I replied—just what you saw. He gave me a look that said he knew better but had decided not to pursue it.

We had more than our share of people problems, and near the top of the list was Jack Owen.

An old associate of Joe Renfield from the Prohibition years, Jack went from one ad agency to another with some Seagram billing in his pocket simply because Father genuinely liked him. He had become a crony of Father's by spending time with him, especially on weekends in my parents' Tarrytown house, where he was more than willing to schmooze while artfully kissing Father's behind.

Jack was a lesser threat to what I was trying to accomplish, and I knew that, as with Vic, a showdown was inevitable. Eventually, Jack fell into a trap of his own making. He decided that Kent cigarettes had

"made it" because *Reader's Digest* had published a story about the benefits of filter cigarettes—less tar and nicotine. He started working on Father to get *Reader's Digest* to do an article on why blends are better than
straights. His reasoning: they contain fewer harmful ingredients,
known as congeners. They are in the product when it is distilled at
lower proof and disappear completely at 190 degrees of proof—95 percent pure alcohol. Our blends were made up of some 65 percent neutral
spirits, as opposed to bourbon whiskeys, which are all distilled at lower
proof. So Owen's assertion was true up to a point. There are fewer congeners in blended whiskey than in straight whiskeys, but the amounts
are infinitesimal. If you overindulge, you are more likely to have a sour
stomach from drinking products distilled at lower proof.

Thinking nothing would ever come of this, I let Jack go on with
his pursuit of the golden calf. But it finally got to be too much; he was
telling Father that he was getting close to his goal, and I started worrying about the fallout should such an article ever find its way into print.

I called Jack into my office and carefully explained the problem.
The thrust of the *Reader's Digest* story was that cigarettes were unhealthy and that perhaps filter cigarettes were less unhealthy. Was he
suggesting we take the position that whiskey was bad for you, and
blended whiskeys were a little less bad?

Maybe he honestly couldn't grasp my point. Regardless, he
wouldn't give up. I then explained the problem to Father, who fortunately understood immediately and shot the whole thing down.

But the whole fiasco didn't seem to affect his relationship with
Jack. I was so disgusted with their "friendship" that I told Father I
would no longer break bread with Jack Owen. If he wanted to invite
him to lunch, that was fine, but I would eat elsewhere. I never violated
that vow, even though Father was tricky at times and would wait until
the very last minute to tell me he had invited Jack to have lunch in his
dining room at 375 Park Avenue.

One Saturday, when Ann and I were at Tarrytown with our children, Father and I went down to the bar in the playhouse to fix a drink
before lunch. He confessed that Jack Owen was coming. I stopped in
my tracks. Okay, I said, but we're leaving.

Father almost pleaded, telling me that Jack was an independent businessman and a loyal, good friend. I angrily replied that he was a leech who made a living out of whatever amounts of Seagram billing he could generate from Father, and that this alone made him the great loyal "friend" he was, because nobody else in the entire organization would give him the time of day. I added that the only reason Father thought Jack was smart was because he had an incredibly clever way of feeding back everything Father said, only in different words, thus agreeing with him while shamelessly kissing his ass.

Father, looking more than pained, protested. "All right," I said, "I'll make a deal with you. I'll stay, on the condition that when Jack arrives and comes down here for a drink, you will say something preposterous. I'll guarantee you that within ten minutes Jack will spit it back in different words."

Father agreed, with a glint of triumph in his eye, and I knew that he was about to bend the meaning of the word *preposterous* way out of shape. Sure enough, when Jack arrived, he did (his exact comment escapes me now). And within ten minutes, Jack regurgitated it.

Perhaps that was a cruel thing to do to Father—time away from the office hung heavily on his hands, and there weren't that many people who would come to Tarrytown on Saturday or Sunday to shoot the breeze. But I didn't like being treated like a child, and I was disappointed that Father would befriend such a fraud. Of course, Sam Bronfman was an insecure man, and Jack was a southerner who really knew how to spread it, so Father was willing to pay the price and ignore what should have been obvious, until his brutal son pointed it out.

Perhaps Father was a sentimentalist, too. As a matter of fact, he once suggested to me that I might like to come over to Tarrytown on a Saturday or Sunday to "schmooze." I carefully explained that while I would go anywhere in the world if he asked me to do something specific, I had a wife and children, and needed to spend my free time with them.

Jack was clever at doing what he knew best—kissing Father's behind. Otherwise, he was stupid. Through his unique understanding of the not-invented-here syndrome, and his ability to make Father think that his suggestions were originally Father's idea, he managed to bring three men into Seagram—none of whom was needed, and all of whom I eventually had to fire.

The first was Bob Bragarnick, a reputed marketing expert who had worked for both Milton Beo, the advertising legend of the time, as well as Charlie Revson. Jack's stated reasoning for hiring Bragarnick was that Seagram needed marketing expertise, and he was right. But his real reason was that he also felt that Bob, out of loyalty, would reward him with some advertising.

There were two other problems with this hire. One, Bob didn't understand that Father was the packaging maven at Seagram, and that you crossed him—on this or any other subject—at your peril. Two, without strong backing from the CEO, you cannot change a company with no marketing history into a marketing-oriented business.

Bob won little support from Father, while he and Vic Fischel quickly became enemies. Though I liked Bob, Seagram politics kept me from being much help. I also knew that we couldn't become a marketing company until I got rid of Fischel and everything he stood for.

The second man Jack Owen hired for Father was Byron Tosi, a Knight of Malta, who was neither a marketer nor an effective salesman. He did have presence, but that was about all. Some time after he came aboard, we were developing a new product for sale by his group, a liqueur called Casanova, to be imported from Italy. Tosi came into my office and suggested that he and I should own the Italian manufacturing company, which would then sell the product to the Seagram import arm, Browne Vintners Company—the company he had been hired to run! For historic reasons, Byron didn't report to Fischel—he reported to me directly. Oscar Weill, his predecessor, had always reported directly to Father.

I gave Byron a lecture on conflicts of interest, but what I should have done was fire him on the spot. That would come some time later.

The third member of the Jack Owen trio was Jack Finneran, a

salesman and a politician. Formerly employed by Rheingold Breweries, he was brought in by Owen and Father to be Fischel's assistant, and perhaps successor or replacement.

Finneran was a decent enough fellow, but not aggressive. When the head of Seagram's sales division retired, Jack should have pursued the job with a passion. But that would have meant lots of domestic travel, decision-making, and bottom-line accountability, none of which Finneran liked. Some time later, when I was finally in a position to ask for his resignation, I told him that his great mistake was in not asking for that specific sales job. He expressed surprise, and quickly volunteered to take it. Of course, it was too late.

———

Still not ready to make my move, I watched all these organizational maneuvers with a jaundiced eye.

I was able to solve some problems, however. Our production division was headquartered in Louisville, Kentucky, with a production liaison officer stationed in New York in case Father wanted to look at samples. This wasn't working as well as it should have. My production background told me that to maintain and improve quality continually we needed key production executives to be close by.

The status quo had a long history. When Father and his brother Harry had built the Louisville plant, it was thought that Harry would live there and run production from its beautiful offices. (They were erected in 1936, when it wasn't costly to do it right.)

But Father and Uncle Harry had had a falling-out. The reasons were never made clear, but I know that Harry was a bit of a shortcutter and that he didn't have Father's devotion to quality. It's also quite probable that Harry, the older brother, resented taking orders, and that Father had to prove in a rather drastic fashion that he was the boss. Uncle Harry sold some of his shares to Father and Allan (who also bought some of Uncle Abe's and Aunt Laura's shares) and moved back to Montreal, where he did well in real estate and other businesses.

Father then hired a man from Hiram Walker to run production:

Fred Willkie, one of Wendell Willkie's brothers (another Willkie brother, Bob, also worked for Seagram). With his sure command of the production operation, Fred became a powerhouse at Seagram. (In a sense, Fred invented domestic vodka by extolling the virtues of grain-neutral spirits, which were used in the Seagram and Calvert blends.) Fred took over in 1942 and remained until he and Father had a falling-out, well after the war.

In truth, they had never spoken the same language. Fred was a petty tyrant with his own public-relations people and his own agenda. His staff was always promoting him as the true force behind Seagram.

For a long time, Fred managed to keep out of Father's way, occupying himself with experiments. He tried to make distillers' dried grain (the refuse from the fermented product after the alcohol had been removed, which was high in protein) into an edible food—it is very sour, and he succeeded in creating different yeast strains that could produce different-tasting products.

But eventually, in 1952, Father got sick and tired of Fred's constant egotistical forays and sent him packing. He then made the mistake of appointing a committee to run the production operation. (Father liked creating committees. The DCL had always had a management committee, and Father thought the sun rose and set by what it did. Of course, this was also a great way to make sure that another Fred Willkie didn't arise to challenge his ego.)

After the horse he had hoped to produce turned out to be a camel, Father asked Adalbert Herman, an overweight Hungarian who was running the Canadian plants, to take over the American operation, too. When Herman retired, I appointed John Izsak, who became vice president for production in the United States. Meanwhile, Canadian production was taken over by a man named Jack Duffy, who had a good background with Seagram in both the United States and Canada.

I decided to bring the senior headquarters staff from Louisville to New York. Father approved of a cost-of-living increase for those who chose to come (most did). I found it a far more efficient arrangement. Having fast, direct access to the production people was a big help in improving the quality of our products, something I had been taught to value. We could taste products together and discuss them.

———

During this time, I also played a role in the creation of what would become the Seagram Building. I capitalize "Building" because that is how I always think of it.

The saga of the Building is a wonderful story of a father who wanted to save his daughter from the sins of living single and divorced in Paris. It is also the story of a daughter who, as an artist, understood quality with every cell in her body. And it is the story of a wife who encouraged her husband to bring his rebellious daughter back and let her supervise the construction of the Building.

Father had purchased a building site for Seagram, a ritzy apartment house located at 375 Park Avenue. During the time-consuming process of buying the apartment house, getting the tenants out, razing it, and preparing the site for construction, he began to survey buildings with an eye to what his own should look like. He seemed quite pleased with the Dominion Life Insurance Company building in Montreal, a drab stone building, solid and uninteresting.

Vic Fischel commissioned Charles Luckman of Lever Brothers to do a drawing and a model of his concept for a building. Three different entrances were specified, one for each of the major sales companies— Seagram, Calvert, and Four Roses. Somehow, the *New Yorker* got wind of this, and declared in an article that the new Seagram Building would, indeed, be based on the Luckman blueprint.

Phyllis read the article with angst and wrote a very long letter to Father telling him what the building should be like. It should "invite people in" and not make them feel that they were walking in a canyon; it should be a monument to him, but also a statement for the future. Father brought that letter to Mother and they discussed it. It occurred to both of them that this might be a way to get Phyllis out from that den of iniquity called Paris. Mother suggested that Father give Phyllis the job of selecting the architect and supervising the building's design. Father agreed, and Phyllis came to New York. She had been a sculptor and a painter, and was quite talented in those two fields, even if she didn't think so. (She's a perfectionist, and probably didn't think she was talented enough.) She found her true destiny in architecture and proved to everyone, including herself, that her skills were indeed formidable.

Father might have thought he was going to have his own way, as was his wont, but he hadn't reckoned with Phyllis, who has great taste and is very articulate, especially when something matters to her. She traveled from one end of America to the other looking at buildings before selecting an architect.

Despite Father's edict of "no stilts" and his admiration for old-fashioned buildings, Phyllis hired Ludwig Mies van der Rohe. Phillip Johnson became his design associate, with Kahn and Jacobs doing the grunt work. Father had taken a liking to Lou Crandall, a builder of great note, and his firm was hired to do the construction.

Phyllis had the good sense to introduce Father and Mies, and they seemed to get along. Mies made Father part of the design team by letting him know exactly what he was planning, and Father learned to respect and even like Mies—though I don't think that he ever went so far as to agree that "less is more."

Because I was the only person who was not cowed by her, my lot was to be the pragmatist. I explained to her that, while her ambition was to build a great building, my job was to save money where possible, and we agreed to solve everything between the two of us without going to Father for arbitration. Though our discussions were always informed by mutual respect, there were, in fact, numerous disagreements. For instance, at one point I was told that Mies was considering using bronze for the skin, but that anodized aluminum would give the same effect more economically. Phyllis prevailed on this point, and most others. Looking back, I'm glad that she did.

Phyllis was deeply involved in the construction of the Seagram Building for several years. It became the great endeavor that launched her distinguished career. Later she went to Yale and then to the University of Chicago, where she continued to work with Mies, and became an architect in her own right. She built the Saidye Bronfman Centre in Montreal, a gift from Saidye's four children in honor of their parents' fortieth anniversary, contributed a great deal of hard work to an array of pro bono projects (including "Save Montreal"), and eventually created the Canadian Centre for Architecture in Montreal, another fantastic building and a world-class institution. But in my eyes, nothing she or anyone else could do will ever rival the beauty and integrity of the Seagram Building.

The day we moved in, I was with Father in his corner office on the fifth floor. I greeted all the employees one by one and introduced each to Mr. Sam. We were so proud of our Building. Company stationery, calling cards, even interoffice memos bore its image.

Though the Building was supposed to be Father's monument, in the end it became a testament to Mies, and to Phyllis's brilliant distillation of what the three-word Seagram motto really means: Integrity, Craftsmanship, Tradition.

Finally, the time came to act. As chairman of the administrative committee, I recommended to Father that Seagram adopt a retirement plan.

Though it may seem odd that we didn't have one, it wasn't so strange when you consider Father's personality and business style. Since he never intended to retire, he didn't think of the need for a retirement policy to cover the other executives (we did have a pension plan).

The top group was getting older. General Schwengel, the figurehead president of Joseph E. Seagram & Sons, Inc., was in his seventies, as was Jim Friel just before his death. Bill Wachtel, the head of Calvert, was in his late sixties, and on and on.

One evening in Tarrytown, in the summer of 1957, I told Father that a retirement policy was essential, because the senior officers were costing the company a lot of money and doing little in return. Father agreed.

"We've got to start with General Schwengel."

"Who," Father asked, "do you propose to take his place as president of the company?"

"Me," I answered.

"Oh, no, my son. That means you would have to consort with all sorts of people, distributors who once were bootleggers. I don't want you to do that."

"Sir, if you were to tell me that I was too young and too inexperienced for that responsibility, I would have to agree. But if you're telling me that the company is not good enough for me to be its president, then it's not good enough to work for at all."

That, of course, was that. In November, the inside board elected me president and chief executive officer of Joseph E. Seagram & Sons, Inc. I looked at Vic Fischel as the words "chief executive officer" were read by the secretary, and saw that he was not a happy man. Vic no doubt knew that there was going to be a very big difference between Frank Schwengel as CEO and Edgar M. Bronfman.

Bearing in mind that Great Britain's Parliament finally took power from the monarchy through the power of the purse, one of the first things I did after assuming my new position was to insist that my initials appear on all salary increases. Hereafter, Vic Fischel would have to come to me to explain every raise in the sales companies.

To further establish authority, I strengthened my oversight of administration. Still, I felt I had not yet proven to my own organization, to the distributors and retailers, and to the industry that I was qualified to run the company.

Enter Calvert Reserve, which had been slipping at the rate of about 10 percent annually for many years. From a high of some 3 million cases just after World War II, it had a current sales level of just under a million cases. In the mid-thirties, it had been America's leading blended whiskey, but it had never achieved the enormous market share or prestige that had come to 7 Crown after Seagram dropped 5 Crown.

Part of the problem was that Father and Seagram were far behind the new marketing curve. Father had built a great business, and no smart-ass MBA was going to tell him what to do. Consumer research? Father just "knew."

In fairness, Father did have great instincts for brands, but terms such as *market position* and *market share* were fairly new concepts, and foreign to him.

Marketing, as a concept, didn't really come into its own until the fifties. Up until then, it was understood that getting the consumer to buy one's products involved two basic elements: selling and advertising. Then along came something called sales promotion, which was a little bit of both—advertising within the retail establishment, placed there by salespeople.

Finally, it occurred to some company that putting products on the shelves and having the consumer take them off required advertising, selling, sales promotion, and public relations. So they rolled all four up into one word, *marketing*. Next they came up with the concept of the brand manager, a specialist in charge of every aspect of the brand, including its composition (the manufacturing process), its pricing, its advertising, its merchandising, sales promotion, its public-relations efforts, and its profitability. Next they established a unified overall sales force, because each salesman would gain strength by representing a whole line of merchandise rather than only a single brand.

From my first days in New York, I had wanted to get more involved in the sales and marketing function at Seagram because it was clear—every business magazine said so—that we were slowly falling. And I knew that between Vic Fischel and Father, we were destined to fall even further behind.

With Calvert Reserve, I had my first opportunity, and a dramatic one at that. Nobody in the wine and spirits industry—perhaps in any other industry—had ever been able to turn around a brand in such decline. But in the spring of 1962 I dreamed of a way to do it, and enlisted the help of Bill Bernbach, a good friend and by far the best advertising executive I have ever met.

On the short side, with a prominent nose and a pair of piercing blue eyes, Bill was a man of enormous ego, and incredibly fluent and convincing. More important, his advertising reflected that persuasive talent. Along with another Jew, Maxwell Dane, and an Irishman named Ned Doyle, he had created the advertising agency Doyle Dane Bernbach. I had admired Bill despite the work that he had done for Schenley Reserve—the "whipped" whiskey campaign—and had asked him to do a campaign for Chivas Regal. This is a story all by itself. I'll tell it later on.

I asked Bill to lunch one day and outlined my plan to overhaul Calvert Reserve. First I would change the name to Calvert Extra. Then I would change the package so that the front label featured drinks, a shot, a whiskey on the rocks, and a highball.

We would put nothing but aged spirits in the blend; this would be the "Extra." Calvert Extra would be sold at the same price as Calvert Reserve, but with no discounting. We would try to obtain permission from the Department of the Treasury to state the age of our spirits on the bottles' back label. However, this was in violation of their normal rules so that, however truthful our claim, it would probably be disapproved. Anticipating this, we then planned to leave the label blank and sue the government for permission to state the contents. If we carried out this plan well, we would obtain terrific publicity about the brand and its aged spirits—just the story I wanted to get across.

I would personally see to the blend and travel the country, putting my personal prestige on the line by introducing the brand at distributor meetings in every market.

One other vital element: we would pick up every unsold bottle of Calvert Reserve from the retailers and replace it with Calvert Extra.

Bill loved the idea, and promised to get back to me, which he did a few weeks later. He had devised a campaign, but was concerned whether or not the whiskey would fit the advertising. He then showed me the composite of the introductory double spread, which was headlined "Introducing Soft Whiskey."

I told him there might be a problem, and went into the blending lab. I tasted each individual part blend (a grouping of like whiskeys from the same distillery) and determined which of them might be just a little bit sharp. Those part blends were then broken down to individual lots, which allowed me to throw out the troublemakers and increase the amounts of those items I thought tasted "soft." The blend was thus reconstituted to taste the way the ad said it would.

Then I went into Father's office, located on the fifth floor of the Seagram Building, next to mine. It was a sunny afternoon, and he was in a good mood until I started my pitch. He looked at me with amazement.

"Why stick out your neck, my son? You have it made. Someday this office will be yours, and you want to take a chance on a job like that?"

"That's precisely why I must do it," I told him. "I want to take on the toughest job I can think of and prove to me, to you, and to everyone that I can do it."

He still looked quizzical, so I proceeded to describe the plan that I had worked out for Bill Bernbach. Father nodded at every phase until I got to the part where we would pick up every unsold bottle of Calvert Reserve.

It wasn't the cost that upset him. It must have seemed to him an admission that something was wrong with the whiskey, a direct attack on his personal integrity.

I explained that, while I recognized the danger of what the public would perceive as the recall of a defective product, there was an even worse scenario that could unfold. Imagine, I said, a distributor's salesman, armed with a handsome sales kit, walking into a retailer's establishment and making his pitch. The retailer replies, "Calvert Extra, huh. Well, come back when I've sold all the Calvert Reserve that I have in stock." End of conversation, end of distribution drive. And why launch an advertising program without distribution?

Now, I told Father, picture another scenario. That same salesman goes into the retailer's establishment and asks, "How much Calvert Reserve do you have in stock?" The retailer confesses that he is not sure, or he gives a rough estimate. The salesman says, "Count the cases and the bottles: we are going to pick them up. I want to talk to you about this new product the company has developed."

"Father," I said, "if the salesman can't sell at least two bottles for every one he is picking up, he isn't much of a salesman. We will get terrific distribution, and then all the other aspects of the campaign can be put in place."

Convinced, he signed off on the plan.

Next, I needed to find the right man to run Calvert and get the campaign rolling. My choice was Bernie Tabbat, with whom I had already worked. Bernie was an executive with our most important sales company, the eponymous Seagram (other sales branches included Calvert, Four Roses, and some smaller concerns). I had first met him in 1951 at the Seagram distributors' convention, and had been much impressed with a presentation he had made. So I got to know him. I tapped him for this new position after we had a perfect meeting of the minds on every aspect of the Calvert campaign.

But when I told Father and Vic, I hit a stumbling block. "No, not Bernie Tabbat!" exclaimed Vic. Father, for reasons I cannot fathom (maybe out of habit), agreed with Vic, who was afraid of someone he couldn't control getting that close to me.

Looking directly at Vic, I replied in a steely voice, "And why not?"

Father, sensing the rising tension and wishing to avoid a confrontation, said, "Vic, I guess it's going to be Bernie Tabbat."

Bernie became the president of Calvert Distillers Company. Because Seagram and Calvert were highly competitive in the marketplace, I felt that I, too, needed a Calvert corporate title. It turned out that we had a manufacturing company which was already incorporated, and I arranged to become its president. Thus, I would be introduced to Calvert salesmen and Calvert distributor salesmen as president of the Calvert Distilling Corporation.

All the pieces had come together. "Look," I said to Father, "you've said often enough that you want your sons to make their mistakes while your eyes are open. Now please promise to not interfere, no matter how hard that might be. If I fall flat on my face, you'll be here to pick me up, but in the meantime, this is my baby."

"Yes, my son," he agreed with some gravity.

But that would not have been Father. He could never leave anything alone. We used to put things into advertisements just so he could change them, a standard technique in dealing with egotistical chief executives.

This time, I hadn't expected any interference. But when the prepublication ad for the "Introducing Soft Whiskey" campaign came across his desk, as all ads did, he picked up the telephone and called Bill Bernbach. "Bill, that's a great ad," he congratulated. "I'd like you to just make one small change. Change the word 'Soft.'"

You think life with Father was easy?

We went from market to market, meeting with the distributors and their salesmen as well as the press, to whom we told the story of the aged spirits and the suit against the government, always insisting that the issue was the right to tell the truth. This strategy generated an enormous amount of media coverage, in turn arousing tremendous public interest. And, as the pickup and exchange began, so did the advertising. Right from the beginning, we had a hit on our hands.

Vic Fischel couldn't stand not being part of the act, and decided to come to the dog-and-pony show we were putting on in Los Angeles. The procession of speakers was fairly straightforward. Bernie Tabbat was master of ceremonies. He introduced me, and I went into my pitch about the new whiskey, the new bottle and label, the pickup and exchange, and my own personal commitment to the whole program. Bernie then explained the specifics of the program and introduced the head of advertising and sales promotion, who showed the ads and the point-of-sale material as well as the salesman's kit, to great applause.

We had to add Vic to the program in Los Angeles, and he was still drunk from the night before. As he babbled on and on, Bernie asked me what could be done. "Watch," I told him, and on a big piece of paper I wrote the words "CLOSE NOW!!!" and held it up in front of Vic. He promptly cut off his remarks, and we went on with the show.

Afterward, I told Vic that I didn't need him for what I was trying to do, and if he went home quietly we could forget the incident.

The last show of that marketing campaign was held in Boston. We went there January 31 and returned February 2. Having forgiven Father for his comment on "Soft Whiskey," I invited him to the show. I also took Ann along since I thought she might be curious as to what I had been doing on the road all those months.

I do believe that Father was impressed with what went on in Boston—the professionalism, the enthusiasm, and especially the freshness of the presentation. It isn't easy to keep a presentation fresh, and I learned to admire professional actors all the more.

What helped greatly was our belief in the campaign, and the fun we had doing it. Father didn't understand the need for all the jokes—all in good taste, mind you—and it was hard to explain that, after months on the road, we had to make it fun or it might have come off as a deadly bore.

Over the next few years, Calvert Extra grew to almost 1.5 million cases from the low of Calvert Reserve's 800,000-plus. I had proven—especially to myself—that I was capable of running the Seagram empire.

The funny thing was that, while I was elated, it really had never occurred to me that I wouldn't succeed, especially after the reactions to the first couple of presentations. We had created excitement and had demonstrated that we were conscious of the problems of the salesmen to whom we were pitching. The applause, the shouts, the smiles and laughs at every meeting told the story.

The success of the Calvert Extra campaign changed the way Father treated me. I honestly believed that he would have preferred that I fail. After all, the great practitioner of the not-invented-here syndrome had been outflanked, and now more than ever, having proven my ability, I was the symbol of his mortality. It also changed my relationship with Vic Fischel. Thereafter, I not only *viewed* him with a certain contempt, I *treated* him accordingly.

One satisfying footnote: At the same time we were developing the market for Calvert Extra, I tapped into an idea I had heard from Bill Wachtel, Calvert's former head. Bill had once suggested that we turn Lord Calvert, a super blend Father created before World War II, into a bottled-in-the-U.S. Canadian whiskey.

Under a quirk in the U.S. tax law, one paid excise taxes on all imported whiskeys as if they were 100 proof. Thus, one could import very high-proof whiskey—about 135 degrees of proof—and pay excise taxes as if it were 100 proof. We could then bottle the goods in this country at 80 proof (thereby saving a lot of tax money) and, at a very competitive price, compete against those 80- and 86-proof whiskeys that came to the U.S. market in bottles and paid excise taxes as if they were 100 proof. Many Scotch and Canadian brands were taking advantage of this loophole, and were doing very well indeed, much to the consternation of the standard brands.

Fritz Siebel, who also designed the Calvert Extra label, created a terrific package, and we sold upwards of a million cases a year of Lord Calvert Canadian until the wrinkle in the law was ironed out. I had become the de jure president of the American subsidiary in 1957, but after I completed the Calvert assignment, in my own head and heart I was at least also the de facto president.

On March 4, 1961, just before the introduction of Calvert Extra, Father turned seventy. To mark the occasion, we had a party for him in New York. I decided, however, that it was in the best interest of the organization to give the company something in his name rather than lavishing him with gifts.

At the time, we had a system of medical insurance that paid for doctors' visits and minor health problems. I reasoned that, while most people could cover the ordinary doctor and dentist bills for their family, a serious illness could incapacitate them both physically and financially. After consulting with experts, we came up with a major medical program to deal with catastrophic illness. I announced the introduction of the plan at Father's party to great applause—except from Father himself, who thought the idea was okay, but that old hungry ego. . . .

I fulfilled one of my greatest dreams during this period: becoming an American citizen.

Because I was married to an American citizen, I was allowed to claim citizenship in three years from the time I applied rather than the usual five. Those three years passed swiftly, and in April 1959 I was sworn in at a private ceremony in a judge's chambers. Before he could ask me any of the standard questions, I told him that I had spent more than two years at Williams College. It would be a terrible indictment of the American educational system should I fail to answer any of his questions correctly, I said—and suggested that he just get out the Bible and swear me in. He thought this over and did exactly that.

Not long after, I invited the judge to lunch at the Seagram offices to meet Father. With a tear in his eye, Father told the judge that, while intellectually he understood my decision to become an American, emotionally he was still not adjusted to it. He loved Canada, the land that had given such opportunity to him and his family.

I must confess that I had no great love for Canada, and really thought of the whole North American continent, north of the Rio Grande, as one big country. I have always been keenly interested in U.S. politics, and I believed that it wasn't proper to get involved in a country's politics if you weren't a citizen.

As it happened, I became a citizen just in time to vote in the election of 1960, which pitted Jack Kennedy against Richard Nixon. I chose to register as a Republican. At that time, the Republican Party of New York was headed by liberals such as Nelson Rockefeller, Jack Javits, Brownie Reid, and John Lindsay. This was not yet the party of the Conservatives.

When I went to the Purchase Community Center to vote, I was told that my name was not on the list of eligible voters. I knew that this was wrong, and inquired whether a remedy was available. I was instructed to go back to the place where I had registered. On Election Day, parents visited children in school, but I told Ann that she would have to go without me—I was determined not only to cast my ballot but to see if the system worked.

Off I went to White Plains, where the clerk tried to dispense with me before discovering that I had indeed registered.

"Okay," I said. "You know that and I know that, but how am I going to convince those little old ladies at the Purchase Community Center?"

He told me to go to a judge and get a court order. All I had to do was tell him my story and swear to an oath. Much to my surprise, it worked. I went back to Purchase, showed them my court order, and voted—after all that trouble—for Nixon!

In my defense, I didn't think that John Kennedy was going to be a great president. Indeed, despite what everybody says, he was not a great president in his first term. On the day before he was killed, I was in Jack Javits's office. Jack wanted me to try and help Nelson Rockefeller win the Republican nomination. "Jack, I can't do that," I said. "I really think that, in his next term of office, Kennedy is going to be a great president, and I want to support him."

Jack called me the day after the assassination. "Edgar," he said, "I'll always remember that you called me before he was killed, not after."

While Father was not thrilled that I had sworn allegiance to a new flag, my actual move to the United States had brought little if any criticism from family members. I had argued that Seagram was doing over 90 percent of its business in the United States, and so that is where I had to be. Charles was happy about it. He and I had agreed long before that I would move to New York. We had both witnessed the terrible fights between Father and Uncle Allan, and he was determined to avoid that kind of confrontation with me. From his viewpoint, my relocation to New York solved the problem. To this day, if Charles wants to move to the most suitable office, and it turns out to be the one Uncle Allan had, he will not touch it with a ten-foot pole.

The only person who pretended that there was any question as to which of us would one day head Seagram was Father. A firm believer in the British policy of divide and conquer, he applied this strategy to Charles and me, and would tell each of us disparaging things about the other. As far as I know, however, there was never any question about Charles's ambitions. True, he and I were equal partners, and he wanted to be treated as such. But he also wanted me, not him, to succeed Father in running the company. I understood this, and now, with the Calvert Extra campaign under my belt, I was ready to take on the greatest challenge of my young career.

CHAPTER 5

TAKING THE REINS:
THE FISCHEL WAR

In 1962, after the Calvert Extra experience, I felt much more secure in my job as president, and decided it was time for me to take over sales and marketing. My original plan was to work with Vic Fischel—as long as he acknowledged that I was his boss. But despite the great success of Calvert Extra, it became clear that Vic had other ideas.

I remember a scene in Father's Chrysler Building office that took place long before I came to work for Seagram in New York. A scene was being shot for a film to be shown at a sales meeting. At one point, Father passed the glass to Vic. The symbolism didn't strike either Father or me at the time, but looking back, it was the perfect metaphor—a dress rehearsal for Vic's hope to succeed Father as head of Distillers Corporation–Seagrams Ltd.

I tried hard to get Vic to understand that his salvation lay in working *for* me, not just *with* me. We had long drunken bouts, and he would come close, swearing eternal love and all that. But I could never sway him from what he saw as his destiny: to follow Father, and then to pass the torch to me. Presumably, age played a part in that scenario. Father was in his seventies, Vic in his late fifties, and I in my thirties. Moreover, Vic thought his relationship with Father was like that of a son.

Father's lack of organization made it even more difficult. He would have ad hoc meetings with Vic (who never did anything important without clearing it with Father) and make decisions in which I was not included. That was Father's way, and I realized that I was not going to change him. He was a great entrepreneur, but not a good manager.

Another sticky problem was the relationship between Father and Vic. As Father grew older, he became even more insecure. He hated being challenged in any way, preferring the company of old cronies and sycophants like Jack Owen—and Vic. While Father understood Fischel's shortcomings, Vic's loyalty was never in question.

Vic was one of the only people with whom Father had a personal bond. True, there were a few others, such as Franz Sichel, Alfred Fromm's partner in the firm of Fromm and Sichel. But Father was essentially a lonely man. He had fought with everyone who had been close to him—his brother Allan, his older brothers Abe and Harry, Laz Phillipps—and he didn't have any close friends.

The story of what happened between Father and Laz is emblematic. Lazarus Phillipps, Q.C., was Montreal's most renowned lawyer. A trustee of the trusts Sam and Allan had set up for their children, he was Father's closest confidant for a long time. But, true to form, the two men got to fighting because they both wanted to be Canada's first Jewish senator. The Liberal Party wouldn't give it to Father because of the Bronfman bootlegging stigma, and Laz was next in line. The original plan was that Laz would run for Parliament, then get a Cabinet appointment and lobby Father into the Senate (an appointed position in Canada, even today). But Laz lost the election—his socialist opponent showed pictures of his home in Westmount, claiming that Phillipps had nothing in common with the electorate in that district, and the voters decided he was right. So Laz decided that, since Sam couldn't get the senatorship, he might as well take it, and the war was on. It wasn't until just before Father's death that I got him to shake hands with Laz and make up.

(I'm reminded of the joke about two Irishmen, Pat and Mike, who were sworn enemies all their lives. When Pat was on his deathbed, the priest asked him if he had any enemies. "Oh, no, Father, except of course for that bastard Mike." Since the priest required him to make peace with his fellow man before he sought peace in the afterlife, Mike was brought in. There was the expected wailing and swearing of eternal friendship, and then Mike started to leave. Pat beckoned him to come back for a second, then whispered in his ear, "Mike, if I don't die, this shit don't go!")

Father's fondness for Vic and his need for companionship made a difficult situation even more intractable. Of course, there was never any doubt in Father's mind as to who would succeed him. But he didn't want my ascent to come at Vic's expense.

It might seem that Father's sentiments should have been irrelevant—after all, I was president and chief executive officer of Joseph E. Seagram & Sons, Inc. But the lines of authority were never clearly drawn because Father, the Deng Xiaoping of Seagram, ignored them. If I wanted to assume control of Fischel's sales operation, I would have to take him on directly, which meant taking on Father.

To grasp the complexity of the situation, you must understand how the sales operation was structured. Vic was president of the House of Seagram, Inc., a wholly owned subsidiary of Joseph E. Seagram & Sons, Inc. Jack Finneran was executive vice president. Within the House of Seagram, Inc., there were three major sales companies: Seagram, Calvert, and Four Roses, each headed by an executive vice president. There were also two less important sales companies headed by vice presidents who reported to Fischel: Kessler, a one-brand company run by Jack Wishny, a relative of Abe Bronfman's wife, Sophie; and General Wine and Spirits, which sold Chivas Regal and Wolfschmidt vodka.

Then there was Browne Vintners, headed by Byron Tosi, which sold Mumm champagne, White Horse scotch, Martell cognac, and other "agency" brands (those owned by third parties), including, believe it or not, Perrier water. This company reported to me. That may sound odd, but from the time Seagram purchased the Browne Vintners Company, the man who ran it—named Oscar Weill—reported directly to Father, and his successors (Weill was later run over in London, probably looking the wrong way) reported to me.

Not only was the Seagram hierarchy confusing, it also lent itself to a wildly inefficient organization with an enormous overhead. Each sales company tracked its own shipments, inventories, and depletions (defined as "sales to retailers," i.e., the amount the distributors, our primary customers, had sold to their retailers). Fischel, however, was not to blame. It was Father's obsession to have competing companies, and in an expanding market it wasn't such a bad idea. Not surprisingly, Father also wanted to be the "President of Presidents." Thus, while bureaucracy in a family-controlled business is theoretically less of a problem than in other kinds of organizations, in this case it was just as bad operationally.

When Vic proposed the concept of "the House of Seagram" sales organization, he had estimated the annual potential savings at $5 million, but he didn't know how to achieve them. First, he didn't understand the nature of bureaucracies: you cannot get people to volunteer to become redundant. Second, he really had no one who could take charge of implementing the necessary changes.

The computer age was just beginning, and we should have been able to cut internal costs steeply. I was intrigued with the possibilities of the computer, but we had nobody in the shop who could explain its potential, and I erred in not getting someone to do just that.

Adding to the crisis atmosphere was the increasing friction between Father and me. The two areas in the company where he still insisted on holding full sway were advertising and packaging, and we battled regularly on both.

Fischel was smart enough not to get involved, but I felt I had to argue with Father. I was convinced that I was right and he was wrong—not in every detail, but certainly in the direction in which we were headed. The world was changing and we were not. Sophisticated techniques were being developed that would revolutionize the way products were marketed.

Father, meanwhile, had his head in the sand. He would spend hours in the packaging department with Gordon Odell, a designer he had brought down from Canada. Gordon, an older man with thinning reddish hair, watery eyes, and a small mustache, had a talent for drawing exactly what Father wanted, but little imagination of his own. Father asked others, often Fischel and me, to join these sessions and would put on the hat of creative genius. Drawing upon his legendary store of foul language, he would hurl invectives at Odell, who would smilingly acquiesce to everything Father demanded.

Father's idiosyncratic nature sometimes led him to pursue ridiculous notions. For instance, in the late fifties, the company bought a great piece of real estate in Chicago, where the Ritz Carlton now stands. Earlier, he had bought a warehouse in Maspeth, New York, and outfitted it with a huge sign (we did use the building to store sales promotion pieces), and he looked at a couple of buildings in Los Angeles for the same purpose. I don't know where he got the idea that putting signs on buildings was terrific advertising, but Vic Fischel encouraged him in this nonsense.

Even if Father had enthusiastically embraced the new ideas that were transforming our industry and every other, the truth is that neither advertising nor packaging is an exact science. There are many ways of testing prospective advertising campaigns, but to use them successfully, you first have to have a sense of the inadequacy of the testing process.

Arthur Politz, a great pollster in his day because of his tremendous math skills, once told me that, before you can test an advertising campaign, you have to have a hypothesis. You cannot simply ask people which of several "somethings" they would prefer, because they won't understand the question. His example was an early job he did for Dr. West's toothbrushes.

In performing a color test on the toothbrushes, Politz discovered that, of all the colors tested, more than 90 percent of respondents preferred either red or blue. But sales figures showed that, despite this demonstrated color preference, they were buying the amber toothbrush. So he asked the question a different way. First, the subject was asked to make a choice among all the colors. Then the subject was asked to choose a free toothbrush to take home. Despite the fact that the respondents overwhelmingly selected blue or red, the color toothbrush most chose to take home was amber, proving that people are most likely to pick what they perceive to be the most popular. Moral of the story: always ask the second question.

In testing packages, you have to ask people to make a choice, and they will, but they will never say "none of the above." So a campaign or a package can win a battle and lose the war.

Given these complications, along with the force of Father's personality and the awe in which he was held, it's no wonder that I had a terrible time with him on advertising and packaging.

Perhaps it seems that packaging, in particular, was none of my business—that it was up to Father, who reveled in it, and to Fischel, who ran sales and marketing. True, except Father was hopelessly behind the times, while Fischel knew as much about packaging as he did about advertising, which was nothing. Even if Vic had had an opinion, he wouldn't have spoken up. He always went along with Father's decisions.

In fairness, Fischel was not a mere flunky. He did have talent of a sort: he was very good with distributors and retailers, and had wonderful interpersonal relationships with many of both. He was a great hero during the years of shortages—which didn't end until the late fifties—because he was fair, and all our customers knew it and trusted him. But he lacked discipline and imagination, and wouldn't be considered for a top management position today.

Other forces no doubt compelled me to challenge Father. I, too, had an ego, as well as deeply held views. And, in a masochistic way, I probably enjoyed taking on Father.

More than that, the continuing decline in our corporate competitiveness promised to make my job even more difficult in the future. I was not prepared to simply sit idly by while the company I would one day run stagnated.

———

To illustrate the problems we faced, a little history is in order. At the zenith of Seagram's market penetration, in 1955 and 1956, one out of three beverage-alcohol drinks in the United States was a Seagram product. Then it went downhill. There were a number of reasons for the drop. First, the difference in quality between our products and those of our competitors had steadily tightened in the two-plus decades since the repeal of Prohibition. It wasn't that we had slipped—on the contrary, we were making better products all the time. Rather, most of the competition's products had improved greatly since the post-1933 era of the unaged whiskeys.

Another reason was the so-called war between blends and straights. Father always believed in blended whiskeys, an idea that originated in Scotland, where blends have been predominant for ages.

The issue of straights versus blends was a moot point during World War II and the Korean War, when little bourbon or straight whiskey was available. (What you could get was generally not very good because of the shortage of barrels.) In those years, Seagram purchased aged stocks of whiskeys and mostly redistilled them into grain-neutral spirits to make more 7 Crown, Calvert Reserve, and Four Roses. Four Roses had been a Kentucky straight bourbon whiskey when we acquired it, but Father changed it to a blend for two reasons: One, blends were quite a bit more profitable than straights, and we indeed made more money in the short run. Two, Father was known as the champion of blends, and since everything at Seagram was so personal with him, he wouldn't sell a brand of straight whiskey.

The redistilling process was expensive, but with the wartime excess profits tax we were paying well over 90 percent in taxes, which meant that market penetration became far more important than profits. After the war, it was a hard habit to break. Indeed, it took my entire business career to change Seagram's focus from volume to profit. (It still might not have happened if my son Edgar hadn't come upon the scene, but that story comes later.)

When bourbon whiskey was once again in plentiful supply, the enormous market share of blended whiskey figured to decline. I suggested to Father that he make Four Roses into a bourbon again, but he was adamantly against it. Instead, we tried to swim upstream by producing blends of straights, which only confused the customer. The effort was unsuccessful, which reinforced Father's negative view of straights.

Of course, we should have been in the bourbon business, but what bothered me was the *process* of the decision, not the decision itself. Father, scaling the heights of unchecked egotism, was convinced that nobody would ever understand the idea of Sam Bronfman selling bourbon. He had the same attitude about doing business in Germany. The reality was that, while Bronfman and Seagram might have been synonymous in Montreal, the rest of the world knew only the company name. What Father never understood was that, while you must have enough ego to make gutsy decisions, you also have to keep some perspective.

Another dimension of the war between straights and blends was the feud between Father and his arch rival, Schenley Industries' Lewis S. Rosenstiel, who was championing straight bourbon whiskeys. Lew had been a partner of the Bronfman brothers during Prohibition, and apparently thought of himself as Sam's fourth brother. He was also a man of enormous ego, and talent to match.

Schenley and Seagram were supposed to have merged after Prohibition, but somehow it was not to be. Father told the story this way: One day, he and Lew were going along the bottling line of the Three Feathers plant in Schenley, Pennsylvania. Father picked up a bottle and said, "Lew, this is hot whiskey!"—meaning it came straight from the still into the bottle. Lew nodded in acknowledgment, to which Father replied, "Lew, we're both going to build great businesses, but you'll take the low road while I'll take the high road."

Seagram's decline also was accelerated by new products entering the marketplace. Father watched with dismay as rum became a factor and Bacardi established itself as a dominant brand. Likewise, he witnessed Smirnoff vodka emerge as a market force, while General Schwengel threw cases of vodka into the swimming pools of American Legion conventions because vodka was "red" and unpatriotic. To make matters worse, Father could have bought Heublein, the purveyor of Smirnoff, but he was unwilling to pay the price. (There was probably never an opportunity to buy Bacardi, a business owned by a Cuban family that had no interest in selling.)

Attempts were made to play catch-up, such as the purchases of Ronrico rum and Wolfschmidt vodka. Uncle Allan bought Wolfschmidt from Sam Morrell, a Latvian Jew who pretended he had a "zecret" (as he pronounced it) formula. This forced us to pay a rectification tax (a tax on blending), which removed what little profit there might have been from the product. (Morrell was shocked when I told him that the secret formula was a couple of drops of citric acid, which we had determined by chemical analysis). The rule in those days—and except for imports such as Absolut, Stoli, and others, it hasn't changed much in almost forty years—was that there were two vodkas: Smirnoff and price. If you wanted the consumer to buy a brand other than Smirnoff, the price would have to be significantly less. The same was true of Puerto Rican rums and Bacardi.

Father did make a great move in the mid-fifties when he bought Myers's rum, a Jamaican product with a distinctive taste. Myers's has gone from strength to strength ever since. In Canada, where rum was a big-seller product on both coasts, Father developed Captain Morgan, named after an old pirate who had sailed the Caribbean. This brand did very well in Canada, then in England, and was introduced into the United States some ten years ago as Captain Morgan Spiced Rum. It now sells more than one million cases a year, and is still growing.

But other golden opportunities were squandered. For instance, Father could have bought Jack Daniel's. There was no question about the price, but he passed it up because he didn't understand the accounting procedures whereby one could write up the inventory and then write off the excess goodwill (which would have thus been part of the cost of the whiskey) against taxes. He just assumed that he knew and, as usual, nobody would contradict him. I learned a valuable lesson: if you don't know, ask.

A product Father should have stayed away from was Leroux, a cordial company in Philadelphia that also marketed Nikolai vodka. He bought Leroux at a price not conducive to profitability, and we struggled with this company for years and years. It made a little money, but we finally sold it in 1991 because it didn't meet the new standards of profitability set by Edgar Jr. By then, it was clear that we were much better off putting the money and sales efforts behind Martell cognacs than playing with domestic liqueurs.

Beyond the poor decision-making about product development and acquisition, a great deal of executive time was wasted during these years on two divisive issues: the Forand Bill and something called "Fair Trade."

The Forand Bill was a piece of congressional legislation intended to allow distillers to keep whiskey in bond for another four years before excise taxes had to be paid (the federal excise tax was then $10.50 a gallon). The original measure had called for taxes to be paid on beverage alcohol within eight years after it was produced, so the final version represented a significant extension.

Many distillers, in particular Lew Rosenstiel of Schenley, had made a lot of whiskey that was unsalable, or that tasted off. (Lew had used laminated barrels instead of white oak in the aging process.) If that whiskey had been forced out of bond, the financial consequences would have been very serious. Lew argued that the law was arbitrary, and that a distiller should be allowed to keep his product in bond as long as was reasonable.

Seagram's General Schwengel, under Father's orders, took this as a personal crusade, insisting that (a) the law was the law; and (b) American-made whiskey got worse rather than better after eight years because of the hot climate in the whiskey-making areas. He tried to line up the entire industry against Schenley, pointing out that the cost of keeping whiskey in barrels would creep inexorably higher if distillers started an age war.

There was some truth to each man's claim. American whiskeys almost never improve beyond eight years because of the climate. But the private-enterprise system surely allows freedom of choice in such matters. Ultimately, both sides underestimated the American public. Taste was what really mattered, and Lew, who never did understand quality, failed in his effort to sell product based on age alone. At one point during the war, Father got really agitated because Lew was advertising his Schenley Reserve with big circles around the ages on the back label to distinguish them from the ages published by 7 Crown. But the public just didn't give a damn.

It seemed to me that the way to beat a rival was to outmarket him, not to use laws that were intrinsically unfair. But there are no Marquis of Queensberry rules in love or war, and Father fought the Forand Bill almost to the death. Nevertheless, it passed, much to his chagrin. I don't think he ever quite forgave Jack Javits for voting in favor, even though Jack's brother was counsel to Schenley. As for Lew, the animosity between him and Father soared to epic scale.

When Lew's son David died in the sixties, I asked Father to write Lew a condolence letter, arguing that, after all, the loss of a son is beyond business rivalry. He took my advice, but there was no response. When I later met Lew at a convention, I reproached him for not acknowledging Father's outreach. He did write Father, invited me to lunch, and actually had the audacity to offer me a job. The luncheon was about sizes—Rosenstiel was on a crusade to let the industry use any size bottle it wanted. We went to a private room in his club, and he proceeded to write all over the tablecloth with a pen, arguing his case. This ended when I said, "Lew (he had asked me to call him Lew), I don't see how this is going to help you. Every retailer has limited shelf space. If there are that many more sizes, he will have to carry Seven Crown in every one of those sizes, leaving less shelf space for other brands like Schenley Reserve." He agreed to back off!

Because of Father's obsession with the Forand Bill, another disaster nearly overtook us. Bill Green—a great friend and at the time the president and chief operating officer of Thatcher Glass Manufacturing Company, a Seagram supplier—suggested to me that we bring Crown Royal into the United States. This was a brand that Father had started in 1939 to honor King George VI and Queen Elizabeth on the first visit a reigning monarch had ever made to Canada. (Father arranged to have a few cases of this beautifully packaged product put on the royal train.) Over the years, many Americans visiting Canada had brought back a bottle or two of Crown Royal, so it was reasonably well known in the United States, even though it had never been sold or advertised here.

Bill was right, of course, but I had to convince both my brother, Charles, and Father. Charles was no problem. "We make an awful lot of money on Crown Royal in Canada," he said.

"How much?" I asked.

"Eighteen dollars a case."

"We'll make thirty-two in the U.S."

"Take all you want," said Charles.

Father also agreed, but insisted that we withhold the certificate of age that was always included in the package. His reasoning: since Crown Royal ranged from ten to thirty-five years old, albeit damn little of the blend was older than ten years, including the certificate would be seen as an admission that age is good—thereby compromising our position on the Forand Bill.

When the first shipments were made in 1964, customers started complaining about the absence of the certificate, and rumor spread that this was not the same whiskey we sold in Canada. Father reluctantly relented, without acknowledging, of course, that he had made a mistake. Today, Crown Royal is a huge and very profitable brand in the United States.

We also squandered much time and energy during the late fifties and early sixties on "Fair Trade," which thankfully is now a part of history.

Seagram, along with the rest of the industry, sells to distributors, who sell to retailers, who sell to consumers. This three-tier system was intact then as it is now. The big difference at that time was the policy that allowed the manufacturer to set the price at which its goods were to be sold by the retailer. (Father loved the line that General Schwengel had created: "A fair profit to the wholesaler, a fair profit to the retailer, and a fair price to the consumer.")

Our people were spending an inordinate amount of time suing retailers who discounted our merchandise—in other words, suing our customers! The theory was that a manufacturer had the right to protect his brand name and its reputation. Discounting supposedly would make the product seem cheap to the consumer and thus less elegant. Prestige was the name of the game. It still is, but not at the consumer's expense: price maintenance is no longer a part of the marketing scheme.

Fair Trade was not universal, however. Governor Nelson Rockefeller discovered when he was appointed vice president of the United States by Gerald Ford that the prices of beverage-alcohol products were considerably less in Washington, D.C., than in New York, which annoyed him. He asked for state legislation under which distillers had to affirm that the prices they received for products sold in New York were no higher than anywhere else. These "Affirmation Laws" spread to many states.

This should have been good news, because it discouraged distillers from offering deals or discounts in other markets unless they did the same in New York. But the industry was unhappy about the Affirmation Laws, so wedded was it to discounting.

Lew Rosenstiel's Schenley Industries, which had the exclusive wholesale rights for Dewar's White Label, did not maintain Fair Trade prices in New York City, among other markets. This brand was sold at cheaper prices than its competition and became the highest-selling Scotch brand in Manhattan, the largest Scotch whiskey market in the United States.

The success of Dewar's was not just a matter of price: it was a traditional Scotch whiskey, with a good reputation and quality to match. When consumers discovered that they could buy it at discounted prices, they did so in droves.

Father and Fischel believed that, in the long run, Dewar's would lose its cachet because of the cheaper price, but it didn't. To this day it is a market leader in the New York market. They were fighting to keep things exactly the same, based on the philosophy that if you are number one, innovation can only hurt you. The truth is that in a competitive marketplace, innovation and continuous improvement are the only way to stay on top. Ask the American automobile companies or IBM.

———·——

While in a very real sense the Fischel War was a struggle over the future of Seagram, it would be misleading to suggest that the company was completely resistant to change. As stubborn as Father was, at times he was capable of broad-mindedness. Two examples come to mind, the first involving Chivas Regal, Seagram's premium brand of Scotch whiskey.

The origins of Chivas Regal date back to the thirties. Five Crown and 7 Crown were market leaders in their respective price ranges. It was discovered on a trademark search that some firm in Scotland owned the name "Four Crown." Panic! A Scottish friend of Father's named James Barclay was commissioned to buy the company, Robert Brown, Ltd. It also had a stock of aging Scotch whiskey and some contracts to buy "fillings," new whiskeys made by independent Highland distillers. After the war, the same Jimmy Barclay told Father that a small company named Chivas Brothers might be available. Chivas Brothers owned only one distillery, Strathisla Glenlivet, but it was the oldest in the Highlands. (The Glenlivet, which the company bought after Father's passing, is the oldest licensed distillery in Scotland, but Strathisla is the oldest distillery.)

Among certain aficionados, Chivas Regal had been known before the war as a twelve-year-old whiskey. Remembering this, Father bought it and began planning the introduction of Chivas Regal into the U.S. market.

I remember sitting in Father's office in 1954 with all sorts of nonsense going on involving the details of the package design, paper for labels, and even glass supplies. It all seemed a bit much, and I finally asked Father what this was all about. He sat me down and told me that the British authorities were eager, to put it mildly, for exports. Meanwhile, here we were with a potential brand and all that whiskey sitting in our warehouses. Swearing me to secrecy, he explained his delaying tactics: he wanted to introduce Chivas Regal as a twelve-year-old whiskey. No one else could possibly produce another twelve-year-old brand for years to come; they didn't have the inventory. In a few months' time, when his whiskeys reached that magic age, he would begin to ship, but not a moment before!

Chivas Regal did indeed make a big splash. But by 1962, the so-called light Scotches, specifically Cutty Sark and J & B, were stealing the market. Chivas, in its dark green glass with a label depicting the ancient accoutrements of the highland castles, was losing ground. I knew this because Herbert Evenson, the executive vice president in charge of Seagram, had shown me the figures.

Chivas had a heavy image and a heavy taste. The formula called for 65 percent malt whiskeys and 35 percent grains. I suggested a different formula, along with a new package and a new advertising campaign.

To his credit, Father agreed to all three, and designed the present package himself with the help of Gordon Odell (there have been only minor changes since). Father had no talent for drawing, but he did have visual skills and knew exactly what he wanted. Above all else, what he wanted was a label that projected dignity. He was a Prohibition-influenced distiller, and dignity was necessary to wash away the stain of that era. It was also essential in his lifelong quest to "be someone."

Once the label was designed, we needed a new advertising campaign. I had not yet met Bill Bernbach (this was before the Calvert Extra campaign), but I admired the work Doyle Dane Bernbach was doing, with the notable exception of its Schenley ads. The campaign for "whipped" whiskey was unsightly and unappetizing, and it made me wonder whether Bill Bernbach could do much for us.

Nonetheless, he seemed to have the kind of creativity I was looking for. This was the man who advertised the Israeli airline El Al with "No Goose, No Gander" and dreamed up the Levi's Jewish Rye campaign (Sammy Davis Jr. and others saying you don't have to be Jewish to like it—but it helps). Father tended to take himself, his products, and his persona too seriously; Bernbach knew how to use humor to get a serious point across.

Bill agreed to meet at Father's apartment at the St. Regis Hotel and make a pitch, but said that he would do no speculative advertising. He would show us the agency's current work and let that speak for itself. I consented to these terms, and Father was taken with Bill and his work. DDB got the account.

It didn't hurt that Bill was Jewish. In those days, very few Jews occupied top positions in advertising agencies. Before he opened his own shop, Bill had been creative director at Grey Advertising, which was headed by two Jews, but I don't recall any other Jewish ad agencies until Doyle Dane Bernbach came along.

(There's a funny story about Jews in advertising: Procter & Gamble used a computer to pick names for new brands, and was about to come out with a new cleaning product. Since the company always did the preliminary advertising work in-house, it was far along with the introductory advertising when some guy at the agency pointed out that DREK, the name the computer had chosen, is Yiddish for "shit." If that someone had been me, knowing of P&G's anti-Semitic hiring policies way back then, I would have kept my mouth shut.)

Father tried to convince Bill that the proper campaign for Chivas was "On a pedestal in every land." He wanted the bottle of Chivas actually on a pedestal with Rome, Athens, London, Paris, etc., as backgrounds. I guess he knew that Bill wasn't going to give him that campaign, because he had his Montreal flunky, Merle M. Schneckenburger, hire one of the Canadian advertising firms to create a few pedestal ads.

Bernbach brought the DDB advertising to my office. The ads were very good, but he had one on the bottom which he kept hiding. (Every marketing executive knows that trick.) I finally asked him what he was concealing. Showman that he was, he told me that he had an introductory ad for the new package, but that he didn't think I would dare run it.

And hence came the ad that literally turned a fading Chivas Regal into the shining star it is today. Bill's concept broke all the rules: it had a ton of copy, and it disparaged the company. The headline read: "What Idiot Changed the Chivas Regal Package?" The copy explained the reasons (you could now see the whiskey, etc., etc.). Its conclusion: "Maybe the Idiot Was a Genius."

"Bill," I said, "we'll run it and I'll take the consequences."

After all, I reasoned with him, if he didn't think the gamble was worth taking (we were talking about Father's wrath), he wouldn't have brought it over. And, besides, it was I who had made the decision to change the package.

Father, busy with his pedestals, didn't object to the ad. (Actually, the only person who gave me hell for the ad was Ann, who said, "Why do you pay good money to call yourself an idiot?") Of course, that didn't keep him from trying to convince both of us that pedestals were far better than the campaign we were about to run.

I agreed to test the two campaigns, and much to my surprise, there wasn't that much difference between them. In-depth group discussions were more favorable to the DDB ads, but not overwhelmingly. It was a prime example of what I've been saying to business schools for years: marketing tools are fine, but they don't replace brains, imagination, instinct, or a combination of the three.

Today, I cannot state categorically that the pedestal campaign would have failed. What is clear is that Father, despite his ego, decided not to stand in the way of an innovative ad strategy, and was richly rewarded for his tolerance.

The other instance of Father stepping back was the time in 1957 when he got a great idea for Christmas packaging. Bottles of Seagram's VO, 7 Crown, and Seagram's Gin were put in silk bags: blue for VO, red for 7 Crown, and gold for Seagram's Gin.

The inspiration came from Crown Royal, which was well known as the whiskey in the purple sack. One thing Father forgot, however, was that Crown Royal's purple sack also came in a box for easy wrapping. Here, there were no boxes, only silk bags (the cost of boxes would have been prohibitive), and the retailers were at a loss as to how to wrap Seagram products in their silken finery.

The bags were a disaster. Whether it was true or not, the retailers were convinced that many consumers didn't want to carry a package that was obviously a bottle. Rather than digging in his heels, Father decided that he didn't want to mess with Christmas packaging any longer: it was no job for a nice Jewish boy!

Chivas Regal and a few other successes notwithstanding, by the early sixties Seagram was adrift. And Vic Fischel was a big part of the problem.

Aside from marketing theories, Vic and I disagreed on other business problems. For example, through my friendship with Bill Green of Thatcher Glass, I had learned how freight impacts the costs of glass shipments to the distillery. It occurred to me that freight must play an even larger role in the cost of shipping case goods to our distributors, given the weight of a case of glass filled with whiskey.

All Seagram's 7 Crown was being shipped from Lawrenceburg, Indiana. I realized that if we shipped to our East Coast customers from our bottling plant in Relay, Maryland, the freight bill would be considerably less.

Vic thought that the savings should go to the distributors, but I disagreed. After all, the investment in plant and bottling equipment had been made not with distributor money, but with Seagram money. This argument didn't convince Vic. Perhaps he wanted to be the big hero with the distributors, or maybe he genuinely believed that he would elicit a greater sales effort by giving them this bonus. Fortunately, as the head of production and administration, it was my decision, and when Fischel appealed to Father, he was quickly overruled.

As my war with Vic escalated, two people came to play a critical role, and their stories figure into the larger drama. The first was Thatcher's Bill Green. Six feet tall, with wavy blondish hair and a devilish smile, Bill was a dapper-dressing lady-killer, not to mention a terrific salesman and top-notch executive. We first met in 1956, when he, his boss, Franklin Pollock (the chairman of Thatcher Glass), and I had lunch together in New York City's Ambassador Hotel. Bill, a great drinker, ordered Seagram's VO, though not to impress me—as I learned later, he loved the taste and had always been a VO man. This, of course, endeared him to me.

Clearly, he was there to sell me a bill of goods, but I was ready to listen to his pitch because it made good sense for Seagram. He proposed a complicated but honest pricing arrangement based on geography: using their plant in Elmira, New York, Thatcher would ship bottles to Seagram in Canada, which would then ship them back to the United States, recovering any duties paid and thereby reducing the cost of glass.

We also initiated talks that led Thatcher to move its head offices from the boondocks up in Elmira to Manhattan—specifically, to the Seagram Building, which was just being completed and was in need of tenants. Father and Mother were off on a Mediterranean trip, and I was in charge of leasing the Building. There had been a move afoot to lower the rent from the six dollars a square foot we were then asking because the space wasn't renting all that quickly, but I had decided that there was no rush. Once you signed a long-term lease for less, you were going to get less for a long time. I remembered Father's telling me about price this way: "The five-dollar whore who takes two dollars will never get five dollars again." Thatcher moved in at the rent we were asking, setting an important precedent.

The rapport between Bill and me was evident at that lunch, and over the years we became close friends. We also did a lot of business together while he was at Thatcher and later, when he set up his own company. (I use the past tense because Bill died of cancer in 1979 at the age of sixty-three. Too damn young.)

All our business deals paid off well. For example, Thatcher wanted to build a flint bottle plant in Lawrenceburg, Indiana, next to its existing amber plant. (Flint is untinted glass used for many distilled spirit products, such as gin, rum, and vodka; amber is dark brown glass, and is traditionally used for whiskey bourbon, blended whiskey, and Canadian whiskey bottles.) Thatcher had originally built the amber bottle factory in Lawrenceburg to service Schenley, the only other bottling house in that small town.

Thatcher didn't have the money to build the new flint operation, and also didn't want to offend Schenley, for whom the plant had been built. Schenley also had a bottling plant in Lawrenceburg, Indiana. To enable them to build this facility—which would save Seagram a lot of money because we bottled some 4 million cases of product packed in flint glass, and glass was priced on an FOB basis—I offered to buy $1 million worth of convertible preferred stock and place it in our pension fund.

The question was, what would happen if Schenley reacted by taking away their business? I considered the matter and agreed to keep Thatcher whole should that happen.

I didn't think that Rosenstiel would get upset over an investment by our pension fund, but I was naive. He took away all the Schenley business, so we made good on my promise. In the end, Seagram not only saved money on the glass we purchased, but the pension fund made a nice profit when Thatcher was eventually bought by Dart.

The other person who figured prominently in the Fischel War was Jack Yogman. When I left Canada for the United States in 1955, I had not yet completed an important project: studying the inventory and determining how large it should be, deciding where the warehouses should be, and reviewing everything else associated with that key aspect of the business.

Just before leaving, I hired Jack Yogman, a young consulting engineer recommended by our new and very bright comptroller Sidney Fread, to finish the job. Two years later, after Jack had completed his report, I gave him a position with Seagram in New York.

Lean, rather short, with a prominent nose, Jack fancied himself a ladies' man. He was very bright and was a good politician, which is not always recognized as a business asset but should be. He moved right up the corporate ladder. During the sixties, as my assistant, he was very involved with U.S. production, then became an executive vice president. After Father died in 1971, he became president and chief operating officer.

Father liked and respected Jack. Thus he became especially useful as a go-between during the Fischel War. Father would complain to Jack that I was putting him in a terrible position by making him choose between Vic and me, his son. Jack would report back to me, then return to Father, attempting as best he could to communicate my position and preserve a modicum of civility.

———

The finale was drawing near. As it did, the executive office atmosphere became highly charged, as the following story illustrates.

Vic often overindulged in the products we sold. On more than one occasion, sitting in the executive bar at the Chrysler Building, he had held forth on Max Drexler, the head of the union that represented our plant personnel, our sales forces, and our distributors' sales forces. There were no secrets in that bar, and Max knew of the invective Vic had heaped on him.

A crisis arose, and the distributors' sales forces in New York City went on strike. We had a wholesale license in New York, and we planned to use it to deliver goods while the strike was being settled. But this required a meeting with Max Drexler.

We convened at the Waldorf-Astoria's Bull & Bear, where Vic was a member. Present at the meeting were Charlie Merinoff Sr., the most important and best-informed distributor in New York, Seagram general counsel Fred Lind, Max Drexler, Vic, and me.

Vic sat to the right of Max, I to the left. After a few drinks, Max decided to get even with Vic and launched into a verbal assault. As the language grew worse, Charlie Merinoff almost swallowed his cigar, and I could see that Fred Lind clearly wanted to be elsewhere. Vic was in great pain, his face florid, his eyes glistening, his mouth twitching. He didn't know whether to rush off, scream, or smack Max in the mouth.

Au moment juste, I put my hand very lightly on Max's forearm and quietly told him that he was forgetting one thing.

"What's that?" he asked.

"That you're my guest." That saved the day. Max calmed down and apologized to me for his bad manners. But the subject we had come to discuss was still not settled, so Max and I agreed to have lunch at the same place the following Friday.

It was a long, long lunch. Max was interested in helping us because he knew there would be money in it for him. But he also wanted a distributorship for his son, Eddie. This was unacceptable to Seagram, and it took a long time to convince him—without insulting his son or casting aspersions on the Drexler family—that the idea wouldn't work.

I finally got back to the office at around four P.M. and, after cleaning off my desk, walked into Vic's office to wish him a good weekend. There was Father sitting with Vic, who had clearly had more than a few drinks.

"What are you doing here? You're supposed to be going home to Mother," I said.

"Son," he replied, "there were times when I had to face the music, and all my brothers ran home to Montreal and left me holding the bag. I wouldn't do that to you."

This high-toned moral justification for doing what he wanted to do angered me. Neither Vic nor Father even asked me how the meeting had gone.

"Father," I said, "if I had known you would be here, I would understand and appreciate what you're saying. The truth is, you are here because you were having a terrific time drinking with Vic."

I then told him that the meeting with Drexler had gone well, and went home to my family.

(Why I should have expected Father to be on that 3:10 plane to Montreal is a good question. In dividing his time between New York and Montreal, he had always waited until the last moment before deciding when he would leave. Uncle Allan, who traveled back and forth to New York with him, was always kept dangling, as was everyone else. This was Father's way of flaunting his importance. Finally, in 1962, when Charles got married and moved out, I told Father that he could no longer do this, since Mother would be alone waiting for him.)

With his decades of employment and his relationship with Father, Vic considered himself part of the Seagram family. Ironically, it was his own flesh and blood that helped seal his fate.

Harold Fischel, Vic's brother, was Southern Division manager of Seagram Distillers Company, the sales arm that sells the company's brand-name products. Harold was not a very bright man. For example, he once walked through a picket line in Miami Beach, thereby poisoning relations between Seagram and the entire union movement. His reason: he wanted to get to his hotel cabana (for which Seagram no doubt was paying).

One day his boss, Herbert Evenson, came to me with a new story of Harold's poor judgment. I told him to fire Harold.

Herb gave me a quizzical look. Assuring him that he needn't worry, I told him that I knew Vic would hit the roof—and that I planned to fire him, too. Herb seemed delighted, and departed to do the deed.

Then the shit hit the fan. Vic stormed into my office and accused me of approving Harold's firing.

I acknowledged that this was true, and told Vic that I saw no job for his brother in my future plans—nor for him.

Shocked, he strode across the hall to Father's office and announced that I had fired him. Father, in a slight panic, came into my office and wanted to know if it was true.

I said that it was. Father asked what exactly I had told Vic.

"That I didn't need him."

"Then you didn't actually say 'you're fired'?"

"No, sir, but my intent was as unmistakable then as it is now. Vic is doing a lousy job, and I want him out of here!"

Stalemate.

Father, of course, would have the last word, but I had made it very clear that if I were countermanded, I would leave the company.

That wasn't what Father had in mind. He had been known to lecture Vic in a crowded room—well, more like scream at him—that this was his company, it was being built for his two sons, and "don't you ever forget it."

A couple of weeks went by, as Father agonized over his loyalty to Vic and the possibility that his son might leave. Father liked Bill Green, and he sought him out, asking why I had done this to him. (He was looking for a way out of the calamity I had caused.)

"Because he loves you," explained Bill. He told Father that I was going to make him proud and would do a great job running the company, but that this would be impossible with Fischel in the picture.

That did the trick. Father came to me and suggested that we keep Fischel as president of the House of Seagram in charge of new business.

Though I knew I had won, I smugly rejected the idea. I didn't appreciate what a sacrifice Father was making in saying those words. Like too many people, I was a little arrogant in my victory. Only later, in subsequent discussions of the Fischel debacle, was I able to tell Father that I had dropped the ax because Vic wouldn't accept me as his boss.

Still, I realized that we needed a "face-saver," so I turned to Jack Yogman. He recommended that we put Wolfschmidt vodka in a separate company, give Vic some equity, and let him sell it under a contract that kept him from doing anything crazy. I asked Jack to present that option to Father so that he could come back to me as if it were his own idea.

Ultimately, Father sent Jack to talk confidentially to Fischel (as if I wouldn't find out), who negotiated for another brand. With seeming reluctance, I threw Carstairs into the pot, and a deal was struck.

In typical Seagram style, I suggested that we have a dinner for Vic and invite the key distributors so that we could put a positive spin on the shakeup. The date was set for June 13, 1963. Father would give the keynote speech.

When the evening came, Father got up and told the following story:

"There was a soldier named Cohen in the British army who was impossible. His commanding officer couldn't stand this fellow and sent him off to India. In due course, he bumped into Cohen one night at the

Savoy Hotel. Lo and behold, Cohen had advanced to officer rank and had a chestful of medals. He called Cohen's new commanding officer and requested an explanation. The reply was forthcoming and direct. 'All I did,' the officer said, 'was give Cohen a gun and tell him he was in business for himself.'"

I didn't think the story was particularly funny but, given the reception it got, I was clearly wrong. Perhaps I was the only person who understood that Vic was getting nothing more than he already had. But if the "gun" was made to sound like something terrific, so much the better for everyone.

Vic found office space in what was then the Union Carbide Building, set up the Victor Fischel Company, and was in business. For a few years he had a marvelous time consorting with distributors whom he invited over to his "hospitality" room, where they drank and played gin rummy. Sales didn't go up much, but no one was the poorer for the enterprise.

More important, the Fischel War was history, and I could now concentrate on my true ambition—to right the Seagram ship and steer it toward a limitless future.

CHAPTER 6

—◆—

FADE TO BLACK: HOLLYWOOD DEALS AND FATHER'S LAST YEARS

When Vic retired to the Union Carbide Building, I figured I was in control. I had already proved myself with the Calvert Extra campaign, and I would now be free to run the U.S. company.

But I forgot about one thing—that Father was still very much present.

It should have occurred to me much earlier on that Father, not Fischel, was my real problem. Indeed, Vic was Father's creation, so the Fischel War in truth was a battle against Father himself—against a certain way of doing business that I could not accept. But I didn't want to acknowledge it.

That was a big error. I really believed that, with Vic gone, Father would soon understand that I knew how to run the company, and that he would do what he had promised: let Charles and me make our mistakes while his eyes were still open.

I had reasoned that if I just got rid of Vic, I could convince Father that I was right on the important corporate issues, as I had about

Calvert Extra. At the very least, I thought that without Vic it would no longer be two against one.

I should have realized that Sam Bronfman would always have one more vote than there were people in the room. And I should have understood that, having seen what I had done to Vic, Father was warier than ever.

In truth, I thought that he would eventually retire, or at least back off. How wrong! Father had no intention of ever retiring. His business was his manhood, and he would never give that away. Perhaps it would have made life easier for both of us if I had understood that, but I didn't.

After Fischel's departure, Father interfered more than ever. As he grew older—he was now advancing through his seventies—he became more strident, more difficult, and more insistent on fulfilling his role as the "President of Presidents." Granted, he had built the company, and he could do with it as he pleased. But from my perspective, there were employees and other stockholders to consider, as well as a family name to protect. And let's face it—my ego was also at stake.

Father also increasingly lost touch with the marketplace, which left me frustrated and upset. Take gin, for example. Father very much wanted to have a brand of gin that would outsell Gordon's, not just to make money, but to make him that much more important, in his own eyes, I suppose. He had produced Seagram's Gin during World War II, but after much experience had concluded that a "golden" gin wasn't going to win the battle. Instead of the slightly tinted gin, he tried to create a Seagram's "white" gin, despite all my protestations that he would only end up confusing those customers who were already drinking Seagram's Gin. As a result, a lot of valuable time and money were wasted. Thank heavens this project never reached fruition. (Today, Seagram's Gin is by far the highest-selling domestic gin in America. Maybe he wasn't all that wrong. But the question remains unanswered. Is thirty years too long to lose money continually on a brand because one man's ego said that Americans wouldn't appreciate a finer product that tasted smoother and looked aged? What actually had happened was that when Seagram's Ancient Bottle Gin was first introduced, some

90 percent of all gin was consumed through the dry martini. If made with Seagram's Gin, it looked like it had too much vermouth, even if it had none at all. Knowing this, I suggested to Father that we lighten the color, in 1957, and he agreed. I said, "Shoudn't we inform Vic Fischel," and his answer was "The sales companies are there to sell what we give them to sell." He really meant "I.")

Next Father became excited about imported gins and decided to design a package based on the "Magna Carta." Need I say more? After exhausting all other options, I finally asked our corporate counsel, Fred Lind, to tell him that the entire legal profession would resent such a use of a sacred historical icon. Father sighed and gave in.

We produced a gin in Canada, Sir Robert Burnett's London Dry, which Father decided to make in the United States on the theory that Americans loved titles. My suggestion was that we make it in England and import it, which I still believe would have made much more sense and might even have been profitable. But Father disagreed, determined to outsell Gordon's with no seeming interest in profitability, just in his dicta. Instead, we spent some money building a "Coffey" still, which the British use to make spirits, or "grain whiskey," as they call it. We had a fairly effective campaign trumpeting the product as "British gin at an American price," with the flags of both countries stressing the point. Sales crept forward, but because of the processing costs and the limited margin, the corporation never made a dime from Sir Robert in the United States. Father thought that imports had little volume, and he refused to believe me when I told him that Beefeater was selling in excess of a million cases per annum. How can you argue with a man who tells you that the official figure just can't be right?

Still looking for a brand name for an imported gin, he compiled a list including London Tower, Big Ben, and Westminster Abbey, all boring and pompous. I hadn't witnessed the problems of a new industry being born out of the ashes of Prohibition, and I couldn't empathize with Father's need for the respectability these names implied.

On a trip to Scotland, we visited a shop in Aberdeen owned by Chivas Brothers that sold biscuits, cheeses, and other such provisions. When Seagram had bought Chivas Brothers, the shop had been retained because it, and hence the company, had the Royal Warrant as suppliers of provisions to Balmoral, the Scottish residence of the Royal Family. Buckingham Palace has since tightened the rules, and we no longer have the Royal Warrant, which certainly did not hamper the sales of Chivas. But again the Royal Warrant appealed to his fragile ego.

Father was in the store checking on the sales of jams and jellies, while I, bored out of my box, had wandered into a little room the shop used for tasting wines and sherries. I discovered a large coffee-table book, *The Chivas Regal Book of London Clubs*, and began to leaf through it.

Father, no doubt annoyed at my lack of enthusiasm for what he was doing, said, "Have you found a name for an imported gin?"

"Yes, sir, I have," I replied to his astonishment. "Boodles." It was the name of a famous London club. He looked disgusted, and we dropped the subject.

A few weeks later, I found Bill Bernbach in Father's office, manfully trying to stay awake as Father read from his list of names for British gins. When the recital finished, I asked Father to try out on Bill the name I liked. In as negative a tone as possible, he said that Edgar had come across this crazy name—Boodles.

Bill sat up. "That's it!" he said. Father, startled, asked why. "Because it's different and intriguing," answered Bill.

At that time, we had a very handsome gentleman by the name of Geoffrey Palau running our United Kingdom sales operation. A veteran of World War II, in which he had lost a leg, Geoffrey had been picked by one of Father's people, and while he didn't do an especially good job, he didn't lose more money than anyone could tolerate. I instructed him to register the name "Boodles" for a gin.

Time went by, and nothing happened. I finally called and asked him where the matter stood.

"Oh, I thought you knew. We have dropped the application because the Boodles Club objected, and Sir Ronald Cumming is a member." Ronnie was then chairman of the DCL, the huge Scottish combine, and a friend of Father's.

I can only imagine why Geoffrey had taken it upon himself to act in this manner. Someone must have brought Father the news that the club had objected and that Ronnie was a member. Father then probably delightedly agreed that the project be stopped, surer than ever that the name was too frivolous, and just forgot to tell me.

But as I sat at my desk, looking at the great package Fritz Siebel had already created for it, I was sick that we had given in so easily. Determined to make it work, I tracked down the best trademark people, and on March 13, I flew to London for a meeting with them.

Geoffrey picked me up at the airport and asked if he could attend the proceedings. Yes, I said, but on one condition—if he opened his damn mouth, I'd throw him out the (expletive deleted) window.

The trademark meeting went well. Our people then met with representatives of the Boodles Club and promised never to sell the brand in the United Kingdom, or to use the club in promoting the brand in America. We also agreed to supply a certain amount of product for the personal use of club members, which probably did the trick. I flew home the following afternoon.

Sadly, despite a great package and a fine gin to put in it, Boodles never achieved the success I had anticipated.

In the fall of 1963, we had a terrible problem in Ohio that could have become the worst nightmare of my life. We had raised prices on all our products, something we now do as a matter of course, but which at that time occurred rarely.

Donald Cook, the director of the Liquor Control Board in the state of Ohio, decided not to accept our price increase. Consequently, we stopped shipping to Ohio, a state that not only wholesaled all its spirits but also retailed them. The state of Pennsylvania, our largest customer, was watching and waiting. For months, there was no movement, as we tried every way imaginable to influence either the director or Governor Rhodes.

To be forced to roll back our prices was unthinkable. It was becoming a *mano a mano* between Donald Cook and me, and I couldn't afford to lose this one.

With the help of the chairman's office at Anchor Hocking, one of our glass suppliers, I secured an appointment with Governor Rhodes. Jack Yogman and I flew to Columbus, but when we telephoned to confirm, we were told that, on the advice of Donald Cook, the governor had canceled our appointment. We had no choice but to fly back to New York. When I returned to my office, I called Father. What would I do if he ordered me to give in and roll back our price increase?

"Dad, the son of a bitch wouldn't even see us!" I said.

There was a pause, and then he replied, "Don't worry, son, we'll sell to somebody else."

Father did have his moments of greatness. He had given me a huge lift at a time when I sorely needed one. Relieved, Jack and I promptly went out and had a three-martini lunch.

But the story didn't end there. Since the governor wouldn't see me, and I couldn't influence him through usual channels, I decided to do something a little more creative. I arranged to spend a week going to every major city in Ohio so that we could sit down with the editors and publishers of the major newspapers to make our case.

I traveled from Columbus to Cincinnati to Akron to Toledo to Dayton, accompanied by a team of seasoned professionals. (We were fortunate to have a company aircraft at our disposal; indeed, a member of our team laughingly told me, "Edgar, you're going to win this war because you have an air force!") We argued that, aside from having the right to determine our own prices, we were also entitled to the proposed increase based on our costs. The pitch was quite effective, but the ultimate outcome of the battle was still in doubt.

Then Don Cook made his big mistake. Governor Rhodes was fighting to get a bond issue passed by the voters, and his office had come up with the slogan "Profit Is Not a Dirty Word in Ohio." Seagram's earnings had just appeared, and Cook, using his Columbus newspaper connections, went on the offensive, asking how we could demand a price increase when our profits were up. The *New York Times* and the *Wall Street Journal* called to get my response. I gave them a paragraph or two, and ended by saying, "And since when is profit a dirty word in Ohio?" Governor Rhodes called Cook, and the day was ours.

———————

That experience notwithstanding, I discovered through the years that if you play by the rules, dealing with politicians and government regulation is not that difficult. Of course, our industry, along with the tobacco industry, has been a favorite target for a long time. Therefore, it's important for us to have good lobbyists working on our behalf in Washington. Generally, I haven't spent too much time on these matters, though on occasion I've had to go to the capital to make our case.

Contributing to political campaigns is essential, so every year I give money to our political action committee. We have to support those elected officials who favor our industry, which means not taxing us to death. It's part of the cost of doing business.

While government interference can be burdensome, I am certainly not one of those laissez-faire capitalists who believes that business should have a totally free hand. On the contrary, I think that government has an important role to play in creating a better society. In this regard, I would describe myself as a liberal, though I don't believe problems can be solved by throwing money at them.

Through the years I've straddled both sides of the partisan divide. In the 1964 election, I voted for Johnson over Barry Goldwater, who represented the extreme right wing of the Republican Party. But in 1972, I voted for Nixon again rather than Senator George McGovern, and lived to regret it. When it comes to the Congress, I tend to support Democrats, because as a rule they care about equality, the environment, and other things that are important to me.

One issue that I've always been very vocal about is racism. In 1964, I went to the White House on behalf of Seagram to make an agreement with President Johnson on equal opportunity in the workplace. This was a landmark in U.S. policy, and a necessary step to address generations of injustice.

Of course, implementing such measures often proves difficult, as I found out firsthand. After returning from Washington, I announced our new policy to the staff, thinking the rest would follow. A year later, however, I discovered that only lip service was being paid to the program, so I informed our senior executives that their bonuses would now be linked directly to the recruitment of minorities. They got the message.

But old habits die hard. Not too long thereafter, I visited the Calvert plant in Relay, Maryland, just outside Baltimore, and discovered that we had a separate dining facility for black employees. The union insisted on it, I was told.

"And where do these employees eat when you paint this dining room, which I assume you do annually?" I asked.

"Well, then they eat with everyone else," came the reply.

I ordered that the plant be integrated immediately. I also told the sales department to convert the segregated dining space into something useful.

My decision wasn't just a matter of good business. I did know that Calvert products were big in the then black market. I had to live with myself, too, and I couldn't if the company I ran was racist. As a Jew who grew up during the Holocaust, I am very sensitive to bigotry of any kind. Throughout my life, I have fought against various forms of discrimination, and I certainly wasn't going to allow it in my own company. Racism has no place at Seagram, and it never will.

———

In 1965, Father decided that Seagram must achieve membership in the One Billion Dollar Club. I didn't think it was all that important and argued in vain that we could wait until the following year. Determined, Father discovered that the revenues from a lackluster resort hotel we owned in British Columbia had not been consolidated in our income statement—and that put us over $1 billion in sales. I had a pen holder built with a bust of my brother and me on each side, and a plaque that read "Thanks a Billion, Dad."

But such moments of detente were few and far between. Father was being difficult about everything I wanted to do. He now ruled by veto, and I would never act behind his back.

Accomplishing anything was so hard that I got into the habit of having Jack Yogman, who was now executive vice president of Joseph E. Seagram & Sons, do the asking. At one point, Father said that if I kept this up it would become Jack Yogman's company, not mine. What would I do then? he asked.

"I'd fire him," I said. And, after Father's death, it did come to that.

As time went on, my restlessness grew. Stymied in my efforts at Seagram, I looked elsewhere for ways to channel my energy and frustration.

On January 20, 1967, I met with a minor television executive named Henry White and a minor movie producer, Claude Giroux. The result was Sagittarius Productions, and thus began my on-again, off-again relationship with Hollywood.

I'd always loved entertainment, and this was my chance to get my hand in the business. More than that, it provided an outlet for my creative drive. Indeed, while there were easier ways to make money than investing in the motion picture/TV industry (or Broadway, as I also found out), participating in an artistic endeavor proved to be uniquely satisfying.

The idea with Sagittarius Productions was to make movies for television and simultaneously release them in foreign markets. Henry would run the company, while Claude and I would put up the money. It was a solid concept, but it didn't work out all that well because the product was mediocre at best. I eventually bought out Claude's interest. I then began to read a lot of scripts and spend time with Henry on casting. If nothing else, it was a great excuse to spend time in England and partake in such indulgences as attending the Cannes Film Festival.

Though our projects ranged in quality from fair to terrible, we made one picture of which I am particularly proud: *Charlotte's Web*, an animated version of the touching children's classic by E. B. White about the friendship between a pig and a spider, featuring the voice of Debbie Reynolds. We visited E. B. White's farm in Maine to see the shed that inspired the work and ate a marvelous rhubarb pie baked by Mrs. White. As executive producer, I determined that whenever a question came up about the script, we should stick to the book. (Film people often try to improve upon the original material, even when it's a masterpiece.)

The firm of Hanna Barbera made the film. I had the pleasure of working with Joe Barbera, who served as producer/director, and seeing how animation worked. He suggested the voices, and expertly so. Paul Lynde was the perfect Templeton the rat, and the rest of the casting was equally superb.

(A funny coincidence: one song in the movie was entitled "Twinkle and Sparkle"—which happened to be the names of the two Norwich terriers Ann had bought for herself and Holly; no one on either side knew about it.)

One other Sagittarius production I regarded highly was our remake of *Jane Eyre*, starring George C. Scott and Susannah York. Scott was a terrific Rochester, and the scenery was very good. We made a little money on *Jane Eyre*, which was repeated on television a few times, and we were very successful with *Charlotte's Web*. I still got annual residuals from the rerelease and video sales of the film, until we bought 80 percent of MCA, and then I turned my interest over to MCA and avoided any potential conflict of interest. We also made *Ash Wednesday* at the request of Frank Yablans, the president of Paramount, which was part of Charlie Bluhdorn's Gulf + Western. Charlie didn't want to do the movie because the star, Elizabeth Taylor, and her husband, Richard Burton, never lived anywhere long enough to pay taxes, which infuriated him. So Yablans asked Sagittarius to make the picture.

This early experience taught me a lot about the film business. On the one hand, it's undeniably seductive—there's a certain thrill to meeting stars, directors, producers, studio heads, and the other intriguing people who inhabit the very different world of Hollywood. Beyond that, I find tremendous satisfaction in watching people go to the theater to see something that I've helped create.

On the other hand, as a businessman it's gut-wrenching to watch a movie being made. The payroll is huge and the process intolerably inefficient. So much time goes into setting up each scene, then after countless takes, everything gets broken down, and off you go to the next shoot and the same delays. God knows how many hours are spent sitting idly by while the star, director, cameraman, or producer has a fit of pique. My son Edgar Jr. experienced the same frustrations when he was producing *The Border* for Universal Studios in 1981.

Despite the frustrations, I soon became more involved in moviemaking. Our longtime friend Leo Kolber also was interested in the motion picture industry. He was a great friend of the late Danny Kaye and was fascinated with the Hollywood scene. Enter a man named G. M. Levin, who owned a big block of MGM stock and had waged at least one unsuccessful proxy battle for control of the company. Leo negotiated with him for the purchase of his stock, but couldn't reach a price we were willing to pay.

To me, MGM was the studio of all studios. I figured that if we could buy out Levin's stock, we would then have a shot at winning control of this fabled entity.

Knowing of our interest, my friend Jim Linen, president of Time Inc., called one day to ask whether I minded if his company bought a 5 percent interest in MGM. The year was 1968, and Jim explained that they wanted to take a look at the "moving image." I was delighted. Father would surely put up resistance if we went forward with an MGM takeover, but it would help to be able to tell him that Time Inc. was involved. (After its experience with MGM, Time went on to start HBO.)

Meanwhile, Leo and I worked on Levin and eventually bought his stock for about $56 million. Not long after, Father came into my office and closed the door, something he rarely did. He invited me to sit with him on the couch, then asked why "we" (meaning the family) had invested all this money in MGM. I went on about the moving image, the MGM library, and the insatiable hunger of television for product.

My answer didn't satisfy him. What he really wanted to know, he told me, was whether we were buying all that stock so that I could meet some girls.

"Father," I said, "nobody has to spend fifty-six million dollars to get laid."

That pacified him, at least for the moment. I was never sure whether his antipathy toward the movies was intrinsic or whether he merely resented my involvement in enterprises other than Seagram, or both. The latter was certainly true, but I believe that Father, being genuinely Victorian, thought there was something immoral about Hollywood. Indeed, he sometimes referred to it as a "whores'" business. Since those days, of course, very large corporations, both domestic and foreign, have made huge investments in the movie business—as the Seagram Company Ltd. would do in years to come.

Now that we had a major interest in MGM, the next step was to get control. Although a proxy battle was possible as a last resort, neither the Time people nor Father would like that, nor would I have. There was a better way to take over the company: through MGM's board of directors. This wouldn't be easy because most of the board members had been selected by Bob O'Brien, the president and CEO. But Bob was going down quickly. He worked only half the day, and word was that he had lost his touch. Leo Kolber and I were on the board, along with two members of Time Inc., and I felt that between us we could convince the others to ease him out.

The night before the vote was spent drinking and checking to make sure that all the other board members were on our side. I awakened the next morning with the awful feeling that I had forgotten something. Slowly it came to me: I had promised my son Edgar that I would discuss the election of 1968 with his class at Collegiate! Business is important, but I had long ago determined to be a far more active presence in my children's lives than my parents had been in mine. There was no choice but to call up MGM and delay the board meeting for two hours.

I forget what excuse I used, but the other members went along. When the board met, we voted to ask for O'Brien's resignation, and the battle was over.

Next, we had to find a new chief executive. I became nonexecutive chairman, but we needed someone to run the everyday business. In the course of that search, I met with perhaps a half dozen potential candidates. Then my friend John Weinberg of Goldman Sachs

& Company suggested that I meet "a brilliant fellow from Minneapolis" named Bo Polk, who just might be available because he was frustrated with his present position at General Mills.

Bo was one of those entrepreneurs who just didn't fit into a stultifying corporate atmosphere. He had tremendous drive and energy, and he seemed the perfect candidate—a solid businessman with a wide-open mind and a desire to do the unexpected. We hired him and gave him a very good contract after he insisted that I might get tired of the movie business, leaving him high and dry. This made sense to me, although I never for a moment thought that it would end the way it did.

Less than a year after we had won control, I received a telephone call from Greg Bautzer, a well-known Los Angeles attorney. Greg was a friend and fellow director of Pepsi–United Bottlers (which became Rheingold), in which our family had earlier bought some stock. He asked if we would be interested in exchanging MGM stock for shares in the San Francisco–based conglomerate TransAmerica. I declined. The principal for whom he was acting was Kirk Kerkorian.

At the time, we were busy putting a team together, and I didn't pay as much attention as I should have. But even if I had, the outcome would likely have been the same. Kerkorian was determined to have MGM, and neither my family, nor I, nor Time Inc. was ready to put up any more money. Though I was upset for Bo Polk—I knew from Greg that Kirk was going to hire Jim Aubrey (who had had a flamboyant career at CBS)—I gave in with reasonably good grace. I gave Bo an office in the Seagram Building, and he set about running an investment company (in addition to collecting on his MGM contract).

Kerkorian suggested that I stay on as non-executive chairman, but clearly there would be no dignity in that. Leo and I did keep our shares, and after the new management built the MGM Grand Hotel in Las Vegas, we made a good profit. The other family members sold their stock right away, however, and ended up losing money.

My sister Minda was bitter, and remained so. I had struggled to convince her that investing in MGM was a good idea, not just a personal indulgence. When Kerkorian came in and she sold her shares at a loss, it confirmed her original doubts. Were she alive today, she would see what a giant force the entertainment/communications industry has become, but . . .

By the same token, there's no doubt that our approach to MGM was fatally flawed. I had no real knowledge of that industry, nor would I give it full time, which clearly was demanded. At one point, Father said to me, "Why are you spending all of your time for fifteen percent of the stock?" And he was absolutely right. I learned very quickly never again to enter a business venture halfheartedly.

One footnote: During my MGM moment, I had the great honor to spend a day watching David Lean on the set of *Ryan's Daughter*. What a genius. David not only was blessed with an unbelievably artistic eye, but he did all the editing himself—which is one of the reasons none of his films ever lost money.

There were other diversions during this period. One of the most memorable came in the fall of 1967, when President Lyndon Johnson repaid the support I'd given his campaign by sending Ann and me to the fourth inauguration of Liberia's President Tubman. My role was to be an ambassador of goodwill, an honor I shared with Supreme Court Justice Thurgood ("Call Me Turkey") Marshall. The leader of the delegation was Vice President Hubert Humphrey.

Hubert was a wonderful man, and I learned to have great affection for him. As a politician, he was a courageous warrior and a great liberal. On the other hand, he knew nothing about the economy other than what he had learned at his father's drugstore in South Dakota.

En route to Liberia, we stopped at Abidjan, the capital of the Ivory Coast. The Department of State had decreed that in French-speaking countries my protocol would be higher than Thurgood's, and vice versa in English-speaking countries. For two days there was a lot of pomp and circumstance, but the best moment came the first night during the gala dinner held at the residence of the U.S. ambassador.

There were some five hundred people in attendance, and I was seated at the head table between two women. On my right was the attractive wife of the deputy chief of mission; on my left was the white French wife of the Ivory Coast Supreme Court's black chief judge. On her left, at the end of the table, was Thurgood. We had been instructed to speak with the person on the right for the first course, and then to the person on the left. Halfway through the first course, I felt a great chill to my left. Sneaking a look, I observed a dreadful silence and two angry faces. Neither spoke a word of the other's language, and the embassy had stupidly not provided a translator.

I asked the lady on my right for permission to straighten out the diplomatic mess on my left, then spent several minutes trying to get a conversation going between Thurgood and the Frenchwoman. Speaking English to him and French to her, then acting as their interpreter, I coaxed some dialogue out of them but no smiles. Frustrated, I hit upon an idea. First, I told them that although they each knew what they had said to me, neither of them knew how I had interpreted it to the other. When they nodded, I reported to them that Thurgood had invited the lovely lady to bed, and that she had accepted. They both burst into laughter, and the crisis was over.

Liberia's ugly history is bound up with that of American slavery. In 1823, during the presidency of James Monroe, a ship was filled with freed slaves and sent back to Africa. They had no idea where they had come from or where they were going. When they landed in what is now Liberia, they proceeded to take over the country and replicate the plantation life they had left in the American South. They became the bosses, and the locals became, if not exactly slaves, then something very close to it.

During our visit, pomposity and ineptitude reigned. Though temperatures climbed above 100 degrees in the shade, we were required to bring full morning dress as well as white tie and a regular tuxedo. Ann and the other ladies in the group had to wear long white gloves as well as long dresses and hats.

The inauguration took place at one P.M. in stultifying heat in a church that was an exact duplicate of a southern one in America. Then we were driven to the Presidential Palace, which had cost the American taxpayer some $100 million, perched atop a hill, to drink warm cocktails while we awaited the arrival of Tubman, his wife, and Ivory Coast's late President Houphouët-Boigny. (During the preinaugural festivities, Hubert could not sit with the great Tubman, who shared his box with Houphouët-Boigny, because Hubert was only a vice president.)

On the way up the hill to the Presidential Palace I noticed that the troops lining the road were carrying submachine guns. "Isn't that a bit dangerous?" I asked our military aide/driver. "You don't think this government is stupid enough to give them any ammunition, do you?" he replied. Some time later, Sergeant Doe found the ammunition and killed Tubman's successor, Tolbert, along with his family and hangers-on. He then appointed himself president, plunging the country into chaos and suffering. Eventually, Doe met the same fate.

Finally, President Tubman and the first lady arrived. They sat at the end of the room, he smoking a small cigar, enjoying the power of making people wait. Then the chief of protocol, an idiot named Morgan, tried fruitlessly to usher the guests upstairs for dinner by instructing us to find our seats on a chart just outside the room in which we were sitting. Everyone gasped in disbelief, and nobody moved. The president then decided that people should be seated by rank, and thus they could, in smaller groups, check the charts. In the meantime, Hubert was speaking with the vice president of Somalia and I was doing the translation—from French to English and vice versa. As soon as Morgan was at the end of the protocol list, he looked up and saw that Ann and I were still there. He looked away, thinking perhaps that he was hallucinating, and that we would go away, and then decided to ignore us. Chester Carter, the American deputy chief of protocol and in charge of our trip, managed to get us seated, but he and I agreed that as soon as Hubert had made his toast, we would get out of there. The three of us found a McDonald's and had a hamburger.

Fortunately, such episodes were balanced out by the good cheer of my traveling partners. One day, while we were onboard Air Force II, Hubert decided to take a nap in the forward compartment, so I sat in his chair to be polite to Muriel Humphrey. She asked if there was anything she could do for me. "Yes, Muriel," I said, "would you peel me a grape?" And she did.

On one leg of the journey, I asked Thurgood just how President Johnson had asked him to be a member of the Supreme Court. He told us that the President had said, "Turkey, what are my friends in Texas going to say to me if I put an uppity nigger like you on the Court?"

"My God," I said, "what did you say to that?"

"I said, 'Thank you, Mr. President.' What the hell did you think I'd say?"

Hubert Humphrey decided that he wanted to spend an extra day and tour around Tunis, the capital of Tunisia. I politely replied that, since January 10 was our fifteenth wedding anniversary, he would either have to throw a party for us or arrange to send us home. He obliged with a party, paid for by Humphrey's close friend Dwayne Andreas, a generous man who subsequently became a good acquaintance of mine.

During our trip, we also met with Ethiopian emperor Haile Selassie, who much preferred speaking French to English. I offered to sponsor a scholarship in agriculture at an American university (it turned out to be Purdue) if he would select an exceptionally bright candidate who could use the knowledge he attained to teach others, which he did. I received a letter from the dean of that school saying that this was the first third world student for whom he didn't have to push aside standards to graduate. I wish I knew what happened to him through the great difficulties that that country underwent!

———

While moviemaking, foreign excursions, and other activities provided some distraction from my troubles at Seagram, I was still chafing under Father's autocratic rule. True, during his last years he spent much time at Safety Harbor, a spa on the West Coast of Florida. But though Father was in New York less and less, his overwhelming personality still pervaded the company, and he was very much the boss right until the end. *Forbes* magazine put it this way: "The trouble was that Mr. Sam grew old and increasingly out of touch with his industry. Like many a strongman-founder, he overstayed his time, either not listening to the unwelcome truth or not being told it by his fearful managers."

Throughout his life, Father had certain beliefs that colored his thinking. One of the most influential was his conviction that Prohibition might return and that the industry should therefore behave in the most cautious, conservative fashion possible. This attitude manifested itself, for instance, in his unwavering opposition to using women in alcohol ads. Father was obsessed with maintaining a solemn, pristine image. He couldn't abide anything that seemed frivolous, such as a name like Boodles—the business had to be taken seriously. But by the sixties, most Americans had long forgotten Prohibition and all its taboos, even if they were old enough to have experienced them . . . even if he hadn't.

In 1969, Father began suffering from prostate cancer. No one, me included, ever told him exactly what illness he had, not even Abe Mayman, his doctor in Montreal. But he suffered a lot.

The cancer was diagnosed in Montreal and confirmed at Mount Sinai Hospital in New York. I was told by the Mount Sinai doctor that the only way Father might achieve some remission would be if his testicles were removed and then replaced with a plastic material. I refused to let that happen. It was intolerable to think of that proud and insecure man undergoing such a humiliating procedure, especially since, in Abe Mayman's view, the operation would do little good.

I have often asked myself whether I was honestly being compassionate or if I just wanted it to be over. I believe the former is true, but I'll probably always be plagued by a little doubt. Not even Abe Mayman was up to explaining everything to Father so that he could decide. Mother also knew the details of Father's illness, and she didn't tell him, either.

Only recently, I learned that Charles had independently come to the same conclusion. This was a relief, because it meant that Charles also agreed with the decision not to operate.

It now seems strange that Charles and I didn't discuss the issue. Charles was in Montreal, I was in New York, and "divide and conquer" was still the rule. Father's enormous personality kept us from talking about it. Nevertheless, the decision, separately endorsed by both of us, seemed to be the right one.

In the summer of 1971, with the July 4 weekend coming up, Ann and I were at her parents' camp at Saranac Lake in New York's Adirondacks. I called Mother, who suddenly insisted that I come to Montreal. Father was getting to be more than she could handle, and she wanted someone there to help her. I went immediately and stayed through the weekend, and spent a lot of time sitting outside in the garden beneath their dressing room window so that the nurse could summon me easily. It was summer and the windows were open.

During the early part of the weekend, Father was well enough to come downstairs for a short while, and we sat together in the sun room. (At Phyllis's insistence, we had installed an electrically operated chair that went from the ground floor up to the master bedroom so that he would not have to walk up the stairs, which was extremely painful.) He looked old but not that weak: some of the fire was still in his eyes, and he seemed more angry about his sickness than sorry for himself. Slowly, he turned his head toward me and asked a question he had never asked before:

"Edgar, why did you involve yourself in making movies? What was your purpose?"

I decided to tell him the truth.

"Father, it became increasingly difficult for me to work with you and for you. The one wonderful thing I had done was the introduction of Calvert Extra, and you were such an egomaniac, you couldn't stand my having had that success.

"One day at lunch, when the subject came up, you categorically stated that the reason Calvert Extra was such a success was that you had made the decision to put grain-neutral spirits in barrels and age them. That wasn't true. We made that decision together because you wanted to advertise the quality of blends and compare them to paintings—a panoply of ingredients, like colors, each designed to contribute to the final taste, the whole being better than the sum of the parts. I suggested that this was impossible so long as there was sixty-five percent white spirits in the bottle. So we decided to age them.

"And you know perfectly well that the aged spirits were only a small part of the mix that made the introduction such a success."

This was not very easy to say, but I knew he was near the end and I felt I could not lie to him, that he should know the truth.

"Well, at least it was something you really enjoyed doing," he said.

What he couldn't understand, and what I couldn't say, was that one of the main reasons I had knocked myself out on the Calvert Extra job was to impress him. I had hoped that he would give me some credit, and perhaps—just perhaps—say those three little words: "I love you."

Father, no doubt thinking about the future of Seagram, was probably relieved that I wasn't running away from the business per se. I went on to remind him that I had enjoyed doing the Calvert Extra campaign until he tried to steal the whole project.

On the Monday following that weekend, I had to go to New York. Jack Yogman and I were trying to buy Monsieur Henri, which had the exclusive agency for all Soviet vodkas (the company also had some wine imports and a Sangria brand in its portfolio). Before leaving, I told Father that I would be back the next day to tell him about it.

"You'll tell me about it if I'm still here," he said. By this time he got up only to use the bathroom, and when he did, his legs, which had been muscular and strong, looked weak and spindly.

When I returned, I explained to Father that there would be no Monsieur Henri deal. Unfortunately, Don Kendall, the CEO of PepsiCo, also had taken an interest—he wanted to bring Pepsi syrup into the Soviet Union while taking vodka out—and it was virtually impossible for us to match his price. Syrup was so profitable that it really didn't matter to PepsiCo if they lost money on the sale of Monsieur Henri products, including Russian vodka.

This turned out to be our last conversation. On July 10, 1971, Charles, Leo Kolber, and I went to eat dinner at Ruby Foo's, a famous Chinese restaurant in Montreal. We returned to Leo's house for a cognac, and when the telephone rang, I went directly to the car, knowing that the end had come. Charles and I raced home to find Mother sobbing and wailing.

I remained calm and mostly oversaw the necessary arrangements. Mother insisted that Father's body be on view in the Samuel Bronfman

House. (This was the building that housed the offices of the Canadian Jewish Congress, the umbrella organization for Canadian Jewry in which he had played such an enormous role.) Phyllis was en route from the Greek isles, and after she arrived, there was a great funeral in the Sha'ar HaShomayim synagogue—an unusual honor in the Jewish tradition accorded only great men.

Charles and I told Uncle Allan that I would become president and that Charles would become executive vice president of Distillers Corporation–Seagrams Ltd. He was very gracious about it.

Things didn't go so well with my sister Minda. We needed to choose a new member for the board of directors, and I wanted Leo Kolber, who I thought would be a real help to Charles. Minda saw the new director as taking Father's place, and she wanted it to be her husband, Alain de Gunzburg. She really didn't want to understand that I was going to take Father's place. (We didn't go into exactly what she meant by that—a Freudian slip?) While rejecting Alain out of hand, I agreed that he would be nominated for the next opening on the board. (Looking back, I might have expanded the board by one director and put them both on. But Minda was always so aggressive that I felt if I let her win one battle, life would quickly become intolerable.)

During the mourning period, we tried to get Uncle Allan to talk about the early days. He professed ignorance, and likely was telling the truth. Allan was at least eight years younger than Father, probably had no memory of Saskatchewan, and certainly had no personal recollection of the family's impoverished existence when they first arrived in Canada.

———

I learned a great deal from Father. For all his faults, he was a great businessman, and he passed on much of his knowledge by example. Perhaps the most important thing I learned from him was a global concept. He talked of doing business all over the world, and I was impressed with that strategy. In our business, Scotch whiskey is made only in Scotland, French wine in France, and so on. To be able to be important manufacturers and purveyors globally was indeed a challenge that I was glad to take up.

First, he knew that quality was of paramount importance, and that it could never be compromised. He took enormous pride in Seagram's products, and that was passed on to me, the best guarantor of high quality. He always strove to create or acquire top-of-the-line brands. "If the point of drinking is to get drunk," Father used to say, "then you're not our customer."

Shortly after Seagram's 5 Crown and 7 Crown became successful brands, Father started the "moderation" campaign. He had seen people—and he was especially concerned about women—overdrinking now that Prohibition was gone. Fearful that the forces that had brought it on could bring it back if people were getting drunk everywhere, he insisted on advertisements such as "We who make whiskey say, 'We don't want your bread money'" or "Some men should not drink," referring to the problem of alcoholism. Seagram now has a more-than-sixty-year history of running ads advising people of the necessity to handle beverage alcohol with care, and now that we have insisted on our right to advertise on television just as beer and wine makers do, we have proposed to the industry that in each such commercial we place a meaningful moderation message.

Though he had no formal business training, Father had great instincts, particularly in the areas of advertising and packaging. There was no such thing as "marketing" when he was building the business, but he grasped the essence of it and single-handedly turned Seagram into the dominant force in the industry.

Father used to talk about the family spirit in the company, and he meant it sincerely. Accordingly, I've always felt that we are one big family. Now, of course, we're one *huge* family, but still I send a note to every employee who has a major anniversary with the company, or an important wedding anniversary.

In 1952, Vic Fischel established the Seagram Family Achievement Association. Its ambition was to keep our distributors close to us by educating and assisting the next generation in every way possible—the sons and sons-in-law. Others have tried over the years to copy us, but except for Seagram, all such attempts have failed. Today, under the leadership of Sam and Edgar Jr., the Seagram Family Association is strong and effective in building that family spirit past our doors to those of our principal customers.

Like Father, I believe it's important that our people feel that I care about them. This explains, I think, why many Seagram employees stay for so long. The feeling is not one of boss and worker, but rather that of a family working together. It's no coincidence that we've had relatively few problems with employee graft and embezzlement, despite the fact that we don't do in-depth background checks, which I consider a terrible intrusion on somebody's privacy.

As for Father's weaknesses, I learned a tremendous amount from him about what *not* to do.

Father let his ego dominate everything. He did things that pleased his vanity, whatever they were. (At one point, he wanted to change his name and that of his children to Bronfman-Seagram.) To him, the purpose of the business was to make him an important person. But the prime purpose of a business is to make money. To make Seagram's name resound would help accomplish that, but not the name and the persona of Sam Bronfman. I determined I was never going to get in that kind of position, and have developed an ability to stand outside myself.

I also saw how many problems Father created by blurring the line between employee and friend. I watched him form personal relationships with people and then have to fire them. It drove him crazy. I have avoided such relationships and in fact have never developed an intimate friendship with anybody who works for me. It could be said that at one time I was close to Jack Yogman, but never to the point of joint holidays, or even dinners with our wives.

Another problem was that Father took himself and his product too seriously, as with the Magna Carta idea. You have to have some sense of humor in life. The essence of humor is being able to laugh at yourself. Father loved to tell jokes, but he couldn't laugh at himself.

Father also had gaping holes in his business knowledge. This would have been okay if he had admitted it, but instead he pretended

to know a lot more than he actually did. His ignorance about accounting is perhaps the best example, and it cost Seagram a lot over the
years. As a result, I made a point of learning as much as I could in areas
in which he was deficient, taking accounting and geology courses. I also
asked questions of those who I thought would know the answers. Father never could.

In his later years, Father refused to relinquish control of those duties that others could do better, such as packaging and advertising. In
the beginning he was magnificent at creating packaging. He designed
the Crown Royal bottle—who could have come up with anything better than the 7 Crown logo? But the sensibilities of one era usually don't
translate to the next, and Father's packaging concepts became increasingly anachronistic. The same was true with advertising. I once told
him that he was advertising to his friends, and they were mostly dead.
You don't advertise to older people, you advertise to younger adults. It
was painfully clear watching Father that old people shouldn't be creating advertising. Each generation speaks a different language. That's
why I don't have anything to do with Seagram's advertising anymore.
In my time, I was good at it, but my peers no longer compose the bulk
of the market.

The insecurity so intrinsic to Father's character kept him from
ever fully trusting anyone. Indeed, he actually was frightened that
Charles and I might orchestrate a coup, since all his Seagram shares
were in trusts of which we, among others, were trustees. So he would
constantly tell us about poor Uncle Allan's troubles with his sons, saying that if he were Allan, he would "bust the trusts."

Father's insecurity, coupled with his ego and horrible temper, also
prevented anyone from offering constructive criticism. Even those
closest to Father were loath to contradict him, and were thus reduced
to sycophants. While this is not all that unusual among CEOs—or anyone in a position of great power—it's very detrimental, and I vowed
early on that I would not make the same mistake.

Finally, Father's uncontrollable temper offered an invaluable lesson in how not to treat people. I was embarrassed by his behavior, and

disturbed as well. He had great potential to be a gentleman, but he never became one.

I'm not sure that Father had a happy life. He accomplished a great deal and truly became "somebody," yet he was always deeply insecure. I remember playing golf with Charles and Father at the Century Country Club near White Plains, New York. If there was another group behind us and they were even remotely near, Father would insist that we let them through.

His wars never stopped. Even if he shook hands with Laz Phillipps in the end, the bitterness remained. And he never resolved his relationship with Uncle Allan.

"We make a great pair," I once said to Father. He asked what I meant, and I replied, "You teach me how to make it and I'll teach you how to spend it." Father's wealth meant very little to him in the material sense; rather, it symbolized "arriving." He did live well, of course, but I don't think he really enjoyed it. He was too driven to appreciate the things money could buy (although he did like the private aircraft). In the final analysis, as I wrote in the Seagram Annual Report to Shareholders in 1971, Father left the world a better place than he found it, and that's about all anybody can do with one's life.

I confess that when Father died, I thought I would inherit the mantle, and more—I thought that his persona would pass on to me. In other words, I thought that I would become Sam Bronfman. Eventually, it occurred to me that I was going to have to prove myself through deeds, and I really wanted to be Edgar.

The problems that I would face were not the same as those Father had encountered at a comparable stage. After all, I inherited a sound company, one that should have been mine to build and grow right from day one. Yet it took a while for me to realize that Father's last years of "veto management" were over, and that I needed to get on with the job. Though I never had thought that I lacked confidence, I must have, because some time passed before I was ready to meet the challenges of innovative leadership.

Indeed, life without Father was not at all what I had imagined it would be. I was numb. Instead of being relieved, I felt guilty about our relationship, especially near the end of his life. It's such a pity, because we could have had fun working together those last years. But he couldn't do anything with anyone else—"we" was just not part of his vocabulary.

And still, his absence left a huge void. For all my rebellion, I deeply missed the discipline he had brought to bear. As I think back, I find it extraordinary that Father played such an overpowering role in my life. While I made every effort to be "free," I needed him desperately. And even when he was gone, I still wanted him to love me—still wanted to hear those three little words, although now I knew that I never would.

CHAPTER 7

ALONE AT THE TOP:
PERSONAL UPHEAVAL AND
PROFESSIONAL CHALLENGES

In the aftermath of Father's death, my personal life quickly went askew. Indeed, for much of the next fifteen years I rode an emotional roller coaster, struggling with difficult relationships and painful separations. The turmoil took its toll on my stewardship of Seagram, at times keeping me from operating on all cylinders. However, I was able to prioritize and concentrate on getting the big picture right. And, as I've learned, therein lies the difference between success and failure.

The first crisis came in September 1971, just two months after Father's passing. Ann and I went on a trip to Jerusalem with our close friends Bill and Judy Green. When we arrived, Ann started a fight. Then she told me she was going home to New York. I replied that if she left, we were through, but this did not dissuade her. So upon my return to New York, I moved into the Seagram apartment at the St. Regis and started divorce proceedings.

In truth, I had been unhappy for some time. While Father was alive, however, I couldn't bring myself to consider divorce, knowing how strongly he would disapprove. I also worried about our five children and what would happen to them if Ann were to get primary custody. When I did file for divorce, I was shocked—though not unpleasantly—that Ann wanted to leave Adam, our youngest, with me.

Though I was the one who had initiated the breakup, it was by no means easy. I had lost the most important figure in my life, and the years that followed were the worst I have ever known. (Fortunately, Ann and I have since become good friends, and we see each other on family occasions.)

When Ann walked out during our trip to Israel, I stopped in London before returning to the States to see Lady Carolyn Townshend. Thus began a disastrous chapter that would leave me even more distraught. Suffice it to say that the death of my father and the divorce from Ann were two enormous emotional shocks. Looking back, I should have waited quite a while before even thinking of another commitment, but I wanted my life to go on, and thought I could replace one wife with another. That didn't work. The marriage ended in a contested annulment, which I won, and I sometimes refer to it as a nonevent. But it did drain me emotionally, and hindered my ability to run Seagram.

Shortly thereafter, another woman, Rita Webb, entered my life. I called her "George" and she later changed her name to Georgiana. It was while we were living together that a terrible thing happened.

In the summer of 1975, George and I were planning our wedding. The ceremony was to be held at the home of my great friends Gretchen and Fritz Siebel, followed by a cocktail party and a buffet-dinner reception at my place in Yorktown Heights. Those plans were spoiled, however, by Mel Byrne and Patrick Lynch, the two men who were later accused of kidnapping my eldest son, Sam. (They were convicted of extortion, but not of the crime I know they committed.)

It all began on Friday night, August 8. Sam ate dinner at Yorktown Heights and then drove to his mother's place in Purchase. Before he could enter the house from the garage, he was accosted by an armed man wearing a ski mask, who blindfolded Sam and led him away at gunpoint to a car on the Hutchinson River Parkway, where his accomplice was waiting.

A little later, Sam called and said that he had been kidnapped, and that his abductors' orders were not to call the police. I immediately contacted the FBI in White Plains and was told to call the local police. (I later learned that the FBI has to be careful about these cases because the large majority of supposed kidnappings involve custody battles in divorce cases.) I did so, and an officer came to the house and spent the night while I awaited further instructions, or whatever else was to come.

The next day, a letter arrived at my old residence on 740 Park Avenue. Thankfully, the doorman remembered me and telephoned my secretary, Maxine Hornung. The letter said that Sam was buried, had a limited time to live, that the kidnappers were desperate Vietnam War veterans, and so on. We were told by the FBI—which was now involved, on the theory that the kidnappers had crossed a state line—that the abductors were copying a case that had received wide publicity. They counseled us not to believe the letter, and that offered some reassurance.

The weekend was spent at Yorktown Heights enduring heavy questioning by FBI agents. We were all weary but cooperated as best we could. Ann was there, too, somehow convinced that Sam's kidnapping was punishment for whatever sins she may have committed.

Since the letter from the perpetrators was sent to New York City, the FBI decided to move our headquarters to our apartment, where the agents took over a bedroom. George was with me and proved a tremendous help in every way. My brother, Charles, came from Montreal and stayed the course. Leo Kolber also came down and stayed for a few days, which meant a lot to me.

At one point, some enterprising reporter checked the municipal records and discovered that George and I had obtained a marriage license. I told her that I might as well give her the ring, but she declined, saying that she didn't want it until *we* got Sam back—a lovely sentiment that I'll never forget.

I received instructions from the abductors regarding the ransom and was ordered to make contact at Kennedy Airport's international arrivals building. I was not keen on going, of course, and the authorities were worried that I, too, might be abducted. Jonathan Rinehart, a good friend who handled Seagram's corporate PR, offered to go in my place. I briefly considered it, but decided that there was too much risk of screwing up the release. Besides, Sam was my son, and I felt that I needed to go.

The kidnappers were truly scared. The one I conversed with at JFK sounded like he thought he was being shadowed. As a result, it took three nights of going to Kennedy before contact was established. The FBI and the NYPD were more than cooperative, and every move I made was monitored, checked, then double- and triple-checked. I was given the code name "Rooster," while Leo McGillicuddy—the supervisor of the FBI's kidnap and extortion squad in New York, who had taken over the operation—was code-named "Irish," as suggested by Charles. That third night, I told Leo that I didn't want such a huge FBI and NYPD presence; it might be picked up by the adversaries. He replied that they didn't want to risk losing me, too. On Friday night, a week after Sam had been kidnapped, we went with what I thought were fewer backup personnel, and the chase was on.

I received commands from the kidnappers to go to different public telephones, first in the TWA building, then in a gas station somewhere out on the highway, and then back at Kennedy. During this surreal journey, there was $2.4 million in the back of the station wagon. They had originally asked for $4.8 million, then reduced the amount by half, for reasons I never understood.

At each telephone, I insisted on being given more time. I convinced the kidnapper that I was not familiar with Long Island or the airport (in fact, I wasn't) because I was always driven there. My hope was to make him feel less anxious about police intervention.

The last place he sent me to was a diner on Queens Boulevard. When I called him, he told me to open the back of Ann's station wagon—they had specified the car I was to use in an earlier communication—and put down the middle seat so that they could see that no one was there. After doing this, I waited at the car instead of returning to the telephone—and almost blew the whole thing. Finally, the chef came out of the diner and told me to go back to the phone (little did I know that he, too, was an FBI agent).

At this point, the kidnapper was really panicked and wanted to call off the meeting. I went into high gear, trying to persuade him that he had not given me proper instructions. Putting the pressure on, I told him that it would be impossible for me to go through all this again. We were so close and I wanted it to be over.

He finally gave me further instructions, and I drove to the place he had specified. He entered the station wagon from the front passenger door and yelled at me not to look at him. I did notice his mask, and I believe that he was wearing slacks and a Windbreaker. I think he also had a gun, but I cannot swear to it.

He directed me where to drive. When we got there, he ordered me to get out of the car. He said to cross the street and wait there exactly twenty minutes, and told me where I could find the station wagon. Before I exited, I managed to hit a switch that activated a radio device hooked up to the FBI. I later found out that it didn't do any good—he switched cars after a block and a half, which I should have known since I had been told where to pick up the car.

I waited on the other side of the street for what I thought was a sufficient period of time, then crossed again. As I reached the spot where I had gotten out of the car, a tall African-American male came out of the shadows. Before I could faint dead away, he identified himself as yet another FBI agent. How they managed to be everywhere is still a mystery to me. We went together to retrieve the car. I asked him to drive—I had had enough of that for one evening—and he took me home. There was nothing more I could do, and I was relieved to be out of the action. My greatest fear, however, was not that I would be harmed, but that I might make a mistake and further endanger Sam.

At the apartment at 960 Fifth Avenue, there was a phone in the room being used by the FBI as an office. I never touched the phone, but when I heard it ring as I was walking by at around two A.M., I picked it up. It was Leo McGillicuddy, who wanted to know if the Rooster would like to speak with his son. It was over.

The rest of the story was also strange. The FBI and NYPD lost contact with the kidnappers' car. That vehicle was being driven by Lynch, the tougher of the two. But they traced the owner through the license plates, and, according to Leo, the arrests were finally made after several snafus and foul-ups. Leo told me that those mistakes weakened the state's case at the trial. (Even so, I was very impressed with Leo, and shortly after he retired from the FBI in 1978, I hired him as chief of Seagram security.)

While I waited for Sam, I sent for George's engagement ring. In the meantime, Seagram medical director Dr. Charles P. Giel came to the house and advised me on how to handle Sam. He said that I had to make him go over the whole thing detail by detail, dredging up everything so that he could get it out of his system.

I followed his instructions. It must have been an awful experience, because at one point Sam said, "Thank God it wasn't Adam!" But he hadn't been molested. He was just scared, filthy, and awfully tired, as well as glad to be free. Unfortunately, the filthy clothes were removed from the room and sent to be cleaned, evidence that might have convicted those two bastards of kidnapping rather than merely extortion.

He showered and shaved, then showered, then showered some more. When, by his standards, he was clean, he ate a large breakfast, and I took him to Yorktown Heights, where the family was waiting. When we arrived, there was a great burst of applause from the crowd that had come to welcome Sam home, and tears of joy and congratulations all around.

The following week, John Loeb, Sam's maternal grandfather, sent me a letter declaring that it probably wouldn't have worked out so well had it not been for my "bravery." I don't know about that; I just did what I had to do.

The kidnappers' lawyer constructed a defense alleging that the whole thing was a hoax and that Sam was part of it. The attorney went so far as to suggest that there had been a homosexual relationship with one of the kidnappers. The filthy clothes might have convinced the jury beyond a doubt that Sam could not have been party to his own kidnapping. Also, the Westchester prosecutor, though a very nice man, was not as good as his adversary.

Such an experience makes you consider both the pleasures and the perils of wealth. The kidnappers got the idea to abduct Sam from the newspaper accounts of my annulment trial with Carolyn Townshend. When you're rich, you are subject to the dangers of blackmail, kidnapping, robbery, and so forth, as well as to the deceptions of money-hungry connivers. You also must tolerate ugly publicity and the hatred of those less fortunate than you, along with the nagging doubt as to whether people like you for yourself or for your money.

On the other hand, as the wag said, I've been miserably poor and miserably rich, and rich is better. I like being wealthy. I like having a farm in Virginia where I can relax, commune with nature, and spend time with friends. I like having a home in Sun Valley, where we ski in winter, and spend glorious summers biking, working out at the athletic club, and living without air conditioning in a latter-day paradise. I love the use of a private aircraft to take me to these places, as well as all over the world. And, like my father, I like "being somebody."

I also like being wealthy because I can help people. I was able to use my position in life to help free Soviet Jewry when there was a Soviet Union. I like being able to help ensure the survival of Judaism, especially in the Diaspora. I like being able to help a young man achieve his ambition of going to college.

Sam's kidnapping was an all-too-real reminder that there are good sides and bad sides to everything. The balance depends on how you live—how smart, how compassionate, and how honest you are with others and with yourself.

———————

After the conclusion of this nightmare, George and I followed through with our wedding plans. It was a gorgeous day, though somewhat marred by the presence of a press corps (which we agreed to see between the wedding proper and the luncheon to follow) as well as a hovering newspaper helicopter trying to shoot pictures. My neighbor, W. Averell Harriman, remarked that someone ought to shoot it out of the sky, and my son Matthew asked if he should go get the gun. Nevertheless, it was a great party, made all the better by the collective relief over Sam's return. Ann was there, as were a host of good friends and George's family from England.

George and I had two children together: Sara, who was born November 21, 1976, and Clare, who was born April 8, 1979. Soon after Clare was born, George decided she wanted a divorce. We parted, and then a few years later, being really naive, I married her again, wanting to keep my young girls with me, but that was not to be, and we divorced again. No real regrets because of Sara and Clare, who are wonderful, loved and loving children.

———————

While my middle-age years were full of emotional upheaval, there was still a company to run. Thus I assumed my new position as head of the Seagram empire, though it would take some time before I fully grew into it.

When I first went on the board in 1955, at age twenty-six, I asked Father what happened at meetings. "What do you think happens?" he said. "We declare a dividend and have a drink."

By 1971 that attitude was clearly passé. So immediately after Father's death, Charles and I set about improving the board of directors by getting some of the top people in Canada to serve as members. (By law in 1971, there had to be a majority of Canadians on all such bodies and each committee thereof. Because we do so much of our business outside of Canada, that no longer applies to Seagram.)

At the time, Charles and I were operating instinctively. Neither of us really understood why we wanted a strong board, but the answer is simple: when you have total power to run a corporation, there is no discipline. I have learned that success in business, and perhaps in most

aspects of life, requires both self-discipline and objectively imposed discipline from outside. A board of directors can provide that necessary
ingredient, but only if the members are strong, independent people.

Today I am proud to say that the Seagram board of directors is the
finest in Canada, and perhaps in North America. Every year, as I toast
the board members for their tremendous help, I sincerely mean it. On
the one hand, they are extremely loyal to the company. On the other
hand, if they don't like something, they will let you know about it, one
way or the other. Because they are completely free to criticize any proposal, there is great value in having to ask their approval for major expenditures. Knowing that, we are always careful to do our homework
before making a proposal to the board.

On at least one occasion, the board expressed unhappiness with a
proposal. We were interested in buying a Mexican brandy company,
but the directors indicated that we should reconsider the idea. Upon
review, we agreed that the criticism was more than justified and abandoned the thought.

The other purpose served by a board of directors is to change
management if it isn't doing as well as it should. I never forget that,
even though Charles's family and mine own a controlling interest, our
duty is to all of the shareholders. If we were incompetent to run the
company, we should not be permitted to do so.

Between 1971 and 1976, my top priority was the expansion of
Seagram's foreign operations. Father had always claimed that he was an
internationalist, but World War II curtailed the overseas opportunities
of North American corporations. Though another twenty-five years
passed before we resumed full-scale efforts abroad, luckily the rest of
the alcohol industry lagged behind Seagram. I recognized now that the
world was quickly becoming a single marketplace. I also realized that,
while in the United States our distributors had played a key role in
building Seagram brands, we could do even better in foreign countries
where we would be able to own and control the primary means of distribution.

Jack Yogman, who loved to make deals, set to work, along with

Harold Fieldsteel, our chief financial officer, and Jim McDonough, the head of Seagram Overseas Sales Company. Together they undertook numerous purchases.

One deal that worked out extremely well was when Jack brought Abdallah Simon into our family of businesses. Ab had had a bad year at Austin Nichols, an important wine importer. He had bought too much of a bad year, and had lost money for his employer. Jack met Ab, and brought him to Seagram, where he set up the Château and Estates Wine Company. Ab had extraordinary contacts with the major Bordeaux producers, as well as the Burgundy wine owners, and he proceeded to build an organization and a business. He was very successful, and when I realized that all the very best of the great houses—Château Lafite Rothschild and Château Mouton Rothschild, Châteaux Haut Brion and Margaux, Cheval Blanc and La Tour—were represented by us, I asked Ab to change the name of his company to include Seagram. I thought the prestige of these great wines would add to the luster of the Seagram name. He was delighted to do so, and in 1983, it became official. Of course, it took a few years for the new labels to hit the market.

Another deal was for Mumm Germany. Seagram owned some 50 percent of Mumm France, so this made good sense. Until the end of World War I, Mumm France had been owned by the Mumm family of Germany. It then became part of the reparations package that Germany had had to pay under the Treaty of Versailles. The jewel, which of course was Mumm France, was taken over by a group headed by René Lalou. The German family was allowed to keep their domestic production for sale in Germany only. There were all sorts of complicated provisions about labels, and the present Mumm Sekt has a special print that looks nothing like the French labels, and only two non-colors, black and white. (Sekt is a type of bland sparkling dry white wine that is about as much like champagne as beer resembles a hearty ale.)

But many of the other deals were not well advised. The trouble with our acquisition program was that it wasn't a program: we were spending money in Europe and South America without any plan to guide us. Moreover, Jack paid no attention to cash flows, and Harold got caught up in the enthusiasm of deal making.

In 1976, Charles, disturbed by the look of our balance sheet, requested a serious review of our debt and cash flow. The analysis provided by Richard Goeltz, our treasurer at the time, painted a frightening picture. As CEO, I should never have allowed the company to put itself in such financial straits, and the analysis served as a much-needed jolt. I finally acknowledged to myself that Jack was a terrible administrator. By that time, he had more than twenty people reporting directly to him. Obviously, that fulfilled a need to have his ego pampered, but it didn't leave him time to listen to his people, or to develop and guide them. And nothing in business is more important than this. Remembering my conversation with Father about Jack, I let him go.

Still, I was hesitant to take full charge, mostly because of my personal problems, and Charles and I decided that we should look for a chief executive "who could take us into the next century," Charles's phrase.

We went to John L. Weinberg, then co-managing partner of Goldman Sachs and a member of our board of directors. John, a close personal friend since the early fifties, is one of the best bankers I ever knew. At his suggestion, we hired Heidrich & Struggles, the well-known executive recruitment firm. In the meantime, I became the interim chief operating officer as well as chief executive officer.

As the months rolled by and we interviewed candidates, I grew more and more uncomfortable with the thought of relinquishing so much control over the company. Having just married George, I was happy for the moment in my personal life and decided I could run Seagram as it should be run.

During a quiet dinner in Montreal with Charles, I told him that I really didn't want to give up my birthright. I was enjoying life at Seagram, I said, and felt ready to guide the corporation myself. I suggested that instead of looking for a CEO, we should look for a COO. Charles replied that if this was my honest intent, he would readily agree. So we shifted gears.

At this point, we were already seriously considering Philip E. Beekman, then president of Colgate, International, for the position of CEO. When I disclosed the change of direction to Gerry Roche, the

Heidrich & Struggles partner helping us with our search, he flashed me a look that said, "You've blown it."

But Gerry came back to us with good news: Phil didn't seem to mind. I was puzzled by this casual attitude, and later asked Phil about it. He told me that because Seagram was a family-controlled company, he felt that titles wouldn't mean very much. Ultimately, he would be reporting to me anyhow.

I understood his point. Each corporation has its own "culture," a special way of doing things, and Seagram is no exception. The company was built so much in Father's image that throughout the industry, Seagram and Bronfman are synonymous. (To wit: One evening, Father and Mother were invited to dinner by Sam Rosenman, the eminent lawyer who had been a speechwriter for FDR. They went to a restaurant called Moskovitch and Lupovitch, and when they arrived, Mr. Rosenman introduced Father to the owner. Not hearing the name, Father said, "Excuse me, but are you Moskovitch or Lupovitch?" "Why should I be Moskovitch or Lupovitch?" the owner replied. "Are you Seagram?")

When Phil became president and chief operating officer, Charles, who had been president, became vice chairman. This left Harold Fieldsteel very disappointed. He thought he should have been named president. But Father had once said, correctly, that you should never ask either your sales manager or your chief accountant to run the company. The first cares only about sales and ignores profits, while the latter will not spend the money needed to generate sales and, in turn, profits.

In spite of his disappointment, however, when I asked Harold what the company needed most, his answer was "marketing." And this was exactly Phil Beekman's field of expertise, and the main reason we brought him aboard.

Phil had started out as a production executive at Colgate, but when he realized the importance of marketing, he set about studying it. He then applied for a transfer, took a cut in pay, and became a marketer. His other great asset was his overseas experience. He was running Colgate's far-flung international operations, had lived in Argentina and spoke Spanish, and knew Europe intimately, so I was confident that he could make sense out of our portfolio of companies and help us generate profits.

Having a president and chief operating officer was very new to Seagram, and it suited not only me but the entire corporation. I don't much like details and am not really suited to being a hands-on operating executive. I enjoy reviewing marketing plans and the bottom line, but I don't have the patience to guide the company managers, nor do I have the basic marketing skills to do that. I'm better at laying out long-term strategy.

Marketing in the early days was all in Father's head. He knew what he wanted to sell and what he wanted the company to be. But it never really found full expression, because he didn't know how to put it in words. It was instinct. He would look at the ads, and that was about it. We had a few other people who were making ads, but advertising isn't marketing. Marketing is the art of defining what you want your brand to be and who you want to appeal to—and then implementing that vision.

Seagram's vision is to define itself as the top of the line. Accordingly, it's not volume that's important, but profit. A sale without profit is a sale without honor. Many companies are destroyed by rivalries driven by egomaniacal CEOs with Napoleon complexes. The trick is to get down to the right size where you can make money.

We've been very successful at establishing a reputation for premium quality. I remember going into a bar with Father not long after we introduced Chivas Regal. Though the place catered mostly to construction workers, it was known to be a big outlet for Chivas. Neither Father nor I could understand why, so we asked the bartender. "A construction worker comes in and he wants a drink," he told us. "For ten cents more, you can ask for Chivas Regal and be a big shot."

The key is creating an image—and then maintaining it. At one point, Bill Bernbach had designed an ad that showed Chivas being served in paper cups. "Bill," I said, "you can't have paper cups with Chivas."

"But, Edgar, everybody . . ."

"Bill, you didn't hear me. You don't associate paper cups with Chivas Regal. Do whatever you want, but no paper cups."

(In this case, image wasn't the only issue; if you serve Chivas in a paper cup, the taste will be altered for the worse.)

In devising marketing strategies, market research can be useful up to a point. But market research is inherently limited by the way in which the question is phrased. People are always asked, "Which do you prefer?" But what if they don't like either one? There is never a "none of the above" line.

I think one of the reasons we've been so successful is that Seagram products actually taste better than most of our competition. It always starts there. You can spend all the time and money in the world on image, but when someone pours a drink it better taste good.

This explains why we've been less successful with our vodka and rum lines. You really can't improve the taste of these products, and by the time we got into those arenas, we were playing catch-up against giants like Smirnoff and Bacardi.

One of the most important elements of marketing is determination. Of course, there are occasional overnight successes, but in general you have to devise a strategy and then stay the course. One of the advantages of having a family-dominated business is that you can take a long-term view with respect to marketing and other aspects of the business.

Of course, it hasn't always worked this way in practice. We once created a brand called Seagram's 100 Pipers Scotch. We had to overcome a couple of problems right from the beginning, the biggest one being that most consumers don't associate Seagram with Scotch. Research led us astray. I guess we asked the question stupidly, because respondents had told us the opposite. We created an ad campaign that I thought was spectacular. It came out of a song that somebody wrote for the introduction of 100 Pipers: if you hear one piper, then it's an ordinary Scotch; two pipers, it's a little bit better; and finally, 100 Pipers. It keeps building and building until it finally penetrates. The ad had a beautiful background with purple and mauve, and it looked like the Scottish hillsides. We were creating an instant tradition, and it might have worked, but Father was too close to his final days and was anxious to have a big success right away. "That'll take forever," he said. Well, that's the nature of the business. You cannot build a brand quickly. However, the offset is that once you establish a brand, it lasts a long, long time.

Unless, of course, you screw it up yourself. Not too long ago, I was in London and was shown a package for Chivas Regal 18. *What?* I thought. *Chivas Regal 18?* We'd spent forty-odd years convincing people that Chivas Regal, a twelve-year-old brand, is the best whiskey they could possibly buy. Then someone decided to introduce Chivas Regal 18, undermining everything we'd done. I wouldn't have objected if they wanted to use the name Chivas along with something else, but not Chivas Regal. When the London people put up a big fuss, I relented and told them that they could try it in some duty-free market in Asia. But it's still a mistake—you don't screw around with a brand like Chivas Regal.

—•—

Phil Beekman turned out to be a wonderful addition to Seagram. Besides being a terrific person, Phil quickly proved himself to be a tremendously hardworking professional dedicated to mastering every detail of the business. His day usually began at six A.M. and rarely ended before nine at night. He did some terrific work for us, introducing marketing disciplines into the company and making sense out of the chaos of our international operations. His hard work set the stage for our future growth.

He also hired Ed McDonnell to run our overseas operations. Ed did a superb job, and in due course my son Edgar placed him in charge of all spirits and wine operations; he also became a member of our board. In April of 1995, Ed announced his retirement and subsequently went into business for himself doing foreign distribution, and is still closely attached to Seagram. He started in the Philippines and I have no doubt he will make good money for us as well as for his family.

During Phil's tenure, we made two more acquisitions: the Scottish single-malt whiskey The Glenlivet and all its subsidiaries, and Sandeman's ports and sherries.

At one point during The Glenlivet negotiations, conducted in Scotland with non-executive chairman Iain Tennant and CEO Ivan Straker, I thought they were being a little greedy. But sometimes you lose perspective in the heat of battle. When I called Charles in Montreal to ask his opinion, he told me to "pay the two dollars," and after a little more negotiating, we agreed on the price. Once again, my view that objective, cool, and collected advice can be invaluable was affirmed.

It was a good acquisition for Seagram. The Glenlivet company sold more than 300,000 cases a year of Glen Grant, a single-malt whiskey, in Italy. By combining the Glen Grant distribution with our brands, Italy became our most profitable subsidiary in Europe.

Seagram also benefited from the purchase in two other ways. First, Chivas Regal could use "fillings" (malt whiskeys distilled by others and matured in our warehouses) from The Glenlivet distilleries, which produce five well-known single malts. Like most popular brands of Scotch, Chivas Regal uses these single malts in its blend, and thus we were able to achieve considerable savings in the cost of the raw material and make sure that, when we needed additional fillings, we would have sufficient supplies even though they were in great demand. Second, I realized that if the consumer wanted to "graduate" from Chivas Regal to an even more prestigious and expensive whiskey, only a single malt would do—and The Glenlivet fit the bill nicely.

Seagram's Sandeman purchase worked out well, too. Ports and sherries have never been very important in the United States. (At the time we bought Sandeman, both Harvey's Bristol Cream, the top-selling brand, and Dry Sack were struggling, despite a very good advertising campaign.) In Europe, however, demand was growing, and some of the markets there had great synergies for us: Sandeman sherries were the leading brand in Holland and, more important, in Germany. Adding them to our product line in both places greatly increased our profitability. Today, Sandeman doesn't quite make the 15 percent return upon which Edgar Jr. insists, but it is not out of reach.

(There is a problem with the basic makeup of port, which I know how to correct, and current Portuguese regulations will allow us and others to make the required changes. In manufacturing port wine, the fermenting of sugar into alcohol is stopped by adding alcohol—hence the appellation "fortified"—to the fermenting mash. By stopping the fermentation, the alcohol allows some of the sugars to remain unconverted, which accounts for port's sweetness. According to the law, which is strictly enforced, no sugar can be added. Unfortunately, the alcohol used for this process is a raw brandy distillate full of congeners that do not sit well in the stomach unless the brandy is either properly aged in oak barrels or distilled at high proof. Thus, port wine, which matures in the bottle, takes forever to age, and after a few glasses people often complain of its aftereffects, such as headaches and upset stomachs.

If high-proof distilled grape spirits were used in the manufacture of port wine it would then require less aging in the consumer's cellar, have the real taste of the grape, and have fewer aftereffects. A large-scale experiment has determined that my surmise was correct—provided you add the high-proof spirits in a diluted form, so as not to shock the fermenting product.)

The Sandeman negotiations were interesting. When Phil Beekman and I went to the Sandeman offices for lunch, we brought along Iain Tennant, former chairman of The Glenlivet group. Iain was now on our board and chaired our U.K. subsidiary. He could testify to the fact that, when we took a company over, we didn't get rid of the management. To the contrary, we integrated their management into our own.

Present at that lunch were the two Sandeman brothers, representing the fourth or possibly fifth generation of their clan. Timothy, the older brother, sat at the head of the table, and David at the other end. They told us that the company was not for sale.

"Then why are we here?" Iain asked.

"When the preeminent figure in the industry wants to see you, it is a pleasure to invite him to lunch," answered Tim.

"Bullshit!" Iain said bluntly. Then, after some verbal sparring, Tim admitted that they might entertain an offer after all.

A deal was eventually struck, and Sandeman became a part of Seagram. Timothy retired a few years later, while David stayed on longer, doing a really top job for us in Europe and America in the area of public and trade relations. Since then, yet another generation of Sandemans has joined the company.

———

Shortly after my father's death in 1971, I was asked by Nahum Goldmann to be involved with the World Jewish Congress, an umbrella organization representing more than eighty national groups throughout the world. In 1979, I was elected acting president, and two years later it became official. Thus the time spent with WJC matters increased dramatically.

How did my activities with the WJC affect Seagram? Ultimately, the answer is unclear. I tried hard to keep the two separate, lest I tarnish my credibility or that of the organization. My circle of contacts expanded through my WJC undertakings, and perhaps Seagram's reputation benefited from the association with the WJC's humanitarian efforts. My work certainly didn't hurt the company, with the exception of the minor and temporary damage we suffered in Austria after the WJC helped expose President Kurt Waldheim's involvement with the Nazis.

My experiences with the WJC is the subject of *The Making of a Jew*, so I will not chronicle in these pages the many adventures I've had while running the world's most important Jewish international organization. Instead, I'll simply share a few lessons learned along the way that have also helped me in my business life.

First, I've discovered how to listen, and why it's so important. At Seagram I was always the boss, even as a young man at the distillery. This fact generally discouraged people from sharing their ideas with me. In a volunteer organization, it's different. No one is scared to contradict you; on the contrary, there tends to be a wide variety of opinions, and you have to justify your position based on its merits. In the latter part of my business career, I have benefited more from this give-and-take process, having learned the value of an open dialogue. I let people know that I'm interested in what they have to say and, even if I differ, listening to them can help clarify my own thinking.

Second, I've found that volunteer work can enrich one's life, providing balance and perspective. Indeed, the WJC was probably the most important thing to me outside of Seagram, offering a chance to develop other aspects of my personality. I don't think it's healthy to concentrate all your energy on business. Those who do become too emotionally tied to it, as I witnessed firsthand with Father. Business demands a lot of energy and commitment, but it is not the ultimate source of happiness or well-being.

Third, my experience with the WJC affirmed a value that had been an unspoken but powerful part of my upbringing: the importance of giving something back. Success in business means little if you divorce yourself from the world. Indeed, one of the best things about wealth and position is that they enable you to make a difference in other people's lives. Both Father and Mother taught this lesson by example through their extensive philanthropic activities. I hope I have passed it on to my children.

CHAPTER 8

EXPANDING THE EMPIRE:
DU PONT, MARTELL, AND
TROPICANA

As a result of our 1981 investment in Conoco/Du Pont, Charles and I took on responsibilities beyond Seagram's core business. Among other things, this meant asserting our rightful position with Du Pont, which proved to be no easy task.

I've always felt that a deal is like a marriage, and that it is therefore essential to consider how you are going to interact with any potential partner. For this reason, I have relied to a great extent on my personal rapport with other executives.

In the case of Du Pont, I had a great deal of respect for Ed Jefferson, the CEO and chairman, as well as most of the people around him. Charles and Andy actually struck up a personal friendship with Ed and his wife, Wunnie. They were courteous and decent, so I felt optimistic about our association.

Unfortunately, Irving Shapiro, who had retired as CEO of Du Pont, still exercised power as chairman of the finance committee, and we were destined not to get along. Thin-lipped, with coal eyes and black-silver hair, Shapiro was not a tall man but stood very erect, underscoring his imperious manner. Irving Shapiro had a real problem letting go, and he treated Jefferson with an attitude that said, "I got you the job as CEO and you should kiss my ass daily."

Shapiro considered himself a member of the duPont family, and once told me a long time before we were involved, when he was still CEO, that he was the link between the days of family management and the current era of professional management. In truth, the real link to the duPont family was Crawford Greenwalt.

A true gentleman in every sense of the word, Crawford had married into the family and eventually risen to CEO. He still had some power at the time we came aboard, and whenever management wanted to do something that Crawford might oppose, they'd ask me to talk to him. In one instance, we were considering forming a political action committee at Du Pont. Crawford hated the idea of a PAC; as far as he was concerned, some member of the family should give the money quietly, as it always had. Of course, he knew this was now impossible.

"Crawford," I said, "I know what you're talking about. I used to do the same thing at Seagram. But we can't do that anymore, there are laws. You have to use a PAC—it's the only way you can do what you really want to do."

Somehow the fact that Procter & Gamble used auditors to make contributions came up. "You know what that is, Crawford?" I asked.

"What?"

"That's a no-PAC PAC. But Du Pont must try and do it honestly, not with subterfuge."

"Edgar, you're absolutely right. Okay, I'm not going to vote for it, but I won't vote against it." And that was his way of giving his blessing. He was a giant of a man.

By the time we arrived, however, the real power struggle was between Shapiro and Jefferson. Shapiro was a staunch defender of the status quo, i.e., "the family runs the company, the family will always run the company." When Jefferson came on, he knew things had to be changed, and he always had to fight with Shapiro. Though Shapiro was a great lawyer, he was neither a great manager nor a great businessman.

Jefferson, originally from Great Britain, came over to the States as a young man and got a job as a chemical engineer. He's a very decent man, and we grew to respect each other. At first, however, he regarded Charles and me warily, assuming that as Jews we were automatically going to be on Shapiro's side. One night at Charles's house, I took Jefferson aside and said, "Look, Jeff, we're on your side." This eased his mind considerably.

Charles and I met with Jefferson and Shapiro, along with each party's counsel, to hammer out a standstill agreement. The idea was to assure them of our intentions so that they wouldn't waste time fighting us. We owned a sizable percentage of Du Pont now, and I wanted them to concentrate on running the business.

More than that, we were very keen on working with management. Otherwise, we'd be on the outside looking in, and life's too short for that. When you're a major shareholder in a company, you should be *part* of it, contribute to the team. If you're not interested, sell your stocks and move on. We played our cards wide open, and in the end Du Pont's top people came to like and respect us.

The standstill agreement gave us two seats on the board and one on the finance committee. That committee no longer exists, but in those days it was extremely important. It had been created to ensure that the Du Pont family, while not running the company on a day-to-day basis, had veto power over all capital expenditures. No outlay of any size could be made unless it was approved by the finance committee. Should one member disagree with the expenditure, it was held over until the next meeting, when questions could be answered and the authorization reconsidered; should two object, it was dead. There were four members of the family on the committee when we came aboard.

The company also was extremely overstaffed. In addition to the finance committee, there was an executive committee composed of managers, and each member had two or three different people reporting to him. By the time we got there, they were already paring down the bureaucracy, but it was still mind-boggling.

Because of the Conoco merger, Du Pont had thirty members on the board (including Charles and me), clearly an unwieldy number. Our strategy was to keep our investment for the long run, and we were content to bide our time, at least for a while. Initially, I served as the

Seagram representative on the finance committee, which met every two weeks in Wilmington, but I soon asked Charles to do the honors. Between Seagram and the World Jewish Congress, I just didn't have the time. In addition, Charles has great diplomatic skills, and with him on the committee, he could play good cop and, when necessary, I could play bad cop.

A few years later, when the time was approaching for Du Pont to renegotiate the standstill agreement, I began making ugly noises. There were a number of things I wanted to rectify, and I was determined to be just as nasty and tough as Shapiro had been in the beginning.

One major bone of contention was that Du Pont kept issuing stock to cover option plans for executives, which forced us to buy shares in the market to protect our 20 percent position, which was important for bookkeeping purposes—we could consolidate our percentage of Du Pont's earnings on our statements. I also felt that we were not being given the kind of attention we deserved. Du Pont was treating us like ordinary directors rather than major shareholders, and failing to consult us on long-term strategy. They believed that all directors were created equal. I believed that some were more equal than others.

We had no desire to try and run Du Pont—Charles and I always believed that it was a special company with good management. We simply wanted the respect due us. I decided that, in the next go-round, we were going to have two members on the finance committee.

Charles suggested that our director and head of Goldman Sachs, John Weinberg, work out a new relationship with Du Pont chairman, Ed Jefferson. John's no pussycat, and I thought it a great idea.

After some protracted negotiations, Steve Banner, our senior counsel and a partner at Simpson Thacher, presented me with a proposal containing two main elements. Number one, our representation on the board of directors and finance committee would match our percentage of Du Pont shares. Two, Du Pont would agree not to issue any more shares without our written permission, and those shares they needed for employee options would henceforth be purchased on the open market. There were other items, but we both knew these were the key issues.

I gave my blessing to the plan, and Steve scheduled a breakfast meeting with Du Pont's banker, First Boston. They agreed in principle on a deal, and that was that.

I don't believe that the members of the Du Pont family ever realized what a favor we had done them. Because of this new agreement, their holdings would no longer face constant dilution.

Now it was time to mend our relationship with Du Pont's management, and nobody could have done a better job than Charles. First, he built a firm friendship with Ed Jefferson, then he established a strong rapport with Ed's successor as chairman, Dick Heckert, and with his successor, Edgar S. Woolard Jr. We remained on good terms with both the Du Pont management and the board right up until the time that we initiated negotiations to sell back our stock. By then, our ownership percentage stood at almost 25 percent, as Du Pont had bought back a large number of its own shares to increase shareholder value.

Though I can't point to any one dramatic act, we made our presence felt at Du Pont. Our role was that of the ever-present thorn that didn't quite prick but could. We kept everyone on their toes, the result being that they probably performed much better and much more efficiently.

As the only outside director of Du Pont who knew anything about the oil business, I was very supportive of Conoco, pushing Ed Jefferson and his successors to invest money in the company. And Charles always backed me up. On another front, my connections came in handy when Du Pont started to operate in Russia. By that time, I knew almost all the top people in the Soviet Union through my involvement with the World Jewish Congress, so I was able to speed things along.

Then there was the transition from Jefferson to Ed Woolard. Ed Woolard is a lovely man, and I became quite fond of him. He's a real country boy—he grew up in a small town in North Carolina, and you can still hear that funny accent. Woolard's very shy and modest, and a real pleasure to be around. Among Du Pont's upper management, he was the only outstanding candidate for chairman. Jefferson knows this and wanted Woolard but, as usual, Shapiro was blocking the way. He just couldn't see an untried and untested man like Woolard coming in and taking over. So we worked out a compromise in which Richard Heckert, a top executive with Du Pont for many years, who was slated to retire at the same time as Jefferson, would stay on for an extra year in the capacity of chairman. I was confident that Heckert would quietly hand the baton to Woolard, and he did exactly that.

Woolard's not an entrepreneur—you don't need to be an entrepreneur to run Du Pont—but he's an excellent manager and he did a terrific job. He made Du Pont tough and lean, taking out layers and layers of fat. For instance, all the directors had offices in the Du Pont building. What did they need offices for? One room where the directors could meet and talk or use a telephone would be quite sufficient. Woolard knew how to deal with this kind of problem.

He also really understood economic globalization and what it meant for the company. He was the one who wanted to build plants in Taiwan, Singapore, South Korea, Australia, and so on. Woolard knew how to use the unstoppable process of globalization to forge a huge operation.

Perhaps most impressively, Woolard is one of the best negotiators I've ever seen. He's tough yet patient and does all of it himself, which is the key to his success.

While the Du Pont venture improved greatly after the first few years, it went through a lot of bad times, too. I remember on many occasions standing up and supporting Ed when we started to downsize. I'd try to make everyone understand how hard it was for him. Downsizing in New York is one thing—you don't even know the guy below you in your apartment building. But in a small town like Wilmington, where Du Pont is based, it's a whole different story. You actually run into the people who lost their jobs and have to look them in the eye.

For Ed it was made even tougher because of his small-town roots. When it was proposed that Du Pont reduce its debt through downsizing, I remember him initially disputing the fact that the company's red ink was getting too high. He was arguing with his heart, not his head.

"Ed, c'mon," I said. "When you were a kid in the boondocks of North Carolina, did you ever think that twelve-billion-dollar debt was nothing? I do believe that Du Pont can handle it, but I'm very conscious that it's getting higher than it should be."

All in all, though, our investment in Du Pont was a satisfying experience. And, as you'll see, it proved to be very profitable as well.

———

In the early eighties, a couple of years after the Du Pont stock purchase, heavy-smoking Harold Fieldsteel was diagnosed with lung cancer and decided to retire. Assuming that his chances of survival weren't terrific, he wanted to cash in his options, along with the other benefits coming to him, in order to get his estate in order. Though I knew I would miss him, I couldn't argue with his logic. (The odds turned out to be better than he thought: Harold lived until January 1995.)

Harold was a genius in his own way, and he had an instinct for the company that was absolutely remarkable. If there was something fishy going on at Seagram, he would invariably get to the bottom of it. In recent years, we've had a couple of suspicious incidents involving inventory, where the warehouses were suddenly filled with merchandise so that sales and profits and thus bonuses would look good. That could never have happened in Harold Fieldsteel's day. He'd look at the shipping reports and say, "Wait a minute, there's something wrong here," then immediately have his guys on it.

Father used to complain that people were getting away with murder on expense accounts (which, of course, happens at all large companies). "Look, Father," I said. "If a guy cheats ten percent on his expense accounts, there's nothing you can do about it. When it gets to thirty-five or forty percent, Harold Fieldsteel will find out so quickly that the guy's head will spin on his way out the door."

Much as I liked him, Harold had an odd habit of bringing unconventional characters into his department. This generally worked out okay, but once in a while it backfired.

A case in point was Tom Hawe, whom Harold had hired as a treasurer. As the British say, Hawe was too clever by half. At one point, he negotiated a deal in Swiss francs. We often deal in foreign currencies because, doing a lot of business in those currencies, we need hedges to protect ourselves. But Hawe's deal was a pure gamble, and it cost the company dearly. I was angry that we had lost money, of course, but I was also furious at Hawe for thinking he had the right to risk the corporation's funds.

Storming into Harold's office, I demanded an explanation. He apologized, but said that he couldn't control Tom.

"In that case," I said, "either give him your job or fire him." Guess his reaction.

When we started looking for Harold's replacement, Steve Banner, then a managing partner of Simpson Thacher & Bartlett (and a Seagram senior officer until his death in May 1995), suggested that I consider David Sacks.

David and I went back a long way. He had been senior tax counsel at Simpson Thacher & Bartlett, and had acted for me when I was making films for Sagittarius as well as during my marital difficulties. At the time of Harold's retirement, David was serving as a senior partner with Lehman Brothers/Kuhn Loeb, but was no longer happy there. Thus, he gladly accepted our offer to become Seagram's chief financial officer.

David is blessed with both street smarts and a strong intellect. (He does crossword puzzles even better than I do.) If he has a flaw, it's that he's more than a little acerbic. Harold Handler, now the senior tax person at Simpson Thacher, was once in David's office with Steve Banner. David said something cutting to Harold, who responded, "That isn't nice." Banner told him that if he wanted nice, he was in the wrong office.

In the early 1980s, Phil Beekman suffered a terrible tragedy: his son and namesake developed AIDS. "Skipper," as he was called, contracted this dread disease at a time when the world was just beginning to understand its horrors. As Phil's friend, I lived through the whole terrifying process with him.

During the course of Skipper's sickness and demise, Phil had a difficult time, and it affected his work. He had gotten where he was by working harder than anyone else. He learned to go without much sleep, and kept meticulous notes, which he studied constantly so that he would always know everything. He'd beat you to death with those details, and since I'm the worst detail man in the world, we made a great combo.

During this awful period, Phil didn't have the physical or mental energy to follow his usual routine, so he resorted to corporate politics. Although he was good at playing this game, he was also transparent.

One day, when Charles and I were having lunch in the executive dining room in New York, he asked, "How much longer are you going to put up with Phil Beekman?"

I hadn't thought the situation was all that obvious to him, and his comment took me by surprise. I agreed that the situation wasn't good, but blamed Skip's death for much of the trouble and said that I was prepared to give Phil six more months to recover. If he didn't, I would recommend that we do something. Charles agreed.

Six months went by without any improvement, and I finally told Charles that I was letting Phil go. This was very difficult for me, and I'm glad that it turned out well for both Phil and Seagram. Not only was I fond of Phil, but he had really gone out of his way to champion my son Edgar Jr., whom I call Efer. (He came by his nickname at the age of fifteen while living in London, courtesy of an advertising campaign pushing eggs for breakfast with the slogan "E for B.") After I asked Edgar to join the company in 1982, Phil brought him in as his executive assistant so that he could quickly get an overview of Seagram operations. Later, Phil fought to have Edgar appointed president of Seagram Europe. He was convinced that Edgar was old enough and smart enough to do the job, and was willing to persuade Charles. I was reluctant to try shoving any of my sons down my brother's throat, but Phil didn't have the slightest hesitation. (More on Edgar's rise through the ranks in chapter 9.)

Nevertheless, I didn't have any choice with regard to Phil's future. Even if he were to pull it together, people throughout the organization had lost a lot of respect for him, and it was clear that he wouldn't be able to operate effectively. I told Phil that Charles and I had lost confidence in him, and he took it like a soldier.

Knowing of our plans, board member John Weinberg had worked out a new position for Phil which was perfect for him in every way. The Kroger supermarket chain had decided to spin off its drugstore business and was looking for an executive to run it. It was renamed Hook SuperRx Inc., and Phil (as well as Goldman Sachs) has an equity interest in the company. With his love of detail and his knowledge of marketing, Phil was the ideal choice. He was able to build its chains into the third largest in the country, and through it all he remained intensely loyal to Seagram. He became one of our largest customers, and worked with our field people to find better ways of attracting consumers to our products.

Charles and I had agreed to consult with each other before naming Phil Beekman's successor. But first I discussed it with Efer.

There were only a few candidates to consider. Among them, Efer strongly favored our CFO, David Sacks, mirroring my own sentiments.

David was then in his early sixties, and it seemed to me that he could do what Phil hadn't done: eliminate the excess staffing that had built up over the years. Under David's influence, Phil had initiated an early-retirement program, much the same as Du Pont had under Ed Jefferson's leadership. But, like Du Pont, we hadn't really cleaned out superfluous layers of management and had some serious surgery ahead of us. It would be painful, as myriad chief executives can attest, but I felt that David could do the job before he retired. His successor, who by then I had decided would be Efer, could then start out with a clean slate.

I wrote Charles a long, carefully reasoned letter describing all the candidates and explaining why Efer and I had concluded that Sacks was the best choice. I had hoped that he would have received that letter while I was en route to London and then follow up with a telephone conversation upon my arrival, but when I called he hadn't received my correspondence.

"Tell me anyway," Charles said.
"David Sacks," I answered.
"Fine," he said. End of discussion.

———•———

During David's watch, we made two acquisitions. The first, Martell, was not his doing. He had had a heart bypass operation and was mostly indisposed during that heated battle. It's just as well, because he might have been against it, which very well could have made it impossible for me to persuade Charles.

The Martell story began in November 1987, when we learned that the family, which controlled a majority of the shares, was possibly willing to make a deal. By that time, however, Grand Met, the U.K. conglomerate that owns International Distillers and Vintners (IDV), also had its sights on Martell and already held a sizable block of stock.

We moved quickly, impelled by my long-standing belief that Martell makes the best cognacs. Efer spent a great deal of time working with the two most interested members of the family, René Martell, the chairman, and Patrick Martell, the general manager. We negotiated a price and were set to close, but then the French government intervened, insisting that the deal go through the Paris Bourse, their stock exchange. Thus a transaction that had been simply between a willing buyer and seller turned into an auction.

During the course of the negotiations, Efer and Steve Banner lived mostly in Paris; Charles and I flew across the Atlantic a couple of times. Grand Met kept raising the ante, and we kept bidding the required 5 percent over them. It was frustrating and difficult. Each time we needed the board to authorize a higher price, we had to hold a transatlantic telephone meeting with directors in Montreal and New York City. The second time Charles and I were in Paris, we promised the board that if Grand Met bid again, it would get the prize. Grand Met did make another offer, but surprisingly announced that it was their final one.

That Friday, with the weekend looming, I called a luncheon meeting of key executives. Efer, who was the first to speak, said that the price was too high and that we could not afford to play the game any longer. This opinion was echoed by Ed McDonnell, president of our overseas operations, and Richard Goeltz, our chief financial officer. That seemed to be that.

As we were eating, I asked what their positions would be if I, as chairman, said that we were going to go ahead. "That would be foolish," answered Ed McDonnell. Everyone was a little shaky, not knowing where I stood.

That weekend, I flew to California with my buddy Dr. Mark Beckman to see my son Sam, who was running Seagram's California wine business. Sam's wife, Melanie, had been diagnosed with breast cancer, and Mark, a gynecological oncologist, had volunteered to help answer Sam and Mel's questions. On Sunday morning, Efer and I discussed the Martell bid by telephone. Though we were thousands of miles apart, we had come to the same conclusion.

For my part, my head told me that the price—almost $1 billion— was too high, but my gut was saying that we had to go ahead. Efer's position was based more on reason. First, he said, we needed a premier cognac in our portfolio because cognac was the big seller in the Far East, the fastest-growing sector in both the world economy and the distilled-spirits market. Second, if we didn't proceed, our employees would think that the Bronfmans had lost interest in the beverage-alcohol business now that we were involved in Du Pont. Moreover, we both knew that, while it might take a little longer than we liked to see a profit, it would eventually come—especially with the synergies of selling Martell, Mumm, Chivas, and The Glenlivet together in the duty-free markets of the Far East, as well as in Europe, North America, and South America. One thing I have learned from a number of wise businesspeople over the years is that if a move is right in principle, some shortcomings in the details will not hurt you in the long run.

Now we had to convince Charles. I called him on Monday morning and said that we had to meet to discuss Martell. He wanted to know what there was to discuss since we'd already told the board that we were not going to bid again. I insisted, and Charles agreed to meet. Two days later he came to New York, and the two of us, along with Goeltz, Banner, and Efer, gathered at the end of the day around the conference table in my office. Efer was brilliant in making his case, and Charles was convinced. At the conclusion of the meeting, I thanked him for his support. "Not at all," he replied. "Thank you for making us do the right thing."

The next job was to convince the board. On the plane to Montreal, Efer and David Sacks (now fully recovered from his bypass operation) were trying to coach me on what to say and which members might present problems. But I knew all the directors, and I was very much aware of the unwritten rule: if Charles and I are both completely behind a project, the board will go along, unless it truly feels we are making a mistake.

Indeed, after Efer's persuasive presentation, one of the directors suggested that perhaps we weren't bidding enough. I laughed and said that Grand Met would stick by its vow not to bid again. I was right, and for a very steep price Martell was ours.

In a subsequent meeting with Grand Met's chairman, Sir Allen Sheppard, I asked why they had shown their hand, but he didn't offer an answer that made sense. They owned a lot of Martell stock, and it would have been in their interest to make us bid as much as possible. As in poker, you should never give anything away when you're trying to make a business deal. If you play your cards right, hopefully the other guy will fold—as indeed we might have if we hadn't known it was their last bid. Perhaps, in truth, he was more interested in getting us to make our final higher bid and sensed that we were ready to drop out unless he made it clear that after that, the game was over.

I am glad to report that never for a moment has anyone connected with our firm regretted the acquisition of Martell. Sales have exceeded our forecasts and, more important, so have profits. Another example, I believe, of the details falling into place if you get the principle right.

A final note on the Martell negotiations: my brother-in-law, Alain de Gunzburg, played a useful role not only as a supporter, but as a great guide through those shark-infested French waters. At one point, we had to see the minister of finance, Edouard Baladur. Alain explained in impressive fashion that our family was partly French, thereby allaying concern that France would be losing a major corporation to foreigners. That was the only time I have ever worn the Legion of Honor, which France awarded me.

A few years later, in the fall of 1991, I met with President Mitterrand on a Tuesday following elections held the previous Sunday, to discuss the World Jewish Congress Conference on Anti-Semitism, Racism, and Xenophobia. I prefaced a remark by noting that our company, Seagram, owned Mumm champagne. He nodded, then said, "Martell, too," sounding none too pleased. But perhaps this was because he and his party had just taken a bath in the elections.

The other major acquisition during David Sacks's tenure was Tropicana. This was very much David's baby, and he played a major role in the negotiations. (I did not.)

Tropicana belonged to the Beatrice Foods empire, controlled by Henry Kravis of KKR, the leverage buyout wizards. (In 1994, Henry married Marie Josée Drouin, one of our board members and a very competent economist.) KKR decided to cash in on its Beatrice investment. Procter & Gamble was interested but it had an antitrust problem because of its ownership of Citrus Hill, a competing orange juice company. Therefore, working through Salomon Brothers, we determined that a bid of $1.2 billion would probably do the trick. The question was whether or not to bite.

We discovered that the brand name Tropicana was even better known and respected than Seagram's 7 Crown. It had tremendous growth possibilities because at the time it was not yet distributed throughout the United States, while much of the rest of the world was still awaiting orange juice. In short, the deal seemed like a good idea all around, and when Charles and I convened a group of senior executives on January 27, 1988, the decision was made to go forward.

There was no trouble with the board members—they understood the wisdom in diversifying beyond the beverage-alcohol business, where growth has been difficult to achieve, into a closely allied field. The vote, taken on April 19, 1988, was unanimous.

One of the reasons for Charles's enthusiasm was our proven success in the "cooler" business. This beverage became a factor several years ago with the introduction of California Coolers, which was later purchased by Brown-Forman (the makers of Jack Daniel's, Southern Comfort, and many other brands, as well as a line of imports). We had decided to compete in that business, but initially had little success. Along came Efer, and through a series of brilliant moves, he elevated Seagram Coolers from a minor position to market leadership, which we now share with Gallo. All other companies, including Brown-Forman, are out of the field or so insignificant that they might as well be. Charles, impressed with our mass-marketing capabilities, reasoned that we could do the same with Tropicana.

There is no question in my mind that Tropicana was a smart acquisition and that we shall eventually make good money from it. We have had some difficulties, not the least of which has been the weather and its vagaries (e.g., Florida freezes) along with heavy fluctuations in the price of oranges. We've had to adjust to the fact that orange juice is an agricultural product with a limited shelf life, both very constricting forces. Because orange juice is highly perishable, considerable technology is required. Orange juice and oxygen do not mix, so the packaging has to be airtight in order to keep the flavor and satisfy health regulations. Airtight packaging is not very environmentally friendly, so our work had been cut out for us.

The company has spent a lot of capital developing the business, and there is considerable work still to be done—increasing the markets for the product, getting a good handle on supply sources, putting a team together to work on overseas expansion. Someday, Cuba will return to the fold of free nations. Then we will have a source of oranges well south of the freeze line, but not as far from our factories as Brazil, which currently supplies us with some of our product. In the meantime, we have expanded the Brazilian source, and the quality of these oranges is as excellent as in Mexico.

The new trade agreement between Canada, Mexico, and the United States will help us significantly with supply. We have also learned to use California oranges. If our European sales grow as much as we hope, and if the economics work to our advantage, we will consider sourcing from there.

We have opened the Japanese market, and I am told that Tropicana is the largest-selling orange juice in Tokyo. We are also market leaders in Canada and in the United Kingdom. When we bought Tropicana, it was already well established in France. We bought out our local French distributor and are striving to increase our sales there substantially.

On a trip to China in September 1992, I ate lunch with the first deputy foreign minister and on the table was a pitcher of orange juice. It tasted fresh and delicious, so there must be orange trees in China. I have since asked our people to prepare for discussions with the Chinese on an orange juice processing plant. What a market that would be! I was back in Beijing in June 1995, and found that the Chinese are very interested in having groves and juice developed. They see it as an important export opportunity. Our recent acquisition of Dole, which fit in very well, has given us a grove in China and a foothold for large development. The main problem is the poor infrastructure in that huge country, in particular the absence of decent roads and commercial refrigeration.

The more we learn about orange juice, the more we realize how much there is to know. What makes it all rewarding is the certainty that Tropicana will eventually prove to be a terrific investment.

David Sacks stayed beyond our normal retirement age of sixty-five, eventually stepping down in 1991. During those six years, he ran a tight ship and did a great job in cutting the layers of fat from our operations. We still remain very close and he continues to act as my personal counsel, just to keep his hand in the pot. He has also served a term as president of the New York United Jewish Appeal/Federation and works hard for Jewish causes.

———

Over the years, there were deals we lost out on or chose not to make. But one of the benefits of maturity is that, when you miss an opportunity, it doesn't seem to hurt as much. My great buddy Bill Green was wont to say, "Show me a good loser, and I'll show you a loser." That's true up to a point, but you can't succeed at everything. Rather than dwell on the past, it's far better to learn from mistakes and then go on to the next adventure.

One of the deals that didn't happen involved Hiram Walker. The Reichmann family was trying to buy the company, and we thought we had an agreement to buy the wine and spirits end. Ultimately, however, Hiram Walker was purchased by Allied Lyons of England. It might have been possible to join with another bidder, but price became an issue, as did related antitrust problems. So the deal slipped away.

I can't say I regret it, though, nor do I feel sorry for the Reichmann family, which became mired in a cash-flow predicament. They didn't treat us very honorably. We had been promised first crack at the beverage-alcohol part of Hiram Walker if they acquired the company, but they never made any effort to live up to that pledge. In fact, when Canary Wharf dragged them under, Paul Reichmann had the nerve to call me and offer us some participation in that white elephant. I was delighted to give him an evasive answer.

We have tried to convince some of our other competitors that where there is no direct conflict, a joint distribution system makes sense, increasing profits for both sides. Unfortunately, our rivals are managed by non-owners who always suspect that such proposals are the first step of a takeover bid.

Though cooperative efforts would be beneficial, Seagram already has the strongest distribution system in the industry. Early on, Father understood the need for a strong distributor organization in the United

States, where in many states brand owners are prohibited from owning the means of distribution, either wholesale or retail. He also started to build a strong distribution network overseas and, when I took over, I intensified those efforts.

One of the greatest payoffs for that undertaking came in the late fall of 1993, when the Swedish government monopoly that makes Absolut vodka awarded Seagram the contract to distribute its prestigious product worldwide. This was a very gratifying victory, reflecting their respect for not only our great distribution system but the quality of our employees. After the announcement, I told Efer and Ed McDonnell that Jan and I wanted to have a dinner in our apartment for all those who had worked so hard to produce that contract. Some forty company members filled my dining room, and it was a thrill to thank them all, from typists to concierges to executives—a great bunch of people in the extended family known as Seagram.

While Seagram and the World Jewish Congress kept me moving at a whirlwind pace, I took the time in November 1988 to have dinner with my late best friend Mark Beckman and his girlfriend, Helen Kelsey. It's a good thing I did, for that dinner changed my life.

Helen invited an artist by the name of Jan Aronson, thinking the two of us might hit it off. She was right on the mark. Soon after, I asked Jan out, and within two months she had moved in with me.

Jan is an artist who works every day at her studio in Long Island City. She is also a former triathlete, and of the many things we share together, a commitment to health and fitness is one of the most important.

Jan and I enjoyed a wonderful relationship right from the start, but after three marriages, I was in no rush to wed again. By 1994, however, the time had come.

The ceremony took place at the Orthodox Fifth Avenue Synagogue. There were four rabbis present, including my great friends Israel Singer and Arthur Hertzberg, along with then–Israeli ambassador to the United States, Itamar Rabinovich, and the late Prime Minister Rabin's closest adviser, Shimon Sheves. My two siblings and all my children came, as did Jan's family.

The reception was held at the beautiful Burden Mansion. Just over 100 people attended, eating terrific food and drinking the best wines (Montrachet Charlemagne and Chateau Lafite '59). Gretchen Siebel, the widow of my great friend Fritz Siebel, masterfully supervised the decoration and catering. It was fantastic to be with all our good friends and our families, and Jan was a radiant bride.

The search for love has been the driving force of much of my life. I have finally found it with Jan. She truly loves me and, as a result, my life is no longer just content, but full of feeling and joy.

CHAPTER 9

PASSING THE TORCH:
EDGAR JR.

The most difficult decision of my life was choosing—or rather naming—a successor.

When I asked Efer to join Seagram in 1982, I already knew that Sam, his elder brother, would not be the next CEO. In fact, it was clear even when they were teenagers that the brilliant, tough-minded businessman in our family would be Efer. He is one of those rare individuals who instinctively understands the business world and always has his priorities in order.

This in no way reflects poorly on Sam, as I later told him. Indeed, Sam is truly the nicest man I know, and my love for him is total. But my responsibility was to choose the right CEO for Seagram regardless of presumed birthright or familial relationship. All my life, I have believed that the job of the CEO is to optimize the value of the business for the benefit of the shareholders, whether those shareholders are family or strangers. And to do this, the CEO has to choose the most qualified people for the task, inside the family or out. To quote the Godfather, this was business. But I did not relish the necessary confrontation.

To set the stage for this painful chapter in my life, let me tell you a little more about Sam and Efer, my two oldest children.

Sam is a fine physical specimen, who stands six feet four, with broad shoulders, a prominent nose, and very curly hair. Moreover, he has a generous, openhearted nature. When he was twelve, we moved to the city and enrolled him in New York's Collegiate School, which had a lot of black and Puerto Rican scholarship kids because I wanted my children to get a glimpse of the real world as opposed to the golden ghetto that was Purchase, New York. He did well there, as he did later at the Deerfield School in the Berkshire Mountains of western Massachusetts, and at Williams College, in Williamstown, Massachusetts.

Sam is a sports lover, and throughout prep school and college, his love of athletics proved to be a great asset, as did his winning personality. He attended Deerfield before it became co-ed, and this may have been a disadvantage when he went on to college. I am a great believer in co-education at the prep school level, because young men and women should get used to being with each other. In Sam's case, when he got to Williams he had to deal with the shock of the opposite sex. Thus, he promptly fell in love with Melanie Mann, whom he eventually married. He had a successful college career and was a first-team tennis and basketball player.

Sam's kidnapping during the summer of 1975 was the Bronfman family's most traumatic experience. I think Sam got through it without permanent scarring. He managed to move on, marry Melanie the following year, and begin a normal life.

Efer is a year and a half younger than Sam. A shade shorter at six feet three, he's blond and very handsome, with a straight Roman nose. He tends to wear Armani clothes. His stride is purposeful, his manner that of both a leader and a lady-killer. As he was growing up, there was always something special about Efer—his calm in a crisis, his ability to deal with his mother's problems, his sense of responsibility for his siblings (he always gave them mature advice, and still does), and especially his awareness of the world around him. While Sam matured as most kids do, Efer was in a hurry to grow up and do adult things. He was a good student at Collegiate. Indeed, considering that he never worked at it, he was terrific. In his senior year, he spent more time running the Collegiate switchboard than attending class.

Efer didn't go to college—he felt it was a waste of time and wanted to get on with his life. He did just that, including his involvement with Sherry Brewer, an African-American woman. I very much wanted for him to end the relationship, because, I told him, all marriages are difficult enough without the added stress of totally different backgrounds. His children, I said, would have problems being accepted by either black or white society. Sherry offered to convert, which, though well intentioned, was not the point.

Efer asked if his marriage to Sherry would make him ineligible for the Seagram presidency. Being a closet liberal, and having respect for the optimism of youth, I told him that one had nothing to do with the other. When they did marry, in 1979, George and I had a reception for them at 960 Fifth Avenue, our home. They had three children: Vanessa, now sixteen, Benjamin, now fourteen, and Hannah, now nine. The marriage ended in 1991, but he works hard at maintaining a good relationship with Sherry and does a superb job with their children. Ben has been bar mitzvahed, and little Hannah has started learning Hebrew.

In 1994, Efer married Clarissa Alcock, whose father was the chief operating officer of the Venezuelan national oil company. Once again, the backgrounds are different, but there's hope. (Isn't that what the wag said about a second marriage—the triumph of hope over experience?)

Both Sam and Efer gained their first professional experience outside Seagram. Following Sam's graduation from Williams, he joined Time Inc., a space salesman for *Sports Illustrated*. He enjoyed the job, and after about a year he was promoted. (I remember he told me that while I had gotten him the job, he had earned the promotion.)

After another year or so, he thought it was time to work for Seagram, and I agreed. At one point, he could have taken a position with the company in Australia as general manager. It would have been perfect for Sam, giving him the kind of experience he needed, and Phil Beekman would have helped him learn how to run a subsidiary. (Sports enthusiast that Sam is, he also would have loved the country.) Unfortunately, he turned it down. I don't think that Melanie wanted to be that far away, and I'm not sure that he did, either.

As for Efer, he immediately started making films. He had caught the bug even earlier while working for my little movie company, Sagittarius Productions, where he met David Puttnam, the respected producer of such films as *Chariots of Fire*. Efer spent a summer in London living with David and his wife, and I think that this was when he fell in love with the film business. He had some success, and produced two plays and two films. The first movie was called *The Bunker*, a grisly tale of men trapped underground at the end of World War II. Too grim to be a commercial success, it was nonetheless a worthy effort and he learned a lot. His second and, as it turned out, last film was *The Border*, with Jack Nicholson. Though the movie was a critical success, it left him frustrated with the film industry. From his standpoint, it wasn't a "business."

I, of course, sympathized with his views on the motion-picture industry, knowing firsthand how frustrating the actual production of a film can be. We had a chat about his future, during which he told me that he was fed up with the motion-picture industry. I suggested that he consider working for Seagram, and after a little discussion it was settled.

Now both Sam and Efer were working for the company, and before long I began sensing a contest between the two over who would succeed me. This was something I was not willing to tolerate.

In a non-family-owned business, competition is good. The winner takes over and the loser gets another job elsewhere. The adherents of the loser swear fealty to the winner, and some of them manage to hang in there. Things then settle down. But it's a whole different story at a company like Seagram. With two brothers vying for the top spot, the loser would stay on, feeling cheated, and as a result he'd be only marginally useful. Having my two sons line up supporters as if it were an election was not good for them, for the corporation, for the family, or for me.

Upset with the looming battle between my sons and knowing that a decision was inevitable, I then proceeded to make a huge mistake. During an interview with a reporter from *Fortune*, I blurted out that Edgar Jr. was the heir apparent.

What I should have done, of course, was discuss the issue with my brother, Charles, then with Efer and Sam. Clearly, the problem was weighing on me, and it made sense to settle it earlier rather than later. But not the way I did it. I was very conflicted. I hate confrontations, and I just wasn't prepared to do this in an orderly manner.

It took Sam a long time to get over the hurt that I had inflicted. I apologized to him for the way I had handled the situation, and eventually he came to understand my decision.

If there's anything to be said in my defense, it is that I didn't extend the drama over succession, as Father did. I blundered badly, but never did I try to manipulate my sons to increase my own sense of importance.

David Sacks, who was by then COO of Seagram, recognized the importance of keeping the family together. He worked out a deal whereby Sam would take over Seagram's Classics, a Palo Alto, California–based company involved in the manufacturing, importing, and marketing of wines. The products include the Sterling Wines of Napa Valley, Monterey Vineyards, Seagram-owned European wines, and Mumm champagnes (also Seagram-owned).

When Sam moved over to Seagram's Classics, it allowed him, his wife, and two kids (Maxwell Peter and Dana Louisa) to relocate to California, Melanie's native state. She was unhappy in New York, and I don't believe she was ever reconciled to the alignment between the two brothers. Maybe time would have cured that, but tragically Melanie was diagnosed with breast cancer in the fall of 1987 and died four years later, in December 1991.

Sam grew up during this ordeal. He is emotionally and intellectually honest with himself and with me. When we got together for lunch after Melanie's death, he explained that, during her illness, he hadn't been able to keep his mind on the major issues of the business and had learned to delegate. I told him that it wasn't as important to be the best businessman in the world as it was to be the best person in the world, and that's what he was. He said that, while he was glad to hear that, he still wanted to be a better businessman and was going to keep working at it.

In fact, Sam has done a first-rate job with Seagram's Classics. He has invested wisely in premium vineyards, thus enabling Sterling to sell even higher-priced premium wines, and has developed a great reputation among the California vintners. I can see the esteem in which he is held when he and I attend the Sun Valley wine auctions, which draw a big crowd of his competitors. In addition to his work with Seagram's Classics, he also markets wines for other companies.

In July 1994, Sam married Kelly Conner, a divorcée with two little girls, the younger of them Dana's age. Sam is also now president of the Samuel Bronfman Foundation. The Foundation was established in 1951 on the occasion of my father's sixtieth birthday. The original purpose was to fund a program on Democratic Business Enterprise at Columbia University. The Foundation funds all sorts of other programs, including Meals on Wheels, the Bronfman Youth Fellowship Program for Canadian and American junior high school kids, and a host of pro bono activities, including scholarships for the sons and daughters of Seagram employees. (There is a cap on how much each employee can earn to be eligible.) With his kind and generous nature, Sam is uniquely qualified to head the Foundation, and I expect that he will be deeply involved with its philanthropic work for many years to come.

Recently, in 1996, Sam was named president of both our wine companies, Châteaux and Estates, as well as Classics. Putting them together will increase efficiencies and the ability to influence fine wine outlets, and Sam's great personality will be a great asset with the French vineyard owners. He is doing a first-rate job with this added responsibility.

While Sam is excellent at what he does, an incident in Acapulco many years ago illustrates in the most flattering way why he would find it difficult to be an effective CEO of the entire corporation. We were playing doubles against a couple. The man had a slight disability, making it hard for him to shift positions easily. Noticing this, I said to Sam, "You can afford to poach at net, because Fred has to telegraph any desire to go down the line." He reprimanded me with his eyes and said, "Oh, Dad." If Efer had been playing, he would have noticed immediately and moved nearer the center of the court.

Luckily, Efer and Sam have succeeded in maintaining a close relationship, as Charles and I did before them. As for my other children, they are not involved in the business, but follow their own paths instead.

———

When Efer decided to join Seagram in 1982, I discussed his eventual role as president. But like everyone else, he had to get some experience under his belt and prove himself, particularly to those who would one day be working for him.

His first position was as executive assistant to Phil Beekman. Much like in other companies, we used the slot of "executive assistant to the president" for advancing promising young executives. (The only problem was that once their "tour" was over, it was difficult to fit the candidate back into the structure. Thus, we have abandoned using the position as a training post.)

After a short time, the job of president, Seagram Europe, opened up. This was one of the tougher assignments in the company, but Efer wanted it badly, and Phil agreed that he could handle it.

I wasn't surprised. There is something about Efer's demeanor which everyone in the organization quickly noted. A very good listener, à la Clinton, he speaks in a soft yet commanding voice. He never seems to lose his cool, no matter what the pressure. (With his temperament, he could be a scratch golfer if he had the time; thank heavens he doesn't!) He's very sensitive to people, but he can be tough when he has to be. (Show me a CEO who can't be tough when necessary and I'll show you a good short sale.)

From the very beginning there was a groundswell of support for him to advance even faster than he did. He did such an outstanding job during his three years in Europe that when it was decided to bring him home to run all spirits sales in the United States, the European Seagram people were deeply disappointed.

During his time abroad, Efer made three important acquisitions. He and his colleagues (in what was then West Germany) bought a company called Matheus Müller. Efer had understoond the importance of Mumm Sekt in the German market. Adding scale could be very profitable, and Matheus Müller fit the bill. Over the years it has paid off handsomely.

Through another two acquisitions, he gave us a leg up in the United Kingdom where our operations were suffering because we had no leverage with the retail trade. Retail outlets were controlled to a frightening extent by the breweries. They owned literally thousands of outlets each, especially the on-premise licensees that carried distilled spirit brands. The DCL, the great Scotch whiskey conglomerate now owned by Guinness and known as United Distillers, gave discounts to its outlets on a combination of its multiple brands—Dewar's, Johnnie Walker, Black & White, White Horse, Haig & Haig, as well as Gordon's gin and Cossack vodka. Thus, the retailers pushed these brands hard, and DCL had good distribution and sales. Even though their discount structure limited their profitability, they were willing to stay with it in order to hold their market share.

Efer found a marvelous way of correcting the situation: he acquired two retail chains and combined them, eliminating their overlaps and nonessential functions. What remained after this rationalization was a chain called Oddbins, which is now worth many times what we paid for it. We were then in a position to do what the U.K. trade calls "reciprocals," which is a fancy way of saying you scratch my back and I'll scratch yours. Overnight, we became a factor in the retail trade in the United Kingdom.

Although we had acquired Sandeman ports and sherries before Efer came on board, it also became his job to integrate these brands, as well as The Glenlivet and its associated companies, into our European operations, so that we could profit from their synergies. He did it with panache. I remember a meeting that he held in San Remo, Italy, at which he asked a former Sandeman executive who was with us to explain to the group just what we had done wrong in trying to fit the pieces together. This was akin to taking down his pants in public, but he was gutsy enough to do it.

When Efer returned to America in 1984, he made an enormous impact. The House of Seagram, our U.S. marketing arm, was bogged down with competing organizational structures and multiple layers of management fat. Not bound by tradition, he reasoned that when sales are expanding it is perfectly natural to have competing sales organizations, but when sales are contracting, as they were in our entire industry, it's important to shrink the sales forces and get rid of the fat. This new broom did indeed sweep clean.

Simultaneously, he began righting a program we had not done well. A new phenomenon known as "coolers" had appeared on the scene. Started by a company called California Coolers, they were light wines mixed with carbonated water and flavoring. What was happening was somewhat like the white wine phenomenon of the sixties, when sales grew impressively not because people were drinking more wine in the traditional way—with their meals—but because they were drinking white wine instead of cocktails. When white wine was eventually replaced by Perrier, wine sales returned to their regular pattern. Similarly, the sale of coolers did not result from an upsurge in alcohol consumption. Rather, coolers profited at the expense of other alcoholic beverages, including beer and highballs. They were extremely successful—for a few years.

Efer's work with Seagram Coolers reminds me of my success with Calvert Extra. He redid everything: the packaging, the flavors, the advertising, the pricing, and the distribution, and triumphed in a terribly fractious and competitive market.

One evening he came to my apartment and told me that he thought he had the perfect advertising campaign. The problem, he said, was that the ad agency wasn't quite sold on it, especially since it was going to be very expensive. He then explained that he wanted to use Bruce Willis, whom I didn't know from Adam's off ox. The TV show *Moonlighting*, in which Willis starred, had just started, and Efer was sure it was going to be a huge success. My advice was to follow his instincts. If the campaign succeeded, we would achieve a major coup and no one would ask about the cost. If we failed, we would lose some money, but not enough to matter in the long run. The risk-reward ratio was in our favor. In business, that is all that matters, since risk of failure can never be entirely eliminated. Those who try to do so end up doing nothing, which generally guarantees failure.

Today there are only two companies left in the cooler business—the giant winery Gallo Brothers and Seagram. Our dramatic turn-around after a dull and inauspicious beginning was due to the marketing instincts and guts of one person, Edgar Bronfman Jr. The campaign was so successful, it convinced my brother Charles that we knew how to mass-market, thus making him comfortable with the acquisition of Tropicana.

There was one key difference between the Calvert Extra and Seagram's Coolers campaigns: the father-son dynamic. While I encouraged Efer to go ahead with his idea, I let him do it on his own and never took credit for his eventual success, as Father did with mine. That experience, like so many others, had taught me what not to do.

In 1988, Efer became a member of the board of directors and executive vice president, U.S. Operations. Eleven months later, in 1989, he became president, chief operating officer of the Seagram Company Limited and a member of the board of directors' executive committee.

I don't believe that I necessarily did Efer a great favor when I asked him to be my successor. There are some obvious satisfactions: the "high" that can come from a well-planned, well-executed business success; the ability to move among the best and brightest businesspeople in the world; the private aircraft that makes such a difference in the effective use of one's time (and, let's face it, in one's comfort level). While none of my children needs a big salary to live a nice life, the pay is good. And having power can be heady, though, as Efer and I have agreed, the day you have to exercise that power, you no longer have it.

But the flip side of the CEO coin is less attractive: aside from the work and the travel, there is the responsibility for expanding the company. This responsibility isn't confined to shareholders; it extends to all stakeholders, including everyone who draws a paycheck, executives and hourly workers alike. The whammy here is that growing the company sometimes requires thinning out the staff. Nothing is harder to do than letting people go, no matter how palatable you try to make it. It's even harder in a company like Seagram, where you feel that every employee is a member of an extended family. Whatever the pay, the CEO really earns it if he does the job he's supposed to do.

Efer is trying to do things differently. He has determined that people are essential to the success of our enterprise and has made human resources a much higher priority than I ever did. My emphasis was on marketing and advertising, going directly to the consumer. Father, bless him, resented needing a staff at all, and he certainly didn't pay attention to company morale. He just wanted everybody to love and admire him.

Of course, morale is a terribly important thing in business, and Edgar devotes a lot of energy to it. He understands that distributors, retailers, salesmen, executives, and workers all play a key role in our industry. For a management team to succeed, all these people have to be well motivated and well directed. (In a recent speech, he said, "People hear what you tell them, but they do what you pay them to do.") He is trying to get people more involved much further down the line than was our custom in the past.

I'm glad that I am no longer involved in the day-to-day management of Seagram. Though I fully support Efer's efforts to increase profit margins through better management of human resources, I no longer have the patience or perseverance to implement such a policy. Likewise, while I understand that such tools as a vision statement can help guide people in making the right decisions, it's not something on which I could imagine spending much time.

Beyond that, I've learned that in business, as in life, change is important. Over the decades, Seagram has been fortunate to attract extremely talented people, all of whom made important contributions during their time. But part of the key to our success is that we always have had an infusion of new blood. The principle of change applies to everyone, even those at the top.

For some CEOs, handing over responsibility to someone else is very traumatic. But I knew it was time. I'm not quite as eager as I once was, and I've learned from hard experience that unless you're completely committed to the job, you shouldn't be there. That's not to say that the business isn't very important to me; it is, and will remain so. But my priorities have changed: much of my energy is consumed with WJC work and other Jewish-related activities, while I also devote a lot of time to my private life with Jan.

Having something to retire *to* instead of *from* is critical. And, of course, with Edgar on the receiving end, passing the torch has been infinitely easier. I knew that the relationship between the two of us was such that if he wanted my help, he would ask.

Indeed, I remember a dinner in Montreal a few years ago. He was describing his effort to visit each major subsidiary every year, the lesser ones every two years. The schedule was impossible. I said, "Do I hear you asking me if I can do some of this for you?"

"Yeah, would you?" he said.

"Sure."

So I found myself traveling again, filling in for Efer and keeping my hand in the pot.

(Frankly, I could do without the traveling, which at best is an unpleasant necessity. I marvel when I hear contestants on game shows— I am addicted to *Jeopardy*—say that they love to travel. Business travel is different. You don't go for the sightseeing or the pleasure; you go because part of your job is to see the troops all over your corporate map. You have to inspire them, listen to their problems, make staff assessments, and do all the other things that contribute to a successful subsidiary. Then there is the unplanned travel—for acquisitions, or putting out fires, or attending a funeral. Unscheduled travel can be even more tiring.

Once you have children, your wife no longer accompanies you as often, if at all, and this creates a strain on the relationship. Yes, it's nice to stand before the shareholders at the annual meeting and report yet another good year, but the effort required to make a company grow is awesome—and best suited to those in the prime of life.)

Has Efer made mistakes? Sure. Some of his personnel decisions, even though well intentioned, haven't been great. Some new product introductions into test markets have been disappointing. But I have learned that while it really would be wonderful to learn from the mistakes of others, we learn best from our own. Therefore I have not told Efer when I disagreed on a hire or a new product. I just hope he's right and that he's listening to his instincts, which are excellent. With experience, those instincts will be finely honed.

As we'll see, he transformed Seagram totally through the purchase of MCA, positioning the company to attain rapid growth as we approach the new millennium. Charles and I agree that he is clearly the ideal leader to take us into the twenty-first century. In this respect, I can say with full confidence that I would hold the same opinion if Efer were not my son. The fact that he is only makes it better for me: I am proud to have a son worthy of keeping the job in the Bronfman family for another generation.

CHAPTER 10

———◆◆◆———

THE SALE OF DU PONT
AND THE PURCHASE OF MCA

Happy in a new marriage, secure about the company's future, and finished with my main tasks as president of the World Jewish Congress, I anticipated calm sailing ahead. I couldn't have been more wrong.

On March 1, 1995, Du Pont's board of directors held a routine meeting in Wilmington. Nothing out of the ordinary occurred until the very end, when a small map showing the Strait of Hormuz and the island of Sirri was passed around the room. It was announced that Conoco was thinking of entering a deal with the emir of Dubai to develop two large oil fields in Iranian waters for the Tehran government. The idea was that natural gas would be piped back to Dubai to extract more oil from their own fields. Presumably, Dubai also would share with Iran the oil produced in these new fields. The investment would be well in excess of $500 million.

Some of the directors, particularly Efer, questioned the advisability of doing business with a rogue state. Outside directors Chuck Vest and Mike Harper were rather vocal in espousing the view that money is money. Charles and I said nothing when Chairman Ed Woolard stated that he was not putting the matter to a vote. We felt that there was plenty of time for discussion.

I later discovered, to my amazement, that Conoco had been working on this deal for more than three years—with Woolard's knowledge. Given the sensitivity of doing business with Iran, one would think that the matter would have been brought before the full board earlier, or at least the relevant committee thereof. It was also revealed that Conoco had long since informed the government of its plans. The State Department had told Conoco that, while the deal was legal because a Dutch subsidiary would be used and none of the oil would enter the United States, it preferred that the company pull out.

The next thing I knew, there was a report in the papers saying that the deal had been made. This was very upsetting. Woolard told me that it was the Iranians who had issued the release—as if it would be a surprise to him that they would do so. (He seemed very naive throughout this entire episode.) He added that the deal would not go through if the Clinton administration disapproved.

Since I had already scheduled meetings with various high-ranking members of Congress on the subject of the World Jewish Restitution Organization, I decided that while in Washington I would try and quash the Conoco-Iran deal. I visited with Bob Dole; Newt Gingrich; Dick Gephardt; Ben Gilman, the chairman of the House Committee on Foreign Affairs; Mitch McConnell, the chairman of the Senate Budget Committee; and Jesse Helms, the chairman of the Senate Foreign Relations Committee. I told each of them that while in the short run it might be good for the shareholders—of whom we were by far the largest—I felt sure it was bad for the country and thus would eventually hurt everyone, including Du Pont. I believed that it was simply wrong to be doing business with Iran. I have learned that, at least most of the time, doing the right thing in business eventually proves to be the most profitable as well. So I asked all my Washington friends to make plenty of noise, hoping that Woolard would bow under pressure.

Our primary concern was that an American company would be making Iran even richer, thereby increasing its ability to fund terrorism on an international scale. I was also worried about the Israeli press, which would accuse Charles and me of doing anything to make money. In the end it could backfire—and harm us.

On Friday evening, March 3, I faxed a letter to Ed Woolard declaring my opposition to the deal and accusing Dino Nicandros, the head of Conoco, of trying to slide it through in an outrageously deceptive manner. I included the list of congressmen with whom I had talked, and further stated that I might press for Nicandros's resignation at the next board meeting.

I understood Nicandros's position. As an oil man, this deal would be a great coup. There was undoubtedly a huge amount of oil involved, and the Japanese and South Koreans (and perhaps others) were at his heels. Moreover, there was nothing illegal about the transaction. Conoco's status in the industry would skyrocket, at least for a while, and Nicandros would gain tremendous respect among his peers. But in my view, the deal crossed the line of what is acceptable. Moreover, it was a direct affront to my work with the WJC and would reflect very poorly on the Bronfman family.

On Monday morning, March 6, Woolard called me, his voice contrite, to tell me that the deal was off. I replied that while I considered Nicandros to be the heavy in the matter, I also felt that he had been somewhat naive. (At that point, I still didn't know that Conoco had been working on the deal for three years.) This was an issue of honor and morality for me, and I had no intention of going easy on him.

That afternoon, Woolard attended a Seagram audit committee meeting (under our standstill agreement, he was on the Seagram board of directors) in New York, and he told his side of the story to Charles and Efer. Charles was sympathetic with Woolard, because I had been so harsh, but Efer handled the situation in a very polite way, reversing any damage Charles might have done. He said that, as far as Nicandros's fate was concerned, Woolard should tell him that the four Seagram directors on the Du Pont board would have to caucus before coming to a consensus.

Clearly, we were unhappy with Du Pont and the terrible publicity the company had received. But by this time, we had already decided to sell our shares back to Du Pont (as I'll soon explain), so it wouldn't have been appropriate for us to act against Nicandros. Otherwise, I think I would have pursued the issue.

Meanwhile, the press jumped on Du Pont and gave credit to the Bronfmans for stopping the deal. In the *Los Angeles Times*, it was reported that "Conoco's withdrawal came after some dramatic behind-the-scenes maneuvering by the Bronfman family, who are active in major Jewish organizations and are strong supporters of the Clinton administration's efforts to isolate Iran." The article went on to say, "As administration officials reviewed the deal in recent days, the Bronfmans conveyed to Du Pont board members their displeasure over the idea of a Conoco deal with Iran."

While it's true that I told Ed Woolard in no uncertain terms what I thought of the deal, the press accounts exaggerated our role in its defeat. Woolard had already decided that the deal was dead, but I think he and Nicandros were waiting for President Clinton to officially bar Conoco from moving forward. That way, they reasoned, Conoco would simply be following the President's orders rather than caving in to political pressure. So Woolard kept dragging his feet with the press, and as the delays continued without a clear statement from Du Pont, they looked worse and worse while the Bronfmans looked better and better.

Finally, on March 14, Clinton announced that he would bar American oil companies from operating in Iranian oil fields. The same day, Conoco officials said they would scrap the deal with Iran, and the crisis was over.

Nevertheless, the question about doing business with Iran occupied news writers for some time after the episode had ended. In a March 22 phone conversation with A. M. Rosenthal of the *New York Times*, I stated that the international community should treat Iran much as it has Iraq. Terrorism is the weapon of the Islamic fundamentalists, whose head office is in Tehran. They have declared war on the West, by claiming that consumerism and secularism are evil and must be wiped out. Until the Western nations decide to take international terrorism seriously, innocent people will continue to be killed. It is possible that Iran can change from within—after all, the difference between a consumer and a non-consumer is the wherewithal to buy. But as long as the ayatollahs are in charge, Iran will be a rogue country, bent on destabilizing the West through terrorism.

———

On Wednesday, March 15, the Seagram board of directors discussed selling our Du Pont shares. Despite the timing, there was no connection with the Conoco/Iran deal. Our management had been studying whether we should keep our position in Du Pont for more than two years, and in fact had hired the Boston Group to take a look at the long-term prospects of the company. Now the moment had come for a decision.

With the help of Goldman Sachs partners Mike Overlock and John S. Weinberg (my friend John L. Weinberg's son), Efer presented the case for selling our stake in Du Pont on a tax-sheltered basis. He had had serious qualms about our investment in Du Pont for some time, based largely on his conviction that the company could not be expected to do much better than track the Standard & Poor 500. Du Pont is a great name, but the basis of its success is research and development; they manage to make the same commodity cheaper than anybody else. For that reason, it won't go on forever. You can't keep technological innovation secret—it's just a question of time.

Efer's belief was confirmed by the Boston Group's analysis. Despite the downsizing and the record earnings Ed Woolard had achieved, Du Pont's growth would be limited by the very nature of its business: the manufacturing of commodities. With the development of new energy sources, the price of one of those commodities—oil—will likely be driven by demand in the not-too-distant future. Added to that was concern about expensive environmental cleanup costs, an inescapable reality for Du Pont.

Beyond these issues, both Efer and I felt that Du Pont was a boring investment. Their business is mostly involved with commodities. Du Pont is still a great company, just not an exciting one.

Charles looked at it differently. He reasoned that Du Pont would be there forever, relieving us of the need to worry about good managers or bad managers at Seagram—as long as we had Du Pont, we would be protected generation after generation. But I feel that unless you're growing a company, you're losing ground, because the rest of the world is always moving forward.

The board was not asked to approve—a formal vote in favor of selling would have had to be made public immediately—but the consensus was quite clear. Toward the end of the month, I traveled to Jerusalem for a day and a half. Despite the problems with the King David Hotel phone system—the queen of the Netherlands had just moved out of the suite, and they had cut off the telephone lines so that no one could ring in—I was in constant communication with both Efer and John L. Weinberg, who was negotiating with Ed Woolard on the sale of our shares back to Du Pont.

On Thursday afternoon, March 30, Efer recommended that we accept Du Pont's final position, which I approved, as did Charles, although reluctantly. The price turned out to be $36.25 a share, or slightly in excess of $9 billion. After Johnny Weinberg had had a chance to deliver the news to Ed Woolard, I put in a call to the Du Pont chairman. I told him that I had learned one thing from Irving Shapiro: if at the end of the negotiations both sides feel some pain in the stomach, it was probably a fair deal. Ed drove a hard bargain, and I wasn't exactly ecstatic about the price—the market on March 30 was 60½—but I do believe that it was fair to both parties. (On the day of the closing, the price actually climbed to 64¼, no doubt because the news of Du Pont buying back our stock had gone public.)

From our standpoint, there were two key considerations. First, unlike in the eighties, when deals were made at the drop of a hat, it would have been difficult to find another buyer for such a huge block. Second, Du Pont consented to structure the buy-back in a very tax-efficient manner, which saved us around a billion dollars. (According to the terms of the deal, we can someday come back into Du Pont if, by an act of God, their stock reaches astronomical heights.) Therefore, we were willing to compromise on price. From Woolard's point of view, he needed a discount to convince his board of directors and the Du Pont family that this purchase was in the best interests of the shareholders.

Could we have gotten more money? The market has gone up smartly since our deal. But MCA would probably have gone elsewhere had we elected to hang on for a better price, and at sky-high prices Du Pont might not have been such a willing buyer. Everyone is blessed with at least 20/20 hindsight. We were able to work out an agreement that met both our needs. So ended our fourteen-year relationship with Du Pont.

Even as we were disposing of the Du Pont shares, we had our eyes on what would become Seagram's biggest prize ever: MCA. But the story of our investment in the entertainment giant begins back in 1990.

A month or so before Matsushita, the giant Japanese maker of Panasonic and other electronic equipment, bought MCA, Steve Banner, Efer, and I had begun discussing the communications/entertainment industry. It was my view, as well as Efer's, that leisure-time activities offer the greatest business opportunities for the next century. As sophisticated technology reduces the need for manual labor, a shorter workweek will become standard, leaving more time for recreation. By combining a strong presence in the entertainment field with our formidable holdings in beverages, we would be ideally positioned for decades to come.

I believed that MCA was the right vehicle for Seagram, while Steve and Efer thought that Time Warner, being more broadly based, would better serve our interests. They had a good point, but my contention was that too much of Time Warner's business was hardware—specifically cable, which was subject to stiff competition and government regulation. The real money, it seemed to me, was going to be made by the owners of content. I also felt that MCA was more manageable in terms of size. But with Matsushita's acquisition of MCA, the argument became moot.

We decided to look elsewhere. Some time passed, and eventually

Efer's friend Michael Ovitz, then the head of Creative Artists Agency, suggested that we talk to Herbert A. Allen, president of Allen & Company, Inc. After consulting with Allen, we settled on Time Warner and purchased 5.7 percent of the company's shares.

Everything went like clockwork. At four P.M. on May 26, 1993, we filed a 13-D with the SEC announcing our share purchases. When the announcement crossed the Dow Jones wire service, I called John McGillicuddy, chairman and chief executive of the Chemical Bank, which had recently merged with the Manufacturers Hanover, to tell him that this was a friendly purchase for investment purposes only. He knew just about everyone and was very close to the Time people. He would spread the word. The night before, I had told Du Pont chairman Ed Woolard about our purchase, and he volunteered to accept press calls—he would gladly tell reporters that we were sincere when we said we were a friendly buyer, and that Du Pont's experience with us had been terrific.

Most of the reviews were raves. *Business Week* wrote that "Edgar Bronfman Jr. has seen the future, and it is multimedia," while *Variety* commented, "At Time Warner, executives were breaking out the Scotch." The analysts were unhappy because they hadn't seen it coming and couldn't figure it out, but the movers and shakers thought it was a great move.

We subsequently increased our stake in Time Warner to almost 15 percent. Unfortunately, Time Warner chairman and CEO, Gerald Levin, persuaded his board to install a poison pill, which made it extremely difficult for us or anyone else to have any say. Efer met with the CEO a couple of times, but no progress was made.

However, in early 1995, our concern over Time Warner's intransigence faded, with the dramatic discovery that Matsushita was willing to sell its interest in MCA. Everyone knew that MCA's top management—Lew Wasserman and Sid Sheinberg—were at odds with their Japanese owners, and vice versa. But through Steve Banner, who had acted for Matsushita in their acquisition of MCA, we learned that the entertainment giant might be available to us.

Efer wasted no time. On March 6, he got on an airplane and flew to Osaka to meet with Matsushita president, Yoichi Morishita. Efer understands the importance of personal contact in business, and he was quickly able to negotiate an exclusive period in which to study the situation and make an offer. He returned three weeks later for further talks, solidifying the feeling of trust with Morishita. The relationship between Efer and Morishita was remarked upon in an article by the *Los Angeles Times* headlined "In the End, MCA Deal Was Simply a Matter of Trust." The piece quoted an unnamed Wall Street executive close to the negotiations who observed, "'While there was no assurance that the gaps could be bridged, there was extraordinary trust and respect. The trust between Bronfman and a man running a $65-billion-a-year company who doesn't speak English was quite remarkable. This was a transaction built by two people who trusted each other.'" The rapport enjoyed by Efer and Morishita was in stark contrast to the acrimonious relations between Matsushita officials and MCA's top brass.

I was delighted with this development. It looked as though it would take years to get some good management into Time Warner. Levin had gone even deeper into cable, and deeper in debt. We were stymied by the poison pill, and it appeared that our investment in the company wouldn't pay off for a long time. MCA thus seemed better and better, and Efer was quite confident that he could "buy it right." Moreover, the timing was perfect, as the sale of our Du Pont stocks promised to free up a lot of capital.

On April 5, 1995, I went to Montreal to have lunch with Mother. She was awake but not quite up to eating, so Charles and I dined together in the breakfast room. He was unhappy about the proposed acquisition of MCA and wanted me to address his concerns. I told him that, while there was no way to promise success, even staid Coca-Cola had bought a movie business—Columbia Pictures—and made a fortune when they sold it to Sony.

Charles wasn't convinced, nor would he be even when we made the final decision. My brother's very smart but also very conservative, while I'm a little more adventurous. He was clearly anxious about the idea of sinking so much money into MCA, which I understood. There's something about Hollywood—the egos, the stars, the hype—that can make you feel uncomfortable. On the other hand, it's a great business if you know how to manage those problems.

Charles and I also were operating from different perspectives. After all, buying MCA represented an enormous opportunity for my son, who was Seagram's CEO. He understood the business and wanted to grow Seagram through a vehicle we controlled rather than through a passive investment. Charles had no such incentive, and was more interested in finding a safe investment—keeping what we had with Du Pont—that would protect the family fortune. But as I reminded him, even his two kids thought we should make the deal.

On April 6, we had a long board meeting at the Seagram Building in New York. First, we had to make a formal decision about whether to sell our Du Pont stock. The vote was unanimous, and we suddenly had almost $8 billion cash in our pockets. Then we had a thorough discussion of the proposed MCA purchase, with Efer laying out the argument in favor. Number one, we were getting a bargain if the negotiations went the way we anticipated. Two, buying another entertainment company, assuming we could find one that we wanted, would entail a hostile bid and a premium. Here we had an opportunity to buy MCA right—the Japanese wanted badly to sell so that they could take the proceeds and reinvest them in their basic business.

No vote was taken at this meeting as the terms of the deal had not yet been finalized. But it became clear that, with the exception of Charles, who intended to go along anyway (and possibly John Weinberg), support for the acquisition of MCA was unanimous.

Efer spent the next day in New York negotiating through counsel with Matsushita. I was in Virginia but must have spoken ten times with Efer. By the end of the day, he had struck a deal, and a very good one at that. To save face for Matsushita, we settled on a final price of $7.13 billion—exactly what they had paid in dollars—for 80 percent of the company. But in fact, they agreed to put money back into MCA and sell us a debt-free company, so the price was thus adjusted to $7.059 billion.

We were very fortunate to be dealing with the Japanese on this transaction. They have a different way of doing business, a different

way of thinking. To them, honor and respect are of paramount importance. Because of this, Matsushita didn't want a long, drawn-out ordeal. We made it clear that just such a scenario would unfold if they
entertained other bids, and that we would pull out. They preferred to
negotiate a deal quietly and keep 20 percent, so we were able to avoid
a bidding war and buy MCA at a very good price. The icing on the cake
was that MCA's record business was worth about a quarter of a billion
more than we paid for it, a fact that came out in due diligence. As for
Matsushita, their 20 percent will someday be worth an awful lot of
money.

Charles had asked me why Matsushita wanted to keep 20 percent.
While my answer didn't satisfy him at the time, I believe that because
the son of the founder was still very much alive and was the company's
chairman, it would have been insulting to sell it all, and thus imply
that he had chaired a bad deal. But with 20 percent and different management, it was thought that this would eventually be a good investment.

On April 9, Efer and I flew separately to Los Angeles—we used all
three G-IVs, as there were a lot of backup staff needed for public relations and dealing with the press. I met Efer at about 1 P.M. in the offices
of Shearman and Sterling, our law firm for this deal (Simpson Thacher
was representing Matsushita). All of us stayed at the Biltmore Hotel,
which my sister Phyllis had helped rebuild many years ago. Efer and I
registered under aliases to avoid being bothered by reporters.

At two P.M. (five P.M. Eastern time), the Seagram board convened
back in New York. John Weinberg abstained from voting on the
grounds that Goldman Sachs had advised Matsushita, even though
counsel had told him it was not necessary. Charles said some nice words
about Efer, and the board quickly spent most of the money we had just
received from Du Pont.

Immediately after the meeting, I called Lew Wasserman, chairman and CEO of MCA. I had known Lew for a long time through various political and charitable activities, as well as my earlier stint in
Hollywood, but only on a very casual basis. Efer and I knew that both
Lew and Sidney Sheinberg, the president of MCA, were very annoyed

that they had been kept in the dark. However, we had signed a confidentiality agreement with Matsushita, so there was no way we could tell Lew, Sid, or anyone else what we were up to. With Matsushita's permission, I had called Lew the Wednesday before to say that we were close to a deal and to assure him that he would be the first to know when it was done.

Now that the sale was official, I asked him and Sid to have lunch with Efer and me, and suggested that he choose a place where he would be most comfortable. He invited us to come Monday to the private dining room at the Universal studio.

After my conversation with Lew, Efer and I called Charles to thank him for his trust and support, knowing that he would have preferred to stay with Du Pont. While I understood my brother's position, I fully sympathized with Efer. You can't ask a forty-year-old to come in as the chief executive officer and tell him that two-thirds of the business is sacrosanct. If you do, you know what kind of businessman you're getting. Du Pont was a fine investment but a passive one. As the third-generation CEO, Efer wanted to build stockholder value far beyond the Standard & Poor 500, and to do that we would have to look elsewhere.

At three P.M., the Japanese arrived at the hotel. After a few speeches, the papers were signed by Morishita and Efer, and we all had a glass of champagne. The deed was done, subject only to due diligence. Interestingly, Michael Ovitz sat at the Seagram side of the table, not the Matsushita side, even though he was being employed by them.

Morishita asked Efer and me to go with him when he called on Lew Wasserman that Sunday afternoon. Fortunately we declined, because as things turned out it would have been a disaster. Wasserman and Sheinberg were already mad at us—and furious with Matsushita—for conducting the negotiations in secret, and we didn't want to start our relationship with two strikes against us.

That evening, we had a celebratory dinner in the hotel, during which I was seated beside Morishita (for Efer was exhausted). Not knowing what to say, I decided to try and make some money. We sell wine and orange juice and other products in Japan, and the translator had told me that Matsushita had some 35,000 workers. "You have a lot of employees," I said. "It would be marvelous if they were acquainted with the products that we sell in Japan. You might suggest to them that they purchase them." He said he'd be delighted to do that, and we talked about making a little brochure that he could pass out to his people.

The next morning, I placed calls to several people, including Bob Strauss, the eminent politician/lawyer and a former director of MCA, who is a longtime friend, and Jack Valenti, president of the Motion Picture Association, whom I have known since his White House days with LBJ. They were both delighted that I had taken the time to inform them of the deal before they read about it in the paper. It had also been recommended that we phone California Governor Pete Wilson, but since I was already scheduled to see him in two weeks, that didn't seem appropriate. (After the MCA deal was announced, the governor's office called to suggest that we meet for lunch on the appointed day to give us more time.)

On Monday morning, Efer and I drove out to Universal City. We were met by Lew and Sid, who ushered us into the private dining room. They were incensed at everyone who had concealed the deal, starting with Michael Ovitz, then the Japanese, and last but not least the two Bronfmans. (Ovitz was working as a consultant for Matsushita, and at the time it looked like he was going to come in and run Universal.)

We tried to explain that our hands had been tied by the confidentiality agreement, but they wouldn't relent. Finally, I had had a mouthful, and suggested that we move on to the topic we had come to discuss—how to make this great company, which they had so ably built, even better. Lew insisted that people wanted to know who was going to run the company. We told him that we hadn't decided. He was perhaps pushing us to say that Sid would run MCA, but that was never a possibility. They also assumed that we had chosen Ovitz, and that we denied. They made it clear that if Ovitz was to get the job, they would be our enemies forever.

When Lew kept pressing, I said, "As far as I'm concerned, Edgar has enough experience and knows enough about this business that we don't have to be in any hurry. And we're not going to make any big mistakes."

Sid then turned to Efer and said, "What would you like us to do?" and the tone of the conversation softened.

I proposed that Lew join the Seagram board, which he at first declined. Soon after, I went with Lew to his office (Efer went with Sid to his), and we spent a couple of hours schmoozing. At one point, we went to use the facilities. He was now in a better mood, so I again suggested that he come on our board.

"Look," I said, "this would send a clear signal to MCA employees that they are going to be protected. Everybody must be really worried that there's going to be a high-scale slaughter. Coming on our board is the easiest way to tell them that's not going to happen. Lew, you're a great guy and I'm very fond of you."

This time he didn't say no. Later on in his office, when it looked as though Sid and Efer were getting along, Lew told me that he would discuss it with his wife, and I promised to call the next day.

Before we left, Sid told us that he wanted Universal to fund a production deal for him. His leverage was that Steven Spielberg has a son-father relationship with him, much as Sid has with Lew. Efer agreed to meet with the director, and also made arrangements to review expansion plans for both the Universal City and Florida theme parks (the latter is owned by MCA in partnership with the J. Arthur Rank group). Then we parted, our relationship with Lew and Sid on a much more positive footing than a few hours before.

I flew back to New York on Tuesday morning and didn't call Lew until Wednesday because of the time difference. When I caught him, he said that he had to discuss his Matsushita contract with Marty Lipton (the famed takeover lawyer who invented the "poison pill") and promised to call me the following day. This sounded like a stall, and that's what it turned out to be, for when he called on Thursday he readily accepted, but asked that there be no public announcement until Sheinberg's situation was resolved. During that conversation, Lew made some nice comments about Efer, who had already held follow-up meetings with MCA executives. "In a very difficult situation," he said, "your son hit a home run."

During the week of April 17 to 21, Efer returned to Los Angeles to finalize Sid and Lew's position. Sid had certain demands we would and could not meet. The Dream Team of Spielberg, Geffen, and Katzenberg proposed a deal to stay at Universal whereby they would get the lion's share of the gross. Lew Wasserman said that any deal he made to be on the Seagram board and remain chairman (not CEO) of MCA would be off if Michael Ovitz took the top job. After being briefed on all this, I said, "Efer, there are two things I have to tell you. Number one, make everybody out there understand that you are a hard-headed businessman who will not be pushed around. And two, remember that with the possible exception of you and me, nobody is indispensable."

Things finally settled down. Efer reached a very good distribution agreement with Dreamworks that could net MCA more than $1 billion over ten years, which sparked an immediate rise in Seagram stock. Sid accepted a production deal with which we could live; under the contract, MCA will finance his new company, which will produce three to four films a year. Lew stepped down as chairman of MCA and agreed to join the Seagram board. And Michael Ovitz decided not to work for MCA.

Ovitz's withdrawal was the most complicated of these matters. On Friday, June 3, Charles came to New York to talk with Efer about the proposed deal that would make Ovitz president of MCA while I was on my way to my weekend place in Charlottesville, Virginia. That afternoon, I said to Efer that though I knew nothing of their conversation, I could guess what Charles had said: Ovitz may be the best there is, but there's no way he could be $50 million better than anyone else. Then I told Efer that, as much as I hated to say it, I agreed with my brother.

Efer went back to Michael and said that he would have to renegotiate the deal. He explained that both his father and his uncle were very unhappy with the terms, and that they were important players. Michael was upset. "That means that you're not in control," he said, to which Efer replied, "Michael, this is a large corporation. My father and brother are big shareholders. That's how corporations work. I suppose that I could push it through if I made all sorts of threats, but that would be very stupid of me and very unhealthy for you."

Though I'll never know Michael's exact reasoning, there's no doubt in my mind that he was worried about having to contend with the Seagram board of directors and two senior Bronfmans, a scenario with which he was unfamiliar. As the *Wall Street Journal* put it, he "would have had to walk away from a unique post where he answered to no one and was in the middle of almost every major deal or negotiation in Hollywood. And even though Mr. Ovitz would have been given broad autonomy at MCA, Edgar Bronfman Jr. . . . . still would have been the boss." The article noted that Michael had gone through the same dance back in 1989, when Sony bought Columbia, eventually choosing to stay with CAA.

Over the weekend, Michael decided to call off the deal. I knew that he'd made the right decision, since the odds were that he and Efer would have been at each other's throat within a year. Michael somehow believed that he was going to have a totally free hand to run MCA, but Efer would never consider abdicating to him, or anyone else, for that matter.

Charles was also glad to hear that Ovitz had dropped out of the picture, but he was still unhappy about our purchase of MCA. One day, he came into my office and sat down.

"I thought as we got older we were supposed to get closer and be better friends," he said.

"Well, that's what's happening," I replied.

"No, it isn't," said Charles.

"What are you talking about?" I asked.

"MCA."

"All right, Charles," I said. "Now the rules are that if you say 'no,' we don't do it. Did you ever say no?"

"Well, no, but . . ."

"Charles, did you ever say no?"

"No. I didn't want to start a family feud."

"There probably would have been one, but if you had said no, we wouldn't have made the deal. Now stop it. We've already made the deal. Let's get on with it."

We did, and that was the end of the issue. That's how our relationship has always been. Since then, Charles's son-in-law has started working for MCA in London, and I think my brother feels better about the situation.

It didn't help matters, however, that we were crucified in the press for buying MCA. Mark Landler, writing in the *New York Times*, commented that Efer is "apparently transforming Seagram from a reliable generator of earnings into a company that will rely heavily on the vagaries of Hollywood." Floyd Norris, in a *Times* column entitled "The Bronfman Follies," wrote, "It certainly appears that Mr. Bronfman Jr. has inherited from his father a willingness to spend billions following Wall Street's current fad. Perhaps Seagram shareholders should have a drink or two while they pray that he also inherited his father's luck." Yet another skeptical *Times* column declared in its headline "What Shiny Toys Money Can Buy" and asserted that our purchase of MCA was motivated by Efer's desire to have a "playground."

The *Wall Street Journal* was no kinder. In a cautionary article titled "Expensive Flops," Laura Landro chronicled the failures of other companies that have entered the entertainment industry. Another piece suggested that our core business might founder because of the MCA deal, saying that Seagram's wine and spirits business was "fighting to stay afloat" in a shrinking market.

One of the few pundits to dissent from the group lynching was economist Joel Kotkin. "On Wall Street and in much of the mainstream business press, Seagram's $5.7 billion purchase of 80 percent of MCA Inc. seems yet another act of folly by a starstruck Hollywood wanna-be," wrote Kotkin in the *Los Angeles Times*. "Yet Seagram's bold move may reflect less naïveté than acumen in taking advantage of the burgeoning industrialization of fantasy."

I was hurt much more by what was said about Efer than what was said about me. He was depicted as a playboy out to get some girls and indulge his interest in film. Anyone familiar with his accomplishments at Seagram would have known that Efer is a serious businessman, and that he would never risk the future of the company to satisfy his personal ambitions.

He worked very hard to make his case with the press, but to no avail. All the "blame" for what was seen as a big mistake fell on his shoulders, as if the deal hadn't been approved by the entire board of directors. The *Wall Street Journal*, with its "Dumb and Dumber" headline, was particularly savage.

I've always had a lot of respect for the press, and I believe strongly in First Amendment protections. But sometimes they take that freedom too far, especially on subjects about which they know little. They didn't do their homework on any of this, and that's what angered me. Of course, I learned long ago not to pay much attention to the pundits. If I had listened seriously every time I was criticized by the press, I would have been useless as a CEO. As a businessman, you have to have faith in your judgment and persevere in the face of criticism, sometimes even ridicule.

Though our stock did drop initially, ultimately we were not affected by the media bashing we received. Indeed, the decline was due primarily to the fact that a lot of Canadian interests sold their shares immediately while Americans were somewhat slow to buy in. Fortunately, the stock rebounded quickly, and concerns about the company dissipated.

Inevitably, the press eventually changed its tune as well. Media pundits began to see what we saw all along—that MCA not only is a movie company, but owned theme parks, music; had exciting deals with Dreamworks SKG, Sega; and much more. It became clear to everyone that we stand to make a lot of money from this purchase. The film library alone generates enormous revenue, benefiting from television's ravenous appetite.

Lingering doubts were put to rest in July 1996, when we made a deal with German broadcasters potentially worth $2.5 billion. The sale includes the broadcast rights to MCA's movie and TV properties, and also establishes lucrative partnerships with the two major German TV companies, the Kirsch Group and RTL. The deal will allow us to move aggressively into international TV. In addition, it provides financing for new television production here at home. In short, the transaction was a bonanza for MCA, dwarfing the deals made by other American studios with German broadcasters.

I firmly believe that, within five to ten years, MCA is going to be a huge, international money earner for our shareholders. To cite just a few examples, we now have what may be the best executive team in the music business, and we are going to be number one in that lucrative field. Our sale to Germany shows the power we have. We will get much bigger and better in television. We are going to have theme parks all around the world, but done well, in a way that will appeal to older people as well. We're building a theme park in Osaka, which was already under way before we came in. We're talking to people in China about building movie theaters and other enterprises. We will expand the personal entertainment side of the business through our deals with Sega, Dreamworks SKG, and MCA. And there is much more.

We're also thinking about the changing consumer profile of the country. As the population ages, the entertainment business will have to adapt. How will the increasing number of older Americans want to spend their leisure time? This is a key question, and careful planning will ensure even greater success. The future looks bright indeed.

On the Seagram side, I am convinced that in five years there will be an upward trend in our business. People will realize that, for most of us, drinking beverage alcohol every day, in moderation, actually can be good for them—not just in terms of longevity, but quality of life as well.

As for Time Warner, we've kept some of our shares and sold some. We're never going to take over the company, especially now that we have MCA. But Time Warner has a great collection of assets, even if it has too much debt and too much invested in cable. In due course, we may sell more and make a lot of money for our shareholders.

———

In some ways, the acquisition of MCA was to Efer what the Du Pont investment had been to me—a huge, controversial deal that transformed and dramatically expanded Seagram. But it was also very different.

We now control MCA, which was never true of Du Pont. Even if we had, I knew I could never manage Du Pont. I don't know enough about the chemical business. On another level, I didn't have the feeling for Du Pont that Edgar has for MCA. To me, at least emotionally, Seagram's core business will always be beverage alcohol—my love of our wine and spirits knows no bounds. So while I was involved with Du Pont, it was never my first priority.

With Efer, MCA is going to demand a tremendous amount of his time and energy. And he loves it. That's really where his heart is, and I understand. He was never immersed as a kid in the world of alcohol production, as I was. At seventeen, I was scrubbing vats in a distillery. Efer started making movies at sixteen, and that's where his greatest knowledge lies. (Conscious of the fact that he's no expert on beverage-alcohol production, Efer has said on several occasions that he wants to find a way to institutionalize me—meaning my knowledge of the business. Toward this end, I've spent some time working with a couple of people in production, and I think it will pay off.)

Indeed, he was more than able to fill the top slot until Frank Biondi joined the company. Efer is *great* with people. It's in his blood.

Bringing in Biondi was an excellent move. As the head of Viacom, Frank was one of the most respected executives in America, and took that company to new levels of success and profitability. Efer also hired a great number-two man, Ron Meyer. Ron, who was second in command under Ovitz at CAA, knows everybody, and everybody knows and loves him. Being an agent, he's fantastic at recruiting good people to work for Universal and making it a place where everybody wants to work.

Another thing is that Efer understands his role. He is very smart about not being all over the papers every day. He understands that it's better to let the people in Hollywood be the big shots. In this particular business, which is so talent-oriented, you have to let people's egos get expressed. He also knows that you have to pay big money to secure that talent, even if the figures seem excessive to many people. Often this means heaping large sums on individuals with dubious personalities, but if they can bring in the crowd, you have to be willing to pay for it.

I'm particularly happy that Efer decided to stay in New York. Out in Hollywood, the egos do run rampant, and someone has to sit back and say no. That's what Efer is doing—staying away from the power, the glamour, the glitter, so that he can look at the company from a businessman's point of view. He's extremely mature for his age and has lived a more intense life than most people, learning a lot as he's gone along.

Buying MCA has utterly altered the destiny of Seagram, and we have Efer to thank for it. Before the acquisition, we were a wine, spirits, and juice company, with a passive investment in Du Pont, which accounted for some two-thirds of our balance sheet. Now we are completely in charge of our own destiny, with the same beverage interests but now also with control of MCA—actually it's now called Universal Studios, Inc.—a wonderful entertainment/communications company with limitless potential.

If Father were alive, he never would have approved the purchase. But things change in life. That's why, when I was sixty-five, I said to Efer, "I've had my turn, now it's yours."

Efer has my total confidence, and I am grateful for the wonderful relationship we enjoy, so different from the one I had with Father. I appreciate what that starved ego accomplished: the business that he built, the devotion he had to quality products, the trusts he created which passed a fortune along to future generations, the example he set in his charitable efforts. But despite all those achievements, he wasn't able to be a warm, affectionate father, thus depriving him of his children's affection.

As a businessman, I tried to build on the foundation Father had laid and, looking back, I'm proud of my accomplishments. Though Father was a great entrepreneur, he was not a good manager, and the company flourished only because our brands were so important. Thus, when I assumed control, my task was not to create great brands, but rather to transform Seagram from a one-man operation into a smooth-running company. This required a fair amount of what is now called reengineering—a fancy name for reexamining the way you do things. Such a process is indispensable if you want to stay on top. My other major challenge was to increase the profitability of the company. This meant reinvigorating the core business through better advertising, marketing, and merchandising, as well as expanding beyond the beverage-alcohol trade. I can say with satisfaction that I achieved both these goals.

With regards to the core business, our market share pulled considerably ahead of our competitors' during my tenure. And, like Father, I maintained Seagram's dominance while sticking to the high road. At my insistence, we never gave our product away; we demanded and received a fair price.

As far as outside deals go, I take particular pride in the Du Pont purchase. The potential downside was unbelievable, but I stuck with my instincts—which is what being a successful businessman is all about. A lot of people approach deals with all kinds of statistics, market research, and so on. When I talk to business groups, I always remind them that, despite all the modern techniques we have, the greatest computer is still the human brain. You have to sort out everything that's coming at you. With experience, this becomes easier, of course, but you have to have the raw material. And you've got to believe in yourself.

Perhaps most important to me is the reputation Seagram enjoys. I worked hard to make the company very special, and I think both our employees and the public consider Seagram to be in a class by itself—not just in the liquor industry but in all the business world.

I also followed in Father's footsteps by devoting myself, through the World Jewish Congress and other endeavors, to the betterment of society. This has become the passion of my later years. When I'm gone, I hope people will remember me not as just a rich man, but as a man who did something to make the world a better place than as he found it.

In my personal life, I have chosen a very different path than

Father's. For while business is important, it is not everything. I have learned that without strong, loving relationships even the highest-paid CEO is destitute. Indeed, there was a time when, despite my wealth and success, I was deeply unhappy. Today, satisfied with my business achievements, still active in the quest for a better world, and blessed by the love of family and friends, I feel I am truly the richest of men.

CHAPTER 11

———◆———

A DISTILLATION

Before I close, I have learned a few things about business and about life which I should like to pass along. My first piece of advice is "be lucky." That's not always easy, but one of the tricks is to recognize opportunity when it knocks. To be able to do that, you must surround yourself with the best advisers you can. Not just your executive staff, but also investment bankers, accountants, and, yes, even lawyers. But be careful—all people have hidden agendas, even if they aren't aware of it. My father wrote in my bar mitzvah letter that every man (I don't know whether, if he were alive today, he would have added "woman") should listen carefully to everyone around him and then make up his mind as to what to do.

———◆———

Be careful of egos, your own as well as those of your fellow executives. Much money is thrown away trying to make a bad decision look good rather than admitting the mistake, and doing something different. Don't get into a bidding contest if you can help it. The winner is either the one with the deepest pockets, or the bigger ego drive, or both. In a bidding war, if you can't help it, try and be as dispassionate as possible. Don't let your emotions rule your intellect. That can be very expensive. While on that subject, never second-guess your fellow executives. It's basically a cheap shot, and if you want them to give you their best, don't tell them later that all along you had seen the flaws in their reasoning but wanted them to learn by making their own mistakes. Slap my face once, you're a fool. Slap my face a second time, I'm a fool.

———•———

Delegate wisely. It's terribly important to fit round holes and square holes with round and square pieces. Because an executive is good at some things doesn't mean he's good at all things. That goes for you, too. You must know the things you are not good at. Get someone you trust to help you with them. While you're at it, nurture your people. A little TLC is always appreciated. If your executive is having an important anniversary, send him and his wife flowers. If he or she is having a company anniversary, send him or her a handwritten note, or maybe buy him or her a drink at the end of the day—in your office, if company regulations don't rule that out. Make it your business to know his wife's or her husband's name, and if they have any problem children, so that you can be compassionate, and not threatening.

———•———

Be careful of consumer research. Remember that almost everyone tries to be polite and there is no answer on the questionnaire for "none of the above." Use your instincts—your brain is the best computer ever, storing data, experiences, and almost-forgotten little things that point it in the right direction most of the time. Use consumer research to check those instincts, but not much more than that. Focus groups are of limited use, and willingness to purchase comes out much higher in a test situation than in real life.

——+——

When you're going through a bad patch, be careful about the decisions you are about to make. Your defenses are likely down, and you are not seeing clearly. When things are rough at home, be extra cautious. Be aware that your executives may have similar problems. It's helpful to have a perception of what's going on in the lives of your close associates.

——+——

Watch your debt position closely. Remember that when things are looking great, debt doesn't seem to be nearly as troublesome as when there is a downturn. My first wife's grandfather, C. M. Loeb, was known to advise that the difference between a man and an animal is that a man has credit, and he ought to use it. That's absolutely true. Some inflation will always be with us, and you will always be paying back debt with cheaper dollars (or whatever the currency) than you borrowed.

——+——

My father's devotion to quality was taken seriously by me, and I have come to realize that the secret to profitability is the margin you can demand for your product, if it is a consumer item. Consumers are willing to pay a higher price if they are convinced that the quality is there, that the product has prestige and has earned it.

——+——

I truly believe that one can be intellectually and morally honest at all times, and you never have to lie to be successful in business. Always earn your self-respect and others will respect you—and your products! As my father put it, "The five-dollar whore who takes two dollars will never get five dollars again." Once you tell a lie, you have lost credibility, and that's your most valuable asset.

———

I have left succession, and succession planning, for the end. That is unbelievably important and unbelievably difficult. First, you have to have made a decision that you will not hang on forever as CEO. Secondly, it's a very good idea to have worked out what you are going to retire to rather than concentrate only on what you are retiring from. In my case, having had a father who stayed on as CEO much too long, for his own emotional reasons, I determined that at age sixty-five I would relinquish the title of CEO. I was extremely lucky in that: (a) I had a marvelous son to succeed me in that position, and (b) I had something exciting and fulfilling to retire to, my pro bono work as head of the World Jewish Congress and the World Jewish Restitution Organization. (Of course that leads to another consideration—how long should I stay as head of those organizations, with all the problems of Jewish organizational life?)

The rule usually is that strong CEOs don't pick strong men or women to succeed them, because strong people are threatening; when climbing the corporate ladder, one kicks a lot of butt to get to the top, and then one remains leery of those whose butts have been kicked. It's necessary, then, to start succession thinking early, and to share it with the board of directors, as insurance that you won't have second thoughts and decide that the corporation just can't get along without you. Aside from changing management if things are going badly, this is one of the most important board functions there is. And speaking of boards, most managers tend to put their friends on the board as a bit of insurance. I know it's getting difficult, but a strong manager needs a strong board to keep him or her honest. Remember that power corrupts, and total power corrupts completely. The way for a CEO to limit his power is by having a strong, well-informed board of directors.

FORWARD AND BACKWARD: CHINA AND RESTITUTION

Since the original draft of this book was written, I have become increasingly engaged in two activities: the expansion of our business into China—one of the most exciting ventures Seagram has ever undertaken—and the increasingly intense efforts of the World Jewish Restitution Organization.

I have always been fascinated by China. As a Jew, I think of it as the only other civilization that has been around as long as ours. As an executive, I know that business cannot for long ignore the world's largest concentration of people.

Indeed, the prospect of commercial enterprise in the most populous nation on earth has tantalized the corporate world for some time. Only in recent years, however, has that possibility become a reality.

For Seagram, China represents a vast market of virtually limitless potential. On the beverage side of the business, we are rapidly expanding our sales of wines and spirits while also forging a lucrative partnership in the area of juice production. Meanwhile, Universal Studios has developed ambitious plans to create a broad array of movies, television, theme parks, retail outlets, and other entertainment ventures. Together, these endeavors promise to yield enormous profits, making China one of the jewels of our international operations in the twenty-first century.

Of course, this is by no means an easy task. The challenges—cultural, political, technological—are daunting, and the process can be painfully slow. But our commitment is for the long term, and if we do things right, it will pay off.

The seeds of our foray into China were sown back in the seventies, when Jim McDonough, then the president of Seagram's Overseas Sales Company, started attending the annual Canton Trade Fair and established a presence for us in tourist spots such as restaurants and hotels. In 1986, Seagram International, guided by Ed McDonnell, painstakingly hammered out a joint venture with the China Distillery Company in Shanghai. But we have soon come to understand that the area between Shanghai and Guangzhou, where there are 200 million Chinese, has developed rapidly, with an economy approaching that of Europe. Like nouveaux riches the world over, they demand the very best, and our sales of Chivas Regal, Chivas Royal Salute, and Martell cognacs have grown impressively. What is important to our company is that Chivas Regal can be made only by us in Scotland, Martell and the great wines the same in France, and so we worry very little about anyone trying to make such products in China. The customer there, as elsewhere, is not interested in cheap imitations.

My own interest in China dates back to 1987 and the formation of the East/West Forum, a think tank I founded and chaired. Though the focus of this scholarly institution was the Soviet empire, it ignited my interest in the Communist world and the question of how to harbor its mostly untapped economic potential.

In 1988, I made my maiden voyage to China. The trip was arranged by my good friend Professor Seweryn Bialer of Columbia University through the auspices of the Beijing Institute for International

Security Studies (BIISS). It offered an extraordinary introduction, which reinforced my fascination with the country and its people.

We stayed at the magnificent Shangri-La in Beijing. I have seen most of the great hotels in the free world, and this one ranks with any of them. Not only was it lavish, it was tastefully done.

How could there be such a luxury hotel in the capital of the People's Republic of China? The Shangri-La was built by foreign-based Chinese, who have played, and will increasingly play, a major role in turning their native land into an economic powerhouse.

I could see from this partnership that, unlike the Soviets, the Chinese were willing and anxious to learn. The mainland Chinese were already making great progress by using the skills of the Hong Kong Chinese and anyone else who could help them achieve their goals. They are a proud and secure people, who know they are more advanced on many levels than other societies and are thus willing to acknowledge their deficiencies and accept the assistance of outsiders.

My first day in China, we were briefed by the U.S. ambassador, Winston Lord, and the top people at the American embassy. We were given a much clearer understanding of the meaning of the Cultural Revolution there—how awful it was and how determined everyone was that it never happen again. The constant dethroning of Chairman Mao was somewhat reminiscent of the constant attacks by Gorbachev and company on Stalin and Stalinism.

I was encouraged to hear Ambassador Lord say that he considered it an important part of his job to help Americans in their attempts to do business in the People's Republic. This, in my experience, is a different view than that held by most embassies. Among other things, we discussed the Chinese appetite for foreign films, presaging future dealings that would come after our purchase of MCA.

One of the main items on my itinerary was a visit to the distillery owned by our partner, China Winery Shanghai. When we arrived, there was a sign at the entrance welcoming me. We were greeted by China Winery's Gong You Pei, as well as by Mao Zhao Xian of the Shanghai Sugar, Cigarette & Wine Corporation. We also met Qi

Minzhi, of Sitco, the Shanghai Investment & Trust Corporation. This outfit is a kind of mini CITIC and took credit for having coordinated the joint venture.

Though the factory had new facilities for bottling soft drinks, it was primitive. We saw a line they had just bought from Japan that extruded the plastic bottles, cooled and filled them, after which they were hand-placed in used shipping cartons.

Next we visited the bottling hall, where they were packing a sorghum product. All the glass we saw was being reused, which certainly slowed down the line, but the glass was consistent in size, about 750 ml. After the labels were scrubbed off, the bottles were washed with a scrubbing brush and then automatically filled, though not very consistently. At two stations, girls were removing misfilled bottles, and they missed a few. The labels were applied in rudimentary fashion. The crown corker was the only efficient part of the line, and even that was slow. Though the temperature was about 100 degrees F, we also went to see the distillery, which was equipped with a tremendous wine-storage area.

During my stay, I delivered a speech before the Academy of Social Sciences on the subject of world economic trends. The main contention of my address was that economic issues were replacing ideology and military strength as the dominant force in international relations. The way of the future was clear: global interdependence. I also spoke bluntly about state-run economies, declaring that monopoly produces stagnation and technological backwardness. Competition, I said, is a necessary ingredient of progress.

Of course, it was clear from this first trip that China was well on the road to reform, though tough sledding lay ahead. Deng Xiaoping had been quoted as saying that, in economic terms, conservatives were the enemy.

Having spent some time in the Soviet Union, it was interesting to compare the two Communist superpowers. In fact, there was little comparison. What they shared was a one-party system, a desire for economic reform, and technological underdevelopment. But the Chinese seemed able to apply the technology they received, while the Soviets, despite advances, weren't able to get them from the lab into the factory. The Chinese had first dealt with the problem of feeding themselves, and the farmers were growing vegetables and bringing them to market. The produce of the collective farms was ignored by the consumers—it was neither fresh nor appetizing.

China, I found, had plenty of perestroika but not much glasnost. (For instance, they had a drastic but effective way of combatting drunk driving: if a police officer smelled alcohol on your breath, he would take your driver's license and rip it up. End of story.)

As for the people, the differences couldn't be more stark. The Soviets were paranoid and xenophobic. Not only did I find the Chinese to be secure about themselves, they were uniformly polite. They seemed fond of foreigners (though in a slightly condescending way) and anxious to please. I was most struck by their industrious nature and entrepreneurial instincts. And again I was impressed by their willingness to learn from the large population of overseas Chinese, who were allowed to invest in exchange for training the local people in business and service.

On the other side of the ledger, the educational system was deplorable. Literacy was low, in part because of the inherent difficulty of the language. It was also clear that the Chinese would have to pay their key people better, including scientists, doctors, and bureaucrats, who were making a pittance compared to many peasants.

Very few businesses were earning any real money in China. But those multinationals that had chosen to stay away from China were making a fundamental error. In our case, I knew we would eventually succeed, and I determined that we should move with all due speed to establish ourselves in as many places as possible. Clearly, it would not be easy, but the future benefits were undeniable.

My second trip to China came in November 1990. On the way, we made a stop in Bangkok, where we had established a very active operation. At the time, we were number two in wine and spirits in Thailand behind Guinness/Moët/Hennessy. Our visit gave me an opportunity to meet the staff and review our advertising efforts.

From there we moved on to China. Our stay was brief and we

spent the entire time in Shanghai, where we focused exclusively on Seagram business. I did have a chance to talk to some young people about the slaughter at Tiananmen Square. They were very restrained in their comments, apparently having learned their lesson about the limits of reform.

This visit included a brief reception at our factory with Mr. Mao and Mr. Gong, our joint venture partners. In attendance were Canada's ambassador to China, representatives from both the U.S. and Canadian consular offices, and the vice mayor of Shanghai. After the appropriate speeches, a lion dance was performed, presumably to bring good luck. We then returned to the hotel, and I invited all the Asian joint venture partners to my suite for cocktails. There was much to toast—by this time, we were doing $750 million of business in the Asia-Pacific region, with a high return on assets.

I went back to China in the fall of 1992. My visit was once again hosted by BIISS, and this time included meetings with Prime Minister Li Peng and many other high officials.

I was greeted as an old friend by General Xu Xin, chairman of BIISS. He hosted a dinner for us, at which Seagram products were served. The general assured me that, in the upcoming Party Congress, the reformers would prevail, and they did. When he mentioned the bloodletting at Tiananmen Square, I let him off the hook by saying that the real mistake was letting the demonstration continue so long, which fueled hopes of real change and forced the army to crush the protest ruthlessly.

I asked the general about the collapse of the Soviet Union and what it meant to the Chinese. He replied that the Chinese were determined not to go down the same road the Soviets had. He then expressed support for our joint ventures in China and responded enthusiastically to the news that we were contemplating more.

The reception was less cordial at a luncheon with the first deputy foreign minister, where I was berated for President Bush's announced sale of F-16s to Taiwan. When he was all through, I tried to give him a lesson in American politics. I explained that the F-16s were made in Fort Worth, Texas, in a factory which employed some four thousand people. That translated into perhaps twenty thousand votes. If President Bush were defeated in Texas in the upcoming election, he would lose the presidency; if he won the election, he would probably rescind the sale. I also forecast that Bill Clinton would win the election, a concept he found very hard to grasp—a sitting president beaten? (On my next trip, I was treated with a little more deference as a result of this forecast.) At this luncheon, I tasted Chinese orange juice and realized that the quality was superb, and it made me think about Tropicana being involved in China.

Another lunch was hosted by Professor Gao Shangquan, vice-minister of the State Commission for Restructuring the Economic Systems. Professor Gao talked about the greater role that the commission would soon play in China. Andrew Muir, our Seagram executive in charge of the region, got a chance to air his grievances when Gao asked about our Shanghai joint venture. Andrew expressed concern about the enterprise, particularly with regard to taxes. The tax rate on imports for the state monopoly was 150 percent, while for the joint venture it was 257 percent. He explained that we were asking only for parity. I added that in order for us to create other joint ventures in China, it would be necessary to adjust the two taxes. Steve Herbits also spoke eloquently about the important role played by American business as the ambassador of goodwill between China and the United States.

Near the end of lunch, Professor Gao talked about fruit juices and their health benefits. I told him that Seagram made orange juice, noting that we were the market leader in Tokyo, and said that if oranges were grown in China, we would be interested in establishing a plant, and producing for the domestic market as well as for export. He promised to look into the matter, and thus the preliminary groundwork was laid for our eventual orange juice venture in China.

Toward the end of the trip came my meeting with Prime Minister Li Peng. After discussing the fall of the Soviet Union and China's recognition of Israel, the dialogue turned to Sino-U.S. relations. The prime minister took issue with the notion that the demise of the USSR had made China less important to the United States. He pointed to the importance of the Chinese market, noting the rising living standards of the approximately 200 million people who live on the country's east coast and the importance of these individuals as a future American market. Mr. Li also brought up the issue of most-favored-nation status, which at the time was the subject of much controversy. Some congressmen, he said, incorrectly believed that MFN helped China and hurt the United States. He cited various figures that contradicted this claim, asserting that Hong Kong might suffer more than China if MFN were revoked. He also made reference to the size and historical ambition of Russia, and suggested that a strategic alliance between the United States and China might be important in the future.

Near the conclusion of our conversation, I told the prime minister that China seemed to be trying very hard to develop an economic model that would give its people the highest standard of living possible. I also expressed my hope that our two nations could learn from each other and become partners in creating a better world.

When Efer assumed day-to-day control of Seagram in 1995, he decided to beef up our China sales force and to make twice-yearly visits to monitor the strategies we had laid out. However, with the purchase of MCA, he was much too busy to go himself, and so in June I found myself heading east once again.

This trip was particularly important, as I had had to cancel a previously scheduled visit because of the MCA negotiations. It was my job to repair the diplomatic damage and persuade our Chinese friends that we were very serious about expanding our business relationship with them.

First, however, we made a stop in Taiwan, where Seagram has established a significant presence. Thanks to some great entrepreneurial work done by Tom Pepper and Yoram Rakover of our Far Eastern team, we broke the monopoly in Taiwan. Our venture there is the most profitable per capita of any subsidiary.

The nouveaux riches are on the rise in Taiwan, and their search for status is reflected in our healthy sales of Chivas Regal as well as Chivas Royal Salute (43,000 cases). We also do very well with the Martell premiums and sell more XO than Cordon Bleu. Martell, which was number nine in the market when we entered the field, is now number one.

Our people in Taiwan were happy to see us. We spent an evening with the executives at an exclusive club, and I told the Chivas Regal story from its very beginnings. They were particularly impressed with the fact that I had been a blender and had reblended Chivas Regal when we changed the package.

From Taiwan we headed to China. The people at CIISS (the first word had been changed from "Beijing" to "Chinese") were more than accommodating. They set up numerous appointments for us, and when we told them that we had been unable to make an appointment with the minister of agriculture, they quickly rectified that omission.

I met again with Vice Minister Liu of their foreign office, and opened the conversation by saying, "Last time we met, you yelled at me about selling F-16s to Taiwan. What are you going to yell about this time?" Of course, I knew: the Chinese were incensed that our State Department had given a visa to President Lee Ten Hiu of Taiwan to travel to the United States and receive an honorary degree at Cornell. Sure enough, I once again became the lightning rod for criticism of American foreign policy, with Vice Minister Liu and his deputy actually going so far as to proclaim that the affair was some kind of plot. I smiled, because I know we are not nearly capable of hatching such a plot.

Perhaps they will someday work out a commonwealth type of relationship whereby Taiwan, like Hong Kong, will become part of China while retaining its own army and legislature.

Our trip included a visit with Vice President Rong Yiren at the Great Hall of the People. We were ushered into a very large reception hall with a ring of chairs in a horseshoe shape and theaterlike chairs on either side. The half-hour meeting was uneventful but politically useful. Like all the other officials whom we met, he was very taken with the idea of Tropicana doing business in China. He talked about the necessity for cooperation in our ventures, with which I heartily agreed, and suggested that I should use my "considerable influence" to improve political relations between China and the United States.

We also had dinner with Lieutenant General Xiong Guang Kai,

assistant chief of staff of the army, at a restaurant in the Shangri-La Hotel. He is a powerful man with a firm handshake who is fluent in English as well as in German. Our delegation spent some time arguing that China could benefit from good public-relations advice and a credible professional presence in Washington. This was well received. After toasting to good relations between our two countries, I got a bit bold and raised the issue of intellectual property rights. I gently pointed out that the army was involved in piracy, and proposed a solution: a joint venture between the army and a company such as Cineplex to build theaters in Chinese cities.

Elaborating on the idea, I suggested that they could start with a city of, say, 500,000 and experiment with this concept. After all, the Chinese population has little to do in the evening, and clean, air-conditioned theater complexes with neon lights, popcorn, and all the other accoutrements might be very popular and profitable. General Xiong seemed to like the idea, and as we were leaving, he promised to get back to me on the matter. I made it very clear that the price for my business consultation was that the army would cease its pirating.

Our meeting with General Xiong provided an interesting end to a fascinating trip. I left with a renewed appreciation for this fantastic country. From the new shops to the faces of the people, one could see that they had come a long way in a short time. By now, it was clear that the reformers were here to stay, and that the business potential in China was enormous. We made progress on most of the issues on our agenda, and I was pleased to find that I had a lot of personal pull with the Chinese.

My most recent trip to China was in November 1996. Accompanying me was a high-level Seagram delegation including Steve Herbits, Frank Biondi, chairman of Universal Studios Inc., and Sandy Climan, executive vice president. The purpose of the visit was twofold: to assess the prospects for further expansion of our spirits and beverages business, and to consider strategies for Universal's growth.

Driving through Beijing, we could see evidence of entrepreneurship everywhere. There are department stores operated by joint ventures with foreign companies, retail shops run exclusively by the

Chinese, and fast-food outlets such as McDonald's and Kentucky Fried Chicken. The next step is to privatize the large factories, and it will be fascinating to watch them do this.

Vice Premier Zhu Rong Ji, one of the top officials in the country, seems to be very involved with this phase of China's reform. There is speculation that he may succeed Li Peng when the latter's term expires. When we met with him, he spoke only through an interpreter, though we were told that he is fluent in English. He greeted me warmly, remarking upon my status as a longtime China visitor. As we all lined up for a photograph, he quipped, "A Universal picture." To his left, in the seat of honor, was General Xiong Guang Kai.

We knew going into this meeting that the vice premier opposes, in principle, the importation of high-priced merchandise such as wine and spirits because of the country's economic problems. Our job was to demonstrate our goodwill.

I started by saying that we were determined always to keep in mind that all our business operations had to be beneficial for China as well as ourselves. Then I carefully broached the subject of high tariffs and smuggling. On the one hand, we have achieved about 35 to 40 percent penetration and have obtained licenses to import through Shanghai and Tianjin (a port an hour and a half east of Beijing on the coast). On the other hand, according to Yoram Rakover, who is in charge of mainland China (and Taiwan), taxes are much too high—the 70 percent tariff and other levies bring it to an intolerable 130 percent.

We explained that our goal is to get the taxes down to 30 percent. We also expressed our concern about the plague of smuggling. The vast bulk of the 300,000-odd cases we sell here are smuggled, because of the high taxes. The present structure could absorb 30 percent. The vice premier appeared quite sympathetic. He asked how much tariff we paid on wine, to which I replied much less than 20 percent. He also was responsive to my argument that China was losing a lot of money as a result of smuggling.

From there I moved on to our interest in developing various entertainment ventures in China, including theaters and a theme park between Hong Kong and Guangzhou. (Virginia Kamsky, our special

China consultant on Universal matters, has already talked to real estate developers, and they seem anxious to form a partnership with us on the theme park project.)

The vice premier told us that Shanghai, and not the south, was the right place for a theme park. This was not surprising, as he was formerly the mayor of Shanghai, which remains his power base. He mentioned that, while he was mayor, he had concluded a deal with Disney and had "given" them a great piece of land in Shanghai, but that nothing had developed. (Michael Ovitz was put in charge of developments in China for Disney, but he failed to overcome their biggest problem, a motion picture about Tibet that China disapproved of. It's somewhat ironic that Mr. Ovitz bought the deal to make that and some other Martin Scorsese films from Universal.)

This led to the contentious question of intellectual property rights, the securing of which is essential for us. The vice premier replied that the IPR question was a serious one in many parts of the world, and that China was doing as good a job as any country in Southeast Asia.

Another issue that came up was the importance of cultural sensitivity. It is our feeling that exporting American entertainment to China is inappropriate, and I assured the vice premier that we respect Chinese tradition and have no intention of trying to import Western culture into a country with a glorious culture of its own. Instead, we want to create entertainment product that is sensitive to Chinese culture. For example, developing characters such as the Monkey King, a central figure in the classic Chinese novel *Journey to the West,* would be an excellent way to promote an entertainment industry suitable for Chinese audiences. The Monkey King character could be central to a TV series, film, retail merchandise, and theme park.

He was very responsive to this approach, which will undoubtedly help build trust and bridge the cultural divide. At the same time, he added that China has a history of absorbing cultures. What they wouldn't tolerate, he said, was pornography or politically subversive material. All in all, it was a productive meeting.

We also had a good talk with the minister of state planning. I urged him to put his weight behind lowering the tariff to 30 percent, and he seemed receptive to the idea. When the discussion turned to the entertainment business, I once again brought up the issue of intellectual property rights. He promised us that the government was doing a great deal, including closing some CD plants, while noting that it is hard to regulate everyone, given the size of the country.

The minister was very enthusiastic about our Three Gorges venture, and indeed the news is very encouraging on the Tropicana-Dole front, as our plans for orange juice production are progressing nicely. While we were in China, we learned that Abbas Bayat was completing negotiations to buy the Dole orange groves in southern China (and those negotiations have been completed). That will be vital to our growth, and in the meantime we are working with the government to get the farmers in the Three Gorges to grow orange trees like those in Florida. At the end of five years—that's how long it takes to develop juice oranges—a processing plant will be built there and refrigerated products will be shipped down the river to Shanghai. That plant should supply China, or the parts that can afford the product, while the southern plant will export, mainly to Japan. It is important for us to control the production of oranges in the south so that the Japanese quality-control people will not find any fault with the chemicals or other substances used.

We met with Abbas Bayat, and he agreed with me that in China businesses must work together. He is also a firm believer in sourcing near the marketplace. But most important, he is a real convert to the idea that China will be his most important country for the production and sales of orange juice. Quite recently, in April 1997, Mr. Bayat resigned. Ellen Marram, the CEO of Tropicana-Dole, has agreed on the importance of this market and is equally enthusiastic.

During our trip we held a press conference to announce the Three Gorges development as well as the purchase of the Dole groves in Beihai. There were thirty-six members of the Chinese press in attendance, apparently a near-record, and they peppered us with intelligent questions. Later during the trip, I was interviewed by Sun Xu of Beijing Television, who queried me about the orange juice business in Beihai and the Three Gorges.

Our trip included a dinner at the Kaminsky Hotel with General Xiong Guang Kai. He is fifty-seven years old but could pass for much younger. After discussing Sino-Russian relations, I asked when China planned to become a market economy. He answered that at a recent meeting of the Communist Party leadership, they had set a target date of 2010.

I also had lunch with Gao Siren, chairman of the Guangzhou municipal Chinese Communist Party. We dined at the White Swan on the Pearl River, and enjoyed a local Chinese red wine. I told him of our spirits, fruit juice, and entertainment operations. On the latter front, I invited him to visit our two U.S. theme parks, but he is a no-nonsense politician, and he told me that he would come only when we started to proceed with our plans. When I explained that the chairman and executive vice president of Universal Studios were looking at sites and wanted to win the cooperation of the local political leadership, he replied that there was no need to see anyone else but him. I hope he's right. After lunch we visited an amusement park that was under construction, but I determined that it did not pose any threat to our plans in the area.

There's no question that Universal will be very involved in China as well as the rest of Southeast Asia. During our trip, the Chinese proposed that we build a theme park with China Central Television as an operating partner. Henderson Land, a Hong Kong real estate developer, discussed building theme parks in Shenzhen, the special economic zone adjacent to Hong Kong. There were also talks about smaller entertainment ventures that could be launched sooner, including projects in Beijing and Shanghai.

I have now been to China five times in eight years, and the country still amazes me. The pace of change is sometimes startling, but the Chinese are determined to modernize their country and have accepted the fact that some dislocation is inevitable. More important, they have come to realize that partnerships with American corporations are essential to their plans and are eager to broaden economic cooperation between our two countries.

For this reason, I firmly believe that China's potential is unmatched anywhere in the world. The obstacles are formidable, but that's what makes any business venture exciting. And as we move into the next century, I am confident that Seagram will be equal to the challenge.

"FOR WANT OF A CHAIR . . ."

Recently, I have received much publicity as a result of our struggle to get the Swiss banks to give to the relatives of survivors what is rightfully theirs. Before we arrived on the scene, the Swiss banks had alternated between denying that there is any such money in their vaults, and paying insignificant sums to some Jewish organizations to go away and let sleeping dogs lie.

Israel Singer, secretary general of the World Jewish Congress and my friend and ally these past nineteen years, was intrigued by this situation. In the fall of 1995, he insisted that I get involved as president of the World Jewish Restitution Organization. This group was founded in 1990 following the collapse of communism in the Soviet Union and Eastern Europe. Communal Jewish property that had been stolen by the Nazis and then by the communist governments of Hungary, Czechoslovakia, Romania, Bulgaria, and Poland, as well as newly independent SSRs such as Ukraine, Belarus, Moldova, and the Baltic countries of Latvia, Estonia, and Lithuania should be returned to the Jewish people. Because of Singer's and my own previous involvement in those countries on the question of Jewish rights—the right to emigrate as well as to live honorable lives there, as Jews—I was asked to be president, and Israel and Uzi Barak of the Jewish Agency became co-chairmen.

Israel managed to get a letter from Israel's then–prime minister, Yitzhak Rabin, naming me as the representative of not only Diaspora Jewry in these matters, but the state of Israel. Thus armed, I led a delegation to Bern, the Swiss capital, on September 12, 1995.

There I used all that I had learned as a businessman to conduct what turned out to be a marathon negotiation. After visiting Swiss

President Kaspar Villager in his office, we walked to a private club for a meeting with the Swiss Bankers Association. There we were ushered into a smallish room with no furniture to speak of, and were left standing pending the arrival of our hosts. After about ten minutes, they stormed into the room, led by the president of the SBA, George Krayer. He proceeded to read me a statement, upon which they had obviously just agreed, which stated that they had done everything imaginable, had come up with 774 dormant accounts (accounts that had not been active in any way since they had been created) that amounted to some 38 million Swiss francs, and what did I have to say to that? I do not know if he expected a negotiation as to the amount of what I immediately considered a bribe. No names were offered to identify these accounts, no information as to which banks had produced them, just an overall figure that I was supposed to take with grace. Then we'd all have lunch and the matter would end.

Instead, I said, "I did not come here to discuss money, I came to discuss process." Once we were seated at lunch, I went on to explain that if they wanted me to tell the world that this was all there was and that there was no more, then I would have to be sure of that, and the only way I could be sure was to be involved in the process of examining the banks themselves.

Two issues were immediately brought up by them: the Swiss bank secrecy laws and their unfailing goodwill, which I must trust. In regard to the first, I replied that it would not be necessary for me personally to audit the banks, but that mutually agreed-upon international auditors could do the job. As to the second, I quoted President Ronald Reagan, who had said to President Gorbachev, "Trust, but verify." At the end of the luncheon we agreed to a committee of eminent persons (their language), consisting of three of them and three of us and a mutually agreed-upon chairman.

There followed a season of foot-dragging. Realizing that this was not getting any easier, Singer and I looked for a lever to pry open the lid of this difficult jar. We decided that the chairman of the Senate Banking Committee, Alfonse D'Amato, Republican of New York, might be an ally, and we arranged to lunch with him in the Senate dining room. He loved the challenge right away. As he and his very capable staff got involved in the subject, his involvement deepened and became more than just a good election issue, but a moral outrage. He met relatives of Holocaust victims who had received moneys due them from France, but had been thrown out of Swiss banks. With the full cooperation of the administration, he managed to get the files of the era declassified. On Tuesday, April 12, 1996, he held the first of the formal hearings into the subject. The Swiss were worried, and they had every right to be. They wanted to meet with me before the hearing, but that was not to be. There was no upside for us, and I wasn't going to listen to any more protestations of goodwill. We told them that I was lunching with the First Lady. "Well, then, he'll be here in Washington." "No, he's lunching with Mrs. Clinton at his apartment in New York."

Actually, I was having a fund-raiser for the upcoming election at my apartment, and the guest of honor was Hillary Clinton. When she arrived, I handed her two pages I had ripped out of *New York* magazine which described the beginning of our struggle with the Swiss Bankers Association. She glanced at the headline and asked, "Edgar, is there any chance we can win with the Swiss banks?" I replied, "Yes, Mrs. Clinton, with your husband's help, there is, and that's why I must see him tomorrow afternoon." I know for a fact that she insisted I see the President, which I did. After listening—he is such a good listener and such a quick study—he asked, "Why is Senator D'Amato holding hearings?" I replied that legislation might prove to be necessary to resolve this problem. "Well, then," said POTUS, "if it comes to that, I will be happy to work with Senator D'Amato on that legislation." As I told the senator later, that was like Esther saying, "I will be happy to sleep with Haman."

The president instructed Chief of Staff Leon Panetta to coordinate an interagency exploration of this period in our history, and Commerce Under Secretary Stuart Eizenstat, who had been the President's emissary on the question of restitution in Eastern Europe, to take charge of this investigation.

We chose, and the Swiss agreed, on Paul Volcker, former chairman of the Federal Reserve, as chairman of the Committee of Eminent

Persons. When he asked me in a telephone conversation why we had chosen him, I replied that he had a great deal of stature, both in size and in the world's estimation. He agreed to the first part (he is six feet ten) and I convinced him that this was an historic opportunity. At the first meeting, which was held in the Bankers Trust Company offices (which had formerly been the offices of James Wolfensohn, now chairman of the World Bank, where Mr. Volcker worked), George Krayer, astounded at the notion that his members, the Swiss banks, would have to pay for the research going on as to what happened during that period, burst out with "Do you expect me to ask my clients to pay to find out what bastards their grandfathers were?" We assured him that, as LBJ said about J. Edgar Hoover, "I'd rather have the S.O.B. inside the tent pissing out than outside the tent pissing in," and that they would have some control of the airing of that information if they were thus involved.

At this and other meetings, the Swiss stalled, stonewalled, and procrastinated. Progress was unbelievably slow. Pressure was needed and was provided by us. We released documents on a steady basis: the accounts Hitler had had for the royalties from *Mein Kampf,* the deposits from his chief tailor, claims from relatives of victims, class-action suits, statements of condemnation from Al D'Amato and the ever-increasing attention being paid by the world's press to this subject.

Meanwhile, activity continued on another front. In 1943, the Quisling government of Norway had sent some sixteen hundred Jews to Auschwitz. Eight hundred returned. What happened to the property of those who were murdered? Some fifty years later, the files were declassified, and a young researcher discovered that the assets of those victims had been auctioned off and the money put into the coffers of the government. This was just after the war, when nobody had any money, and the auctioned properties went for a fraction of their real value. The Norwegian government set up a commission to examine what had happened and what restitution was owed, and that report was due in the spring of 1997.

Because of this fine example, the WJRO and the World Jewish Congress agreed to have joint meetings in November 1996 in Oslo.

The Swiss cameras were there, and the pressure kept building on the Swiss. When asked what I thought they could do, I replied that since there were Holocaust victims dying every day, some in dire straits, an interim fund to alleviate their suffering would go a long way to raising the Swiss image in the eyes of the world.

On December 9, 1996, Ambassador Thomas Borer came to New York and lunched with Israel Singer and me. The long and the short of that meeting was that he suggested a fund of between 300 and 400 million Swiss francs to alleviate the sufferings of Holocaust survivors. When asked when the funds could be announced, he answered, "Not before February." "Why so long?" "Because now it's the Christmas season, and then everyone will be skiing, and there are many people I must convince." This was not a firm offer, then, and I insisted that we would have to keep doing what we had been doing until such a fund could be formally announced.

The next day, Representative Jim Leach of Iowa, chairman of the House Banking Committee, held a hearing. I testified, along with others, and was as critical of Switzerland and its banks as ever. Israel Singer met with the three major banks in Switzerland during this time, and convinced them the pressure would not go away, that the world was taken with this, the last chapter of World War II and the Holocaust, and would never let up until a conclusion was reached. We consulted with Richard Holbrooke, a friend of long standing, and a former assistant secretary of state who had brokered the Bosnian peace settlement and had received the Goldmann medal, the highest honor the World Jewish Congress can bestow. Holbrooke now works for CS (Crédit Suisse)–First Boston. Holbrooke stated to the chairman of Crédit Suisse that the Swiss banks were going to have a hard time keeping clients if they were perceived to be black hats.

Finally, Crédit Suisse and two other major banks initiated a break in the log jam. But as always throughout this epic, the Swiss managed to make two major mistakes. One was that on New Year's Eve, 1996, the outgoing president of Switzerland, Jean-Claude Delamuraz, accused us of being blackmailers and extortionists because we had suggested an interim fund for the relief of Holocaust survivors. The second was when a young guard found someone shredding papers at the United Bank of Switzerland, a clear violation of the law. Then the guard was sacked as well as arrested! They can be stupid, especially in terms of public relations!

The government finally woke up, and announced a donation of 100 million Swiss francs to the fund that had been set up by the banks, members of industry, and the insurance companies for the benefit of Holocaust survivors, to be paid out forthwith; and announced further that they wanted to create a fund of 7 billion Swiss francs, the income from which would go to alleviate the survivors' conditions now, and in the future the horrible conditions of man's inhumanity to man.

At a glatt kosher luncheon at the Four Seasons restaurant in New York on March 13, 1996, Foreign Minister Flavio Cotti spoke, and I followed, with these remarks:

"Mr. Foreign Minister, ladies and gentlemen: this is an extraordinary session. I commend you, Mr. Foreign Minister, for your remarks and for the inspired program you have placed before your parliament and your people.

"Some facts that we must all recognize: During the Second World War, Switzerland paid an enormous moral price for its neutrality, and caused others to pay with their lives and sometimes their fortunes.

"Switzerland came out of World War Two a much richer country than when it began.

"Switzerland has now seen fit to use some of its resources to set up a humanitarian fund. As these moneys alleviate pain and suffering for all living victims of the Holocaust, I am sure that this decision will go a long way to making the Swiss people feel good about themselves, and changing the world's opinion about Switzerland and its willingness to face its past so that it can have a bright and honorable future.

"I congratulate the government, the banks, and the business community for setting up a fund to directly aid the neediest Jewish Holocaust survivors. It was because of those poor unfortunates, many of whom are dying every day, who cannot wait for the outcome of the Volcker Commission report, that we suggested such an interim gesture.

"I am amazed at the treatment that the rest of the world bestowed on European Jews at the end of World War II. The Russians were coming and all humanitarian thought and decency seem to have abandoned the Allies, as death camp survivors found themselves in DP camps. The question of what happened to the Jewish property of Holocaust victims throughout Eastern and Western Europe must also be examined. All European countries must now look back, just as Switzerland is looking back, squarely facing a period of shame.

"What is there left to be done? The work of the Volcker and of the Bergier commissions must go on with all deliberate haste. We must find out the truth! Those who have just claims must be satisfied, either with what they are entitled or with a valid explanation of what happened to the properties entrusted to Swiss banks. Switzerland's activities in support of either side during World War II must be given the light of day.

"Furthermore, Switzerland, with its new openness, must become a standard for the rest of Europe. Poland and the Czech Republic must take heed. No one, and I mean no one, can be allowed to profit from the ashes of the Holocaust. Commissions are being set up in Sweden, France, Portugal, Spain, Holland, and Belgium. We must learn what happened to the properties of the victims of the Holocaust. France must fairly address its Vichy government and its egregious behavior.

"I am particularly grateful to Senator Alfonse D'Amato. He and the staff of his Senate Banking Committee played a key role in opening classified files and getting us to the point at which we have arrived today. I must thank Secretary Stuart Eizenstat, who, under the direction of President Clinton, has done an enormous task in assembling the truth about America's behavior in that same period. We will study that report, and put it in context with the reports of the commissions of inquiry being carried on in Europe, so that in the not too distant future, the last chapter of the Holocaust and World War II can be written, and truth and justice will prevail."

Secretary Eizenstat's report was released on May 7, 1997. It detailed that the Swiss did not give back the looted gold and other looted property in their vaults. It confirmed that victim gold had been smelted down and mixed in with the ingots of bank gold. It also confirmed that, by financing the Third Reich as they had, the Swiss had prolonged the war by at least a year. Since at least a hundred thousand people were being killed every day in the camps and on the battlefield, it is a simple calculation to come to the realization that the Switzerland of 1943 through 1945 was directly responsible for perhaps more than 5 million deaths, in the camps and on the battlefields.

It has been a difficult period. Many people have accused us of creating anti-Semitism, but I don't believe that Jews create anti-Semitism—anti-Semites do. The answer isn't to say "Don't make trouble" and hide our heads in the sand. The answer is to be proud of our heritage, of our tradition, to stand tall, and to insist that we have the same rights and obligations as everyone else. We may not earn the friendship of others, but we will demand their respect, not because of our newfound strength, which is transitory, but because of our enormous contributions to civilization, which are permanent.